SPECTRUM

Grade 3

GEORGIA Test Prep

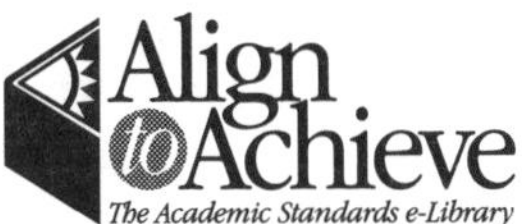

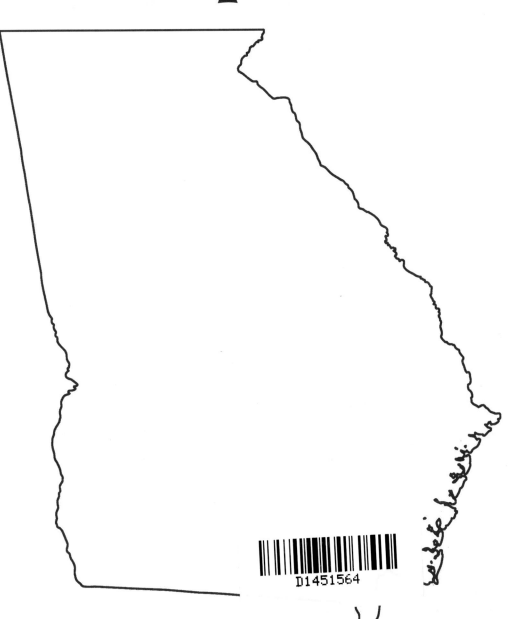

SPECTRUM

Frank Schaffer Publications®

Spectrum is an imprint of Frank Schaffer Publications.

Send all inquiries to:
Frank Schaffer Publications
3195 Wilson Drive NW
Grand Rapids, Michigan 49534

ISBN 0-7696-3473-7

3 4 5 6 7 8 9 10 COR 11 10 09 08 07 06

Table of Contents

What's Inside?

This workbook is designed to help you and your third grader understand what he or she will be expected to know on the Georgia third-grade state tests.

Practice Pages

The workbook is divided into four sections: English/Language Arts, Mathematics, Social Studies, and Science. Each section has practice activities that have questions similar to those that will appear on the state tests. Students should use a pencil to fill in the correct answers and to complete any writing on these activities.

Georgia State Standards

Before each practice section is a list of the state standards covered by that section. The shaded *What it means* sections will help to explain any information in the standards that might be unfamiliar.

Mini-Tests and Final Tests

Practice activities are grouped by state standard. When each group is completed, the student can move on to a mini-test that covers the material presented on those practice activities. After an entire set of standards and accompanying activities are completed, the student should take the final test, which incorporates materials from all the practice activities in that section.

Final Test Answer Sheet

The final tests have separate answer sheets that mimic the style of the answer sheets the students will use on the state tests. The answer sheets appear at the end of each final test.

How Am I Doing?

These pages are designed to help students identify areas where they are proficient and areas where they still need more practice. Students can keep track of their mini-test scores on these pages.

Answer Key

Answers to all the practice activities, mini-tests, and final tests are listed by page number and appear at the end of the book.

Frequently Asked Questions

What kinds of information does my child have to know to pass the test?

The Georgia Department of Education provides a list of the knowledge and skills that students are expected to master at each grade level. The activities in this workbook provide students with practice in each of these areas.

Are there special strategies or tips that will help my child do well?

The workbook provides sample questions that have content similar to that on the state tests. Test-taking tips are offered throughout the book.

How do I know what areas my child needs help in?

A special *How Am I Doing?* section will help you and your third grader evaluate progress. It will pinpoint areas where more work is needed as well as areas where your student excels.

Georgia English/Language Arts Content Standards

The English/language arts section measures knowledge in four different areas:

1) **Reading**

2) **Writing**

3) **Conventions**

4) **Listening, Speaking, and Viewing**

Georgia English/Language Arts Table of Contents

Reading Standards

Reading, writing, speaking, and listening skills are necessary tools for effective communication. The mastery of these skills is essential for enrichment and lifelong learning. Children must develop their ability to read with fluency and understanding in order to build their knowledge of the world.

Fluency

ELA3R1. The student demonstrates the ability to read orally with speed, accuracy, and expression. ***(See page 8.)*** **The student:**

a. applies letter-sound knowledge to decode unknown words quickly and accurately.
b. reads familiar text with expression.
c. reads third-grade text at a target rate of 120 words correct per minute.
d. uses self-correction when subsequent reading indicates an earlier misreading within grade-level texts.

Vocabulary

ELA3R2. The student acquires and uses grade-level words to communicate effectively. ***(See pages 9–13.)*** **The student:**

a. reads literary and informational texts and incorporates new words into oral and written language.
b. uses grade-appropriate words with multiple meanings.
c. recognizes and applies the appropriate usage of homophones, homographs, antonyms, and synonyms.
d. identifies the meaning of common idioms and figurative phrases, and incorporates them into oral and written language.
e. identifies and infers meaning from common root words, common prefixes (e.g., *un-, re-, dis-, in-*) and common suffixes (e.g., *-tion, -ous, -ly*).
f. determines the meaning of unknown words on the basis of context.

What it means:

- Students should be able to use several different strategies to help them determine the meaning of unfamiliar words. An important strategy in determining meaning is knowing **homophones** (words that are pronounced alike but are different in meaning and spelling), **homographs** (words that are spelled alike but are different in meaning or pronunciation), **antonyms** (words that mean the opposite), and **synonyms** (words that mean the same).
- **Figurative language** is language used for descriptive effect. It describes or implies meaning rather than stating it directly. Similes and metaphors are types of figurative language.
- Students should recognize the meaning of common word beginnings, or prefixes, such as *un-, re-,* and *pre-,* and endings, or suffixes, such as *-less* and *-ful.*

Comprehension

ELA3R3. The student uses a variety of strategies to gain meaning from grade-level text. ***(See pages 14–27.)*** **The student:**

a. reads a variety of texts for information and pleasure.
b. makes predictions from text content.
c. generates questions to improve comprehension.
d. distinguishes fact from opinion.

Reading Standards

e. recognizes plot, setting, and character within text, and compares and contrasts these elements between texts.
f. makes judgments and inferences about setting, characters, and events and supports them with evidence from the text.
g. summarizes text content.
h. interprets information from illustrations, diagrams, charts, graphs, and graphic organizers.
i. makes connections between texts and/or personal experiences.
j. identifies and infers main idea and supporting details.
k. self-monitors comprehension to clarify meaning.
l. identifies and infers cause-and-effect relationships and draws conclusions.
m. recalls explicit facts and infers implicit facts.
n. identifies the basic elements of a variety of genres (fiction, nonfiction, drama, and poetry).

What it means:

- **Genre** is the type or category of literature. Some examples of genres are fiction, nonfiction, and poetry. Each genre is categorized by various differences in form. For example, nonfiction differs from fiction in that it presents facts or tells a true story.

o. uses titles, table of contents, and chapter headings to locate information quickly and accurately and to preview text.
p. recognizes the author's purpose.
q. formulates and defends an opinion about a text.
r. applies dictionary, thesaurus, and glossary skills to determine word meanings.

What it means:

- Students should know how to use a dictionary to look up words and know that the dictionary provides other information about words besides definitions.

Name ______________________ Date ______________

English/ Language Arts

ELA3R1

Developing Fluency

Testing

Sign on the door? It's already been hung.
We're waiting until the bell has rung.
Pencils sharp and faces gone pale,
It seems like a prison—academic **jail!**

I studied until I'd had enough.
I hope the math is not too tough.
Numbers and symbols churn through my brain—
Why is place value causing me **pain?**

Their, there, they're. . . our or *hour,*
Ever think little words could hold so much power?
Can you see that knowing which one is right
Is a **worry** keeping me up all night?

The capital of Arkansas? Easy, that's a breeze!
Boise? Boston? Bismarck? My mind is a freeze!
The continents—name them all, then find them on a map.
I'm feeling very anxious here; I think this is a **trap!**

Science? The *atmosphere* in here is creating such a **force**
My brain cells are starting to *erode,* of course!
And who is *predator* and who is the *prey*?
I'm under a *microscope* in every way!

Testing!

DIRECTIONS: Reread the poem more than once. Then answer the questions.

1. What emotion is the speaker trying to show by saying "faces gone pale" in line 4?

Ⓐ fear
Ⓑ confidence
Ⓒ anger
Ⓓ happiness

2. You can guess that the speaker—

Ⓕ doesn't care about school very much.
Ⓖ wants to do well in school.
Ⓗ likes to do math—especially place value.
Ⓙ enjoys test taking.

3. Which subject would *not* be on the test?

Ⓐ math
Ⓑ science
Ⓒ social studies
Ⓓ music

4. What do you think is written on the "sign on the door"?

____

____

5. How do you think the author of this poem feels about testing? Why do you think so?

____

____

____

STOP

Name ______________________ Date ______________

Vocabulary Development

DIRECTIONS: Read the passage and answer the questions that follow.

Making Clay Move

Beginning in about 1990, claymation became very popular. *Animators* have used this clay animation to make several famous movies and TV commercials. However, claymation is not a new idea. In 1897, a claylike material called *plasticine* was invented. Moviemakers used plasticine to create clay animation films as early as 1908. Animators could use the plasticine models for scenes that could not be filmed in real life.

Here's how claymation works. First, an artist makes one or more clay models. Moviemakers pose each model, take a picture, and then stop. Next, they move the model a tiny bit to a slightly different pose. Then they take another picture. They continue the pattern of taking pictures, moving the model, and taking pictures again. It can take hundreds of pictures to make a few seconds of film. The idea of moving models and using stop-action photography came from a French animator named George Melier. He once had a job as a magician and called his work "trick film."

Today's animators use different kinds of clay. They can also use computers to speed up the claymation process. But the basic idea of clay animation has not changed in over a hundred years!

1. This story is mostly about

Ⓐ the history of claymation films.
Ⓑ George Melier, a French magician.
Ⓒ making models out of plasticine.
Ⓓ today's animators and how they work.

2. What is plasticine?

Ⓕ a type of plastic model
Ⓖ a claylike material
Ⓗ a French animator
Ⓙ the idea of moving models

3. What do you think "stop-action photography" is?

Ⓐ making everyone stop while a photo is taken
Ⓑ moving a model, taking the picture, then moving the model again
Ⓒ using magic tricks to make the camera work
Ⓓ a camera that stops after the picture is taken

4. What is an animator?

Ⓕ someone who works with actors
Ⓖ someone who makes clay sculptures
Ⓗ someone who invents clay materials
Ⓙ someone who makes animated films

5. Which two words are used to make the word *claymation*?

Ⓐ clay and movement
Ⓑ clay and maker
Ⓒ clay and animation
Ⓓ clay and photography

Name ______________________________ Date ______________

English/ Language Arts

ELA3R2

Vocabulary

Using Words with Multiple Meanings

DIRECTIONS: For numbers 1–4, read the two sentences. Then choose the word that fits in the blank in both sentences.

1. **The tree had rough ________ . The dog wanted to ________ all the time.**
   - Ⓐ branches
   - Ⓑ yap
   - Ⓒ bark
   - Ⓓ jump

2. **Did the baby ________ the toy? Mr. Lee wanted to take a ________ .**
   - Ⓕ sleep
   - Ⓖ lose
   - Ⓗ ruin
   - Ⓙ break

3. **Dad gets a ________ every week. I want to ________ my math homework.**
   - Ⓐ note
   - Ⓑ redo
   - Ⓒ check
   - Ⓓ payment

4. **Use the ________ to make the hole. The ________ at the party was delicious.**
   - Ⓕ shovel
   - Ⓖ dig
   - Ⓗ punch
   - Ⓙ rake

DIRECTIONS: For numbers 5–8, find the answer in which the underlined word is used in the same way as the word in the box.

5. **This [kind] of plant is rare.**
   - Ⓐ Mrs. Rodriguez is kind.
   - Ⓑ The kind man smiled.
   - Ⓒ I like this kind of cereal.
   - Ⓓ No one thinks that person is kind.

6. **The knight will [bow] to the queen.**
   - Ⓕ She tied a big bow on the gift.
   - Ⓖ I know that I should bow to my dance partner.
   - Ⓗ Did you see how the bow matched her dress?
   - Ⓙ A bow is made of ribbon.

7. **Put your [hand] on the table.**
   - Ⓐ Give Mr. Johnson a hand.
   - Ⓑ The band deserves a hand for their music.
   - Ⓒ I have to hand it to you.
   - Ⓓ Please give your little sister your hand.

8. **You need to do it this [way] .**
   - Ⓕ The king sat way up on the throne.
   - Ⓖ The recipe shows the way to make a cake.
   - Ⓗ He found his way home.
   - Ⓙ I don't know the way to the school.

Name ______________________ Date ______________

English/ Language Arts

ELA3R2

Vocabulary

Synonyms, Antonyms, and Homophones

A **synonym** is a word that means **nearly the same** as another word. A few synonyms for the word *great* are "big," "wide," and "large."

An **antonym** is a word that means the **opposite** of another word. A few antonyms for the word *great* are "little," "narrow," and "small."

A **homophone** is one of two or more words pronounced alike but different in meaning, origin, or spelling. A homophone for the word *flour* is "flower."

DIRECTIONS: Write three **synonyms** for each word in numbers 1–6.

1. **pretty:** ________ ________ ________
2. **hot:** ________ ________ ________
3. **old:** ________ ________ ________
4. **early:** ________ ________ ________
5. **light:** ________ ________ ________
6. **remove:** ________ ________ ________

DIRECTIONS: Write three **antonyms** for each word in numbers 7–12.

7. **pretty:** ________ ________ ________
8. **hot:** ________ ________ ________
9. **old:** ________ ________ ________
10. **early:** ________ ________ ________
11. **light:** ________ ________ ________
12. **remove:** ________ ________ ________

DIRECTIONS: Write two **homophones** for each word in numbers 13–15.

13. **to:** too two
14. **cent:** scent sent
15. **for:** ________ ________

Name ______________________________ Date ______________

English/
Language Arts

ELA3R2

Vocabulary

Using Figurative Language

Polar Bears

With fur like a snowstorm
And eyes like the night,
Two giant old bears
Sure gave me a fright.

They came up behind me
As quiet as mice,
And tapped on my shoulder.
Their paws were like ice.

As high as a kite,
I jumped in the air,
And turned around to see
Those bears standing there.

"We're sorry we scared you,"
The bears said so cool.
"We just came to ask you
To fill up our pool!"

DIRECTIONS: Fill in the blanks to complete the similes from the poem.

1. **paws like** ______________________
2. **fur like** ______________________
3. **as high as a** ______________________
4. **eyes like** ______________________
5. **as quiet as** ______________________

DIRECTIONS: Write your own similes using these words as a guide. Compare two things by using the words *like* or *as.*

6. **a lunch *as*** ______________________ ***as*** ______________________
7. **a friend *like* a** ______________________
8. **a coat *as*** ______________________ ***as*** ______________________
9. **a winter day *like* a** ______________________ ______________________
10. **with** ______________________ ***like* sunshine**

Name ______________________________ Date ______________

English/
Language Arts

ELA3R2

Vocabulary

Root Words, Prefixes, and Suffixes

DIRECTIONS: Choose the best answer.

1. **Find the word in which only the root word is underlined.**
   - (A) carpet
   - (B) barrel
   - (C) playful
   - (D) release

2. **Find the word in which only the root word is underlined.**
   - (F) older
   - (G) unsafe
   - (H) roomy
   - (J) fully

3. **Find the word in which only the suffix is underlined.**
   - (A) bundle
   - (B) mostly
   - (C) careless
   - (D) pronoun

4. **Find the word in which only the prefix is underlined.**
   - (F) pretend
   - (G) allow
   - (H) between
   - (J) unknown

5. **Which of these words does not have a suffix?**
   - (A) runner
   - (B) untied
   - (C) hairless
   - (D) washable

6. **Which of these words does not have a prefix?**
   - (F) defrost
   - (G) nonstop
   - (H) fixable
   - (J) prepay

7. **What does the prefix *un-* mean in the word *unsafe*?**
   - (A) over
   - (B) not
   - (C) in favor of
   - (D) before

8. **What does the suffix *-less* mean in the word *hopeless*?**
   - (F) full of
   - (G) like
   - (H) place
   - (J) without

9. **Find the word that means "to play again."**
   - (A) playful
   - (B) replay
   - (C) player
   - (D) display

10. **Find the word that means "to see beforehand."**
    - (F) bifocal
    - (G) microscope
    - (H) present
    - (J) preview

Name ______________________ Date ______________

English/
Language Arts

ELA3R3

Comprehension

Making Predictions and Inferences

DIRECTIONS: Read the passage and answer the questions that follow.

It's as black as ink out here in the pasture, and I'm as tired as an old shoe. But even if I were in my bed, I don't think I'd be sleeping like a baby tonight.

Last summer for my birthday, my parents gave me my dream horse. Her name is Goldie. She is a beautiful palomino. I love to watch her gallop around the pasture. She runs like the wind and looks so carefree. I hope I'll see her run that way again.

Yesterday, after I fed her, I forgot to close the door to the feed shed. She got into the grain and ate like a pig, which is very unhealthy for a horse. The veterinarian said I have to watch her like a hawk tonight to be sure she doesn't get colic. That's a very bad stomachache. Because he also said I should keep her moving, I have walked her around and around the pasture until I feel like we're on a merry-go-round.

Now the sun is finally beginning to peek over the horizon, and Goldie seems content. I think she's going to be as good as new.

1. **What will the narrator most likely do the next time she feeds the horse?**
   - Ⓐ She will feed the horse too much.
   - Ⓑ She will make sure she closes the feed shed door.
   - Ⓒ She will give the horse plenty of water.
   - Ⓓ She will leave the feed shed open.

2. **How much experience do you think the narrator has with horses?**
   - Ⓕ Lots. She's probably owned many horses before.
   - Ⓖ This is probably her first horse. She doesn't have a lot of experience.
   - Ⓗ She's probably owned a horse before this, but not many.
   - Ⓙ I can't tell from the story.

3. **Based on the passage, which of the following is most likely true about the narrator?**
   - Ⓐ She really does not care much about Goldie.
   - Ⓑ She is devoted to Goldie and will be dedicated to helping her.
   - Ⓒ She will not want to have anything to do with horses in the future.
   - Ⓓ The story does not reveal anything about the narrator.

Name ______________________________ Date ______________

English/
Language Arts

ELA3R3

Comprehension

Distinguishing Fact from Opinion

DIRECTIONS: Read each passage and answer the questions that follow.

Example:

It had snowed all night. "Hurray!" said Jeffrey. "No school today! Snowstorms are the greatest!"

"Not only do I have to get to work," said Mom glumly, "but I also have to shovel snow."

Candy barked. She loved to play in the snow. She was as happy as Jeffrey.

Which one of these statements is an opinion?

- (A) Mom had to shovel snow.
- (B) It had snowed all night.
- (C) Snowstorms are the greatest.
- (D) The dog was happy.

To help you identify some opinions, look for words like *believe, feel,* and *think.*

History Lesson

The students looked at the Web site about Thanksgiving. "I think that the Pilgrims were very brave," said Chad.

"When they came to Massachusetts, there were no other settlers from Europe," Keisha said. "I bet they probably felt lonely here."

"Their first year was a difficult one," Mr. Perez added. "Many of the Pilgrims became ill."

"I think I would have wanted to go home!" said Ang. "I would have felt that even boarding the Mayflower was a big mistake."

1. What opinion did Keisha express?

- (A) The Pilgrims were the only European settlers in Massachusetts.
- (B) The Pilgrims had a difficult first year.
- (C) The Pilgrims wanted to go home.
- (D) The Pilgrims probably felt lonely.

2. What fact did Keisha state?

- (F) The Pilgrims were the only European settlers in Massachusetts.
- (G) The Pilgrims were brave.
- (H) The Pilgrims made a mistake by boarding the Mayflower.
- (J) The Pilgrims had a difficult first year.

3. Which two characters in the story expressed only opinions?

- (A) Chad and Keisha
- (B) Mr. Perez and Keisha
- (C) Chad and Ang
- (D) Ang and Mr. Perez

4. Which character expressed only facts?

- (F) Chad
- (G) Keisha
- (H) Mr. Perez
- (J) Ang

Name ______________________ Date ______________

English/
Language Arts

ELA3R3

Comprehension

Plot Elements

DIRECTIONS: Read the story fragments below and answer the questions that follow.

Rollerblading

A. Suddenly, Jason heard a loud crash on the other side of the park fence. "What was that?" asked Tashara.

B. It was a sunny spring day, and Jason couldn't wait for Tashara to show him how to use his new rollerblades at the park.

C. From around the corner limped Michael, covered with twigs and leaves. "I don't think we have to worry about show-offs anymore," Jason said with a smile.

D. Almost as soon as they got to the park, however, Michael raced by the slower skaters with a mocking sneer. "Show-off," Jason said.

1. Which section presents the main conflict (problem) in the story?

Ⓐ A
Ⓑ B
Ⓒ C
Ⓓ D

2. Which section shows the climax (most exciting part) of the story?

Ⓕ A
Ⓖ B
Ⓗ C
Ⓙ D

3. Which section shows the resolution (end) of the story?

Ⓐ A
Ⓑ B
Ⓒ C
Ⓓ D

STOP

Name ______________________________ Date ______________

English/
Language Arts

ELA3R3

Comprehension

Describing Setting

DIRECTIONS: Read the passage and answer the questions that follow.

Anna's Favorite Time

The wind blew softly, rippling the grasses across the prairie. Everywhere that Anna looked, she saw sky. She picked up the heavy iron pot and placed it back on the fire. As the sun began to set, she was glad for the shade of her sunbonnet. The sky lit up with pink, orange, and gold. Anna stirred the stew while she looked at the beauty all around her. She knew that Pa and the others would be hungry when they returned, so she decided to prepare the meal. She climbed into the back of the covered wagon and searched through the food box for the tin plates and cups. Before the sun had slipped over the horizon, the stew was ready and everyone gathered around the fire for a warm meal. It was Anna's favorite time of day.

1. This story most likely takes place in __________ .

- (A) a made-up time
- (B) the past
- (C) the present
- (D) the future

2. One clue that tells the time period in which the story takes place is that __________ .

- (F) Anna is cooking in a heavy iron pot
- (G) Anna climbs into the back of a covered wagon
- (H) Anna decides to prepare a meal
- (J) everyone gathers around the fire

3. The setting of the story is __________ .

- (A) the prairie
- (B) the mountains
- (C) the city
- (D) the ocean

4. This story takes place at what time of day?

- (F) early morning
- (G) lunchtime
- (H) afternoon
- (J) early evening

5. One clue that tells what time of day the story takes place is that __________ .

- (A) the wind blew softly
- (B) the sun began to set
- (C) Pa and the others would be hungry
- (D) it was Anna's favorite time of day

6. One detail that does not give a clue about the time period in which the story takes place is that __________ .

- (F) Anna wore a sunbonnet
- (G) the plates and cups were made of tin
- (H) they ate around the fire
- (J) none of these

STOP

Name ______________________ Date ______________

English/
Language Arts

ELA3R3

Comprehension

Comparing Characters

DIRECTIONS: Read the two passages and answer the questions that follow.

A Day on the Trail

Dylan's Story:

Today was the day I had been waiting for—our class nature hike. Before we left the bus, Mr. Evans told us the person who found the most items on the list would get a prize. A lot of the kids didn't understand that they needed to be quiet to see any wildlife. I stayed behind the group and moved very slowly down the trail. I found sixteen different leaf specimens and did scratch tests on five different rocks. I was sorry when we had to leave, but I was thrilled to win a field microscope!

Danny's Story:

Today was the day I had been dreading—our class nature hike. My mother could barely drag me out of bed. On the bus, Mr. Evans handed out lists we were supposed to fill in. As if the hike itself wasn't bad enough, I lost my canteen right away; then I ripped my T-shirt on a bush. I did manage to find a couple of rocks, but only because I tripped on them. I didn't see even one animal. By the time we got back to the bus, I was hot, dirty, and tired. To make things worse, I was covered with poison ivy.

1. Write in the name of the character described by each phrase.

Ⓐ __________ thrilled to win a microscope

Ⓑ __________ saw no animals

Ⓒ __________ got up late

Ⓓ __________ found five different rocks

2. Whose day was exciting, interesting, happy, and good?

____

____

3. The two characters reacted very differently to the same setting. Which character's reaction was most like yours would be? Why?

____

____

____

____

____

____

____

STOP

Name ______________________ Date ______________

English/
Language Arts

ELA3R3

Comprehension

Identifying Main Ideas

DIRECTIONS: Read the passage and answer the questions that follow.

Example:

At 5:00 P.M., we were called to the home of a Mr. and Mrs. Bear. They found that the lock on their front door had been forced open. Food had been stolen and a chair was broken. Baby Bear then went upstairs and found someone asleep in his bed.

What is the main idea of this paragraph?

Ⓐ Someone broke a lock.

Ⓑ Someone stole some food.

Ⓒ Mr. and Mrs. Bear's house was broken into.

Ⓓ Baby Bear found his bed.

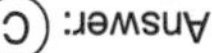

Look back to the item to find each answer, but don't keep rereading the story.

Pioneer Diary

Today, we left our dear home in Ohio forever. Soon we will be a thousand miles away. The distance is too great for us to ever return. Oh, how Grandmother cried as we said goodbye! Uncle Dan and Aunt Martha have bought our farm, so it is no longer our home. All we have now is what is here in our wagon.

When we drove past the woods at the edge of our fields, Papa said to me, "Ellen, take a good look at those trees. It will be many years before we see big trees like that again. We will have to plant trees on the prairie." I felt like crying, just like Grandmother, but I wanted to show Papa that I could be brave.

1. What is the main idea of this story?

Ⓐ Ellen feels like crying.

Ⓑ Ellen wants to be brave.

Ⓒ Ellen and her father are moving to the prairie.

Ⓓ Ellen's father has sold his farm.

2. How do you know the place to which Ellen is moving?

Ⓕ Her grandmother cries.

Ⓖ Her father says they will have to plant trees on the prairie.

Ⓗ Her father has packed a wagon.

Ⓙ Ellen is keeping a diary.

3. Why does Ellen say she is leaving "forever"?

Ⓐ In pioneer days, people were not allowed to go back home again.

Ⓑ In pioneer days, the trip out West was thousands and thousands of miles.

Ⓒ In pioneer days, it was too far for people to travel back and forth for visits.

Ⓓ In pioneer days, people did not sell their farms.

STOP

Name ______________________ Date ______________

English/ Language Arts

ELA3R3

Comprehension

Organizing Supporting Details

DIRECTIONS: Use the passage to fill in the topic sentence below. Fill in the rest of the ovals with supporting details.

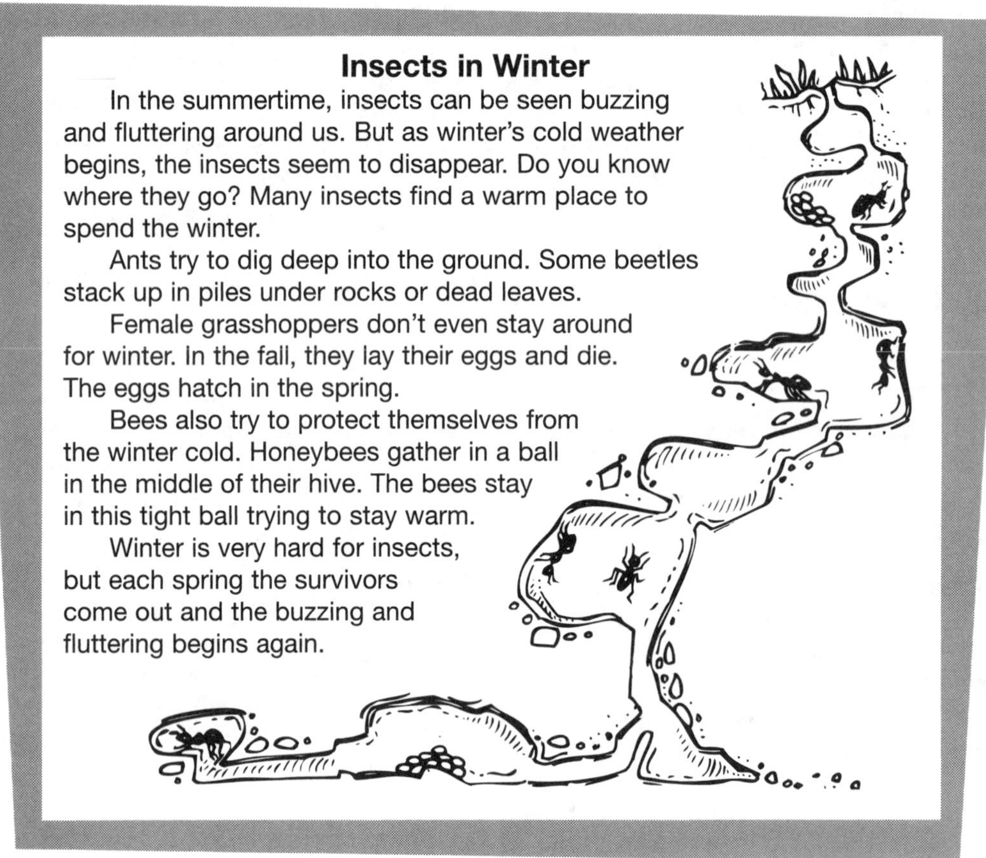

Insects in Winter

In the summertime, insects can be seen buzzing and fluttering around us. But as winter's cold weather begins, the insects seem to disappear. Do you know where they go? Many insects find a warm place to spend the winter.

Ants try to dig deep into the ground. Some beetles stack up in piles under rocks or dead leaves.

Female grasshoppers don't even stay around for winter. In the fall, they lay their eggs and die. The eggs hatch in the spring.

Bees also try to protect themselves from the winter cold. Honeybees gather in a ball in the middle of their hive. The bees stay in this tight ball trying to stay warm.

Winter is very hard for insects, but each spring the survivors come out and the buzzing and fluttering begins again.

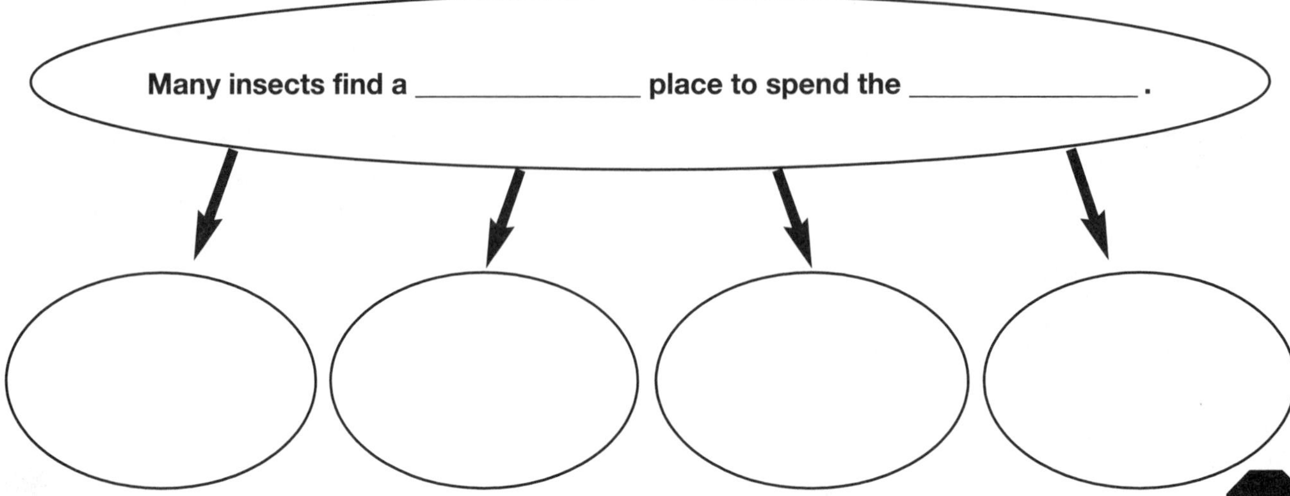
Many insects find a ______________ place to spend the ______________ .

STOP

Name ______________________ Date ______________

English/
Language Arts

ELA3R3

Comprehension

Identifying Cause and Effect

DIRECTIONS: Read the passage and answer the questions that follow.

Bonnie Blair

Speed skater Bonnie Blair is the only American woman to have won five Olympic gold medals. She is known as one of the best speed skaters in the world.

Born on March 18, 1964, Bonnie was the youngest in a speed-skating family. Her five older brothers and sisters were champion skaters who encouraged her. They put a pair of skates over Bonnie's shoes when she was two years old because there weren't any skates small enough for her tiny feet.

As Bonnie grew, she trained hard six days a week, always pushing to improve her time. Bonnie kept this up until she was the world's best female speed skater. She won her first Olympic gold medal in the 500-meter race in 1988. In 1992, she won both the 500-meter and the 1,000-meter Olympic races in Albertville, France. She repeated her victories in 1994 in Lillehammer, Norway.

Bonnie's Olympic successes made her famous all over the world. Bonnie retired from speed skating in 1995 to focus on other competitions.

1. What was the effect of Bonnie being born into a speed-skating family?

____

____

____

____

2. What caused Bonnie's brothers and sisters to put skates over her shoes?

____

____

____

____

3. What was the effect of Bonnie's practice and hard work?

____

____

____

____

STOP

Name ______________________ Date ______________

English/
Language Arts

ELA3R3

Comprehension

Identifying Genres

DIRECTIONS: Read the following passages and answer the questions.

My Backpack

My backpack's so heavy
It must weigh a ton.
With thousands of books—
My work's never done.
My arms are so sore
I can't lift a pen.
My breath is so short
I need oxygen.
When I stoop over,
It makes me fall down.
I think I'll just stay here
All squashed on the ground.

1. This passage is which genre (type) of literature?

- (A) poetry
- (B) fiction
- (C) nonfiction
- (D) drama

2. What clues helped you decide what genre it is?

- (F) It tells a story.
- (G) It includes stage directions.
- (H) It has rhyming words.
- (J) It gives details and facts about something real.

Salt and Pepper

Salt and Pepper were born in the same month and lived together at Peterson's Pet Shop. Salt was a white kitten, whose cage sat in the front window beside a black puppy named Pepper. The two were best friends.

One day, Manuel and his father came into Peterson's Pet Shop to purchase a kitten. Manuel chose Salt because she was so playful.

Several weeks later, Lorinda and her mother stopped by the pet shop to look at the puppies. "Oh, Mama," said Lorinda. "This little black puppy has such beautiful eyes and he likes me already."

"He seems great," said her mother. "I hope he gets along with our neighbor Manuel's new white kitten."

"Oh, I think they'll be best friends," Lorinda replied. "Won't they be cute together? Just like salt and pepper!"

3. This passage is which genre (type) of literature?

- (A) poetry
- (B) fiction
- (C) nonfiction
- (D) drama

4. What clues helped you decide?

- (F) It tells a story.
- (G) It includes stage directions.
- (H) It has rhyming words.
- (J) It gives details and facts about something real.

Name ______________________ Date ______________

On Stage

ART: Dad, when can we visit Sizzle?
MR. BOUIE: Sizzle may not even recognize us.
ART: *(very surprised)* She'd never forget me!
MR. BOUIE: She may not want a visit. You know she'll look different now.
ART: I know she's expecting. *(getting excited)* Do you think she'll have more than one?
MR. BOUIE: *(sitting down on the living room couch)* Probably not. They usually have one at a time.
ART: I can't wait to see it! *(walking behind the couch so his dad can't see him)* Poor Sizzle. She hated it when we took her to the zoo.
MR. BOUIE: Yes, but later she seemed to notice us only when we brought her bananas.
ART: I don't blame her; we abandoned her! It was Uncle Jack's fault. *(biting his nails, but walking in front of the couch)* I wanted to keep her!
MR. BOUIE: Now don't blame Jack. You were delighted when he brought her home. *(sees Art biting nails)* Art! *(shouting)* How many times do I have to tell you to stop doing that?

5. This passage is which genre (type) of literature?

- Ⓐ poetry
- Ⓑ fiction
- Ⓒ nonfiction
- Ⓓ drama

6. What clues helped you decide what genre it is?

- Ⓕ It is a made-up story.
- Ⓖ It includes stage directions.
- Ⓗ It has rhyming words.
- Ⓙ It gives details and facts about something real.

The Heart

Have you ever imagined that your heart looked like a valentine? Your heart is really about the size and shape of your fist. Every time your heart beats it pumps blood to your body. Your heart never rests. It beats 100,000 times a day.

One part of your heart sends blood to all parts of your body. The blood carries the oxygen that your body needs to live. Another part of the heart takes in the blood coming back from your body and sends it to your lungs for more oxygen. Then, the fresh blood is pumped back to your body again.

7. This passage is which genre (type) of literature?

- Ⓐ poetry
- Ⓑ fiction
- Ⓒ nonfiction
- Ⓓ drama

8. What clues helped you decide what genre it is?

- Ⓕ It is a made-up story.
- Ⓖ It includes stage directions.
- Ⓗ It has rhyming words.
- Ⓙ It gives details and facts about something real.

Name ______________________ Date ______________

English/
Language Arts

ELA3R3

Comprehension

Using Text Formats

DIRECTIONS: Read the table of contents and index. Then answer the questions.

TABLE OF CONTENTS

INDEX

1. In which chapter would you look for information about butterflies?

Ⓐ chapter 3
Ⓑ chapter 4
Ⓒ chapter 5
Ⓓ chapter 6

2. What is the title of Chapter 3?

Ⓕ *Animals Around the World*
Ⓖ *Creatures of the Sea*
Ⓗ *Rodents*
Ⓙ *Insects and Spiders*

3. To find out about rain forest animals, turn to pages ________ .

Ⓐ 60–64
Ⓑ 103–107
Ⓒ 39–41
Ⓓ 14–15

4. Which chapter would you read to learn about rats?

Ⓕ chapter 1
Ⓖ chapter 2
Ⓗ chapter 3
Ⓙ chapter 4

5. If you wanted information on blue whales, you would turn to page ________ .

Ⓐ 60
Ⓑ 61
Ⓒ 62
Ⓓ 64

6. Where would you look to find information about the Seattle Zoo?

Ⓕ chapter 1
Ⓖ chapter 2
Ⓗ chapter 3
Ⓙ chapter 4

7. Which of the following would make the best title for this book?

Ⓐ *The Complete Guide to Animals and Insects*
Ⓑ *Understanding the Insect World*
Ⓒ *All About Reptiles*
Ⓓ *Discovering Sea Creatures*

STOP

Name ________________________________ Date ________________

English/
Language Arts

ELA3R3

Comprehension

The Author's Purpose

DIRECTIONS: Read the passage and answer the questions that follow.

Animal Mysteries

As long as people have studied animals, they have wondered about why animals act certain ways. Animal behavior can be a real mystery.

One mystery has to do with some animals' strange behavior before earthquakes. Horses and cattle stampede, seabirds screech, dogs howl, and some animals even come out of hibernation early before an earthquake begins.

Another mystery involves birds and ants. No one can explain why a bird will pick up an ant in its beak and rub the ant over its feathers again and again. This is called "anting," and birds have been known to do this for an hour without stopping.

One animal mystery is very sad. For hundreds of years, some whales have swum into shallow waters and mysteriously grounded themselves on a beach where they might die. Reports of beached whales occur about five times a year somewhere in the world.

1. Which sentence best summarizes the author's feelings about animals?

- (A) She is curious about animals.
- (B) She understands animals completely.
- (C) She does not like animals.
- (D) She wishes animals were quieter.

2. What word(s) in the passage helped you guess how the author felt about animals?

____

____

3. The author most likely has written this passage to _________ .

- (F) study animal behavior before earthquakes
- (G) explain why whales beach themselves
- (H) explain why birds rub ants on their feathers
- (J) tell readers about some interesting animal mysteries

Name ______________________________ Date ______________

English/
Language Arts

ELA3R3

Using a Dictionary

Comprehension

Remember, dictionary entries can tell you more than just the meaning of a word. They also can help you say a word correctly and tell you if a word is a noun, verb, adjective, adverb, or pronoun.

DIRECTIONS: Use the dictionary entries to answer numbers 1–3.

save [sāv] *v.* **1.** to rescue from harm or danger **2.** to keep in a safe condition **3.** to set aside for future use; store **4.** to avoid

saving [sā´vĭng] *n.* **1.** rescuing from harm or danger **2.** avoiding excess spending; economy **3.** something saved

savory [sā´və-rē] *adj.* **1.** appealing to the taste or smell **2.** salty to the taste

1. The *a* in the word *saving* sounds most like the word _________ .

Ⓐ pat
Ⓑ ape
Ⓒ heated
Ⓓ naughty

2. Which sentence uses *save* in the same way as definition number 3?

Ⓕ Firefighters save lives.
Ⓖ She saves half of all she earns.
Ⓗ Going by jet saves eight hours of driving.
Ⓙ The life jacket saved the boy from drowning.

3. Which sentence uses *savory* in the same way as definition number 2?

Ⓐ The savory stew made me thirsty.
Ⓑ The savory bank opened an account.
Ⓒ This flower has a savory scent.
Ⓓ The savory dog rescued me.

DIRECTIONS: Use the dictionary entry to answer numbers 4–5.

beam [bēm] *n.* **1.** a squared-off log used to support a building **2.** a ray of light **3.** the wooden roller in a loom *v.* **1.** to shine **2.** to smile broadly

4. Which use of the word *beam* is a verb?

Ⓕ The beam held up the plaster ceiling.
Ⓖ The beam of sunlight warmed the room.
Ⓗ She moved the beam before she added a row of wool.
Ⓙ The bright stars beam in the night sky.

5. Which sentence uses the word *beam* in the same way as the first definition of the noun?

Ⓐ The ceiling beam had fallen into the room.
Ⓑ The beam of the loom was broken.
Ⓒ She beamed her approval.
Ⓓ The beam of sunlight came through the tree.

Name ______________________________ Date ______________

English/
Language Arts

ELA3R3

Using a Thesaurus

Comprehension

DIRECTIONS: Use the sample thesaurus to answer questions 1–4.

head [hed] *n.* **1.** skull, scalp, *noggin **2.** leader, commander, director, chief, manager **3.** top, summit, peak **4.** front **5.** toilet, restroom (on a boat) **6.** come to a head, reach the end or turning point **7.** heads up, watch out, duck, be careful **8.** keep one's head, stay calm, *roll with the punches

head [hed] *v.* **1.** lead, command, direct, supervise

Key: *adj*. adjective, *adv*. adverb, *n.* noun, *v*. verb, *slang

DIRECTIONS: Choose the best synonym to replace the underlined word in each sentence.

1. The brain is inside the <u>head</u>.

- (A) front
- (B) top
- (C) summit
- (D) skull

2. Michael asked if he could come aboard our boat and use the <u>head</u>.

- (F) summit
- (G) manager
- (H) toilet
- (J) scalp

3. Captain Blaine was the <u>head</u> of the army.

- (A) commander
- (B) top
- (C) peak
- (D) front

4. "Noggin" and "roll with the punches" are both examples of

- (F) verbs
- (G) nouns
- (H) slang
- (J) adjectives

5. How is the underlined word used in this sentence? She was chosen to <u>head</u> the Art Club.

- (A) noun
- (B) verb
- (C) slang
- (D) adverb

6. What would be another way to say "Watch out!"?

- (F) keep your head
- (G) come to a head
- (H) heads up
- (J) roll with the punches

7. How is the underlined word used in the sentence? She was able to keep her <u>head</u> when everyone else was panicking.

- (A) adjective
- (B) adverb
- (C) verb
- (D) noun

STOP

Name ______________________ Date ______________

English/
Language Arts

ELA3R1–ELA3R3

For pages 8–27

Mini-Test 1

Reading

DIRECTIONS: Read the passage and answer the questions.

A Microscope

Have you ever looked into a microscope? A microscope is an <u>instrument</u> that helps us see very small things by <u>magnifying</u> them. Scientists and doctors can use microscopes to study parts of the body, such as blood and skin cells. They can also study germs, tiny plants, and tiny animals.

1. In this passage, what does the word *instrument* mean?

- (A) a tool
- (B) a drum
- (C) an office
- (D) a paper

2. Which of the following is a synonym for *thrilling*?

- (F) long
- (G) boring
- (H) exciting
- (J) interesting

3. Which of the following is an antonym for *continue*?

- (A) stop
- (B) go on
- (C) roost
- (D) sleep

4. Find the word in which only the prefix is underlined.

- (F) <u>pre</u>view
- (G) de<u>cide</u>
- (H) <u>ale</u>rt
- (J) mon<u>ster</u>

5. Find the answer in which the underlined word is used in the same way as in this sentence.

Don't <u>break</u> the glass!

- (A) We are going to Florida during our spring <u>break</u>.
- (B) David took a <u>break</u> from his work.
- (C) I wish you would give me a <u>break</u>.
- (D) She had to <u>break</u> open her piggy bank.

DIRECTIONS: Read the passages and answer the questions.

Sign Language

Sign language is used by people who are not able to hear or speak well. They use their hands instead of their voices to talk. Their hand signals may be different letters, words, or whole ideas.

Sign language is used by other people, too. Have you ever watched a football or basketball game? The referees use hand signals to let people know what has happened in the game. Signs can mean "foul," "time out," or can let players know when a play was good.

Guess who else uses sign language? You do! You wave your hand for *hello* and *goodbye.* You nod your head up and down to say *yes* and back and forth to say *no.* You point to show which way to go. Sign language is used by people everywhere as another way of communicating.

6. This passage is which genre (type) of literature?

- (F) poetry
- (G) fiction
- (H) nonfiction
- (J) drama

Name ______________________________ Date ______________

7. What is the main idea of this passage?

- Ⓐ Sign language is used by people who cannot hear well.
- Ⓑ Sign language is important to many sports.
- Ⓒ Sign language is not used in all countries.
- Ⓓ Sign language is used by people everywhere.

8. Which sentence is an opinion?

- Ⓕ Sign language is used as another way of communicating.
- Ⓖ Sign language is very interesting.
- Ⓗ Sign language is used in sports.
- Ⓙ Sign language is done with hand signals.

The Runner

Alanna loved to run. She ran to school and she ran home. She ran to the library and to her friends' houses. One day she ran downstairs and said, "I think I'll train for the marathon this summer to raise money for the homeless shelter." She knew that the winner would get a trophy and $1,000 for the shelter.

Alanna started to train for the marathon. She bought a new pair of running shoes. She ran on the track and on the sidewalks. After a month, her knees started to hurt. The pain got worse, and her mother took Alanna to the doctor. "You have runner's knees," said the doctor. "You have done too much running without warming up. You'll have to do some exercises to strengthen your knees."

Alanna had to slow down for a couple of weeks. As she exercised, her pain decreased. Soon she was able to run again. At the end of August, her friends stood cheering as Alanna broke the tape at the marathon.

9. What word best describes Alanna?

- Ⓐ smart
- Ⓑ athletic
- Ⓒ musical
- Ⓓ stubborn

10. What is the setting at the end of the story?

- Ⓕ Alanna's home
- Ⓖ the doctor's office
- Ⓗ the marathon
- Ⓙ Alanna's school

11. What is the plot or problem in the story?

- Ⓐ Alanna loses the marathon.
- Ⓑ Alanna runs on the sidewalk and ruins her shoes.
- Ⓒ Alanna runs in too many places and hurts her knees.
- Ⓓ Alanna runs without warming up and gets runner's knees.

DIRECTIONS: Use the sample index for numbers 12–13.

O

12. You will find information about what topic on page 365?

- Ⓕ ocean temperatures
- Ⓖ density of the ocean
- Ⓗ waves
- Ⓙ the octopus

13. On what pages will you most likely find information about mining the oceans for minerals?

- Ⓐ pages 175–176
- Ⓑ pages 368–369
- Ⓒ pages 373–375
- Ⓓ pages 371–372

STOP

Writing Standards

The student writes clear, coherent text that develops a central idea or tells a story. The writing shows consideration of the audience and purpose. The student progresses through the stages of the writing process (e.g., prewriting, drafting, revising, and editing).

ELA3W1. The student demonstrates competency in the writing process. ***(See pages 31–39.)*** **The student:**

a. captures a reader's interest by setting a purpose and developing a point of view.
b. begins to select a focus and an organizational pattern based on purpose, genre, expectations, audience, and length.
c. writes text of a length appropriate to address the topic or tell the story.
d. uses organizational patterns for conveying information (e.g., chronological order, cause and effect, similarity and difference, questions and answers).
e. begins to use appropriate structures to ensure coherence (e.g., transition words and phrases, bullets, subheadings, numbering).
f. begins to use specific sensory details (e.g., strong verbs, adjectives) to enhance descriptive effect.
g. begins to develop characters through action and dialogue.
h. begins to use descriptive adjectives and verbs to communicate setting, character, and plot.
i. begins to include relevant examples, facts, anecdotes, and details appropriate to the audience.
j. uses a variety of resources to research and share information on a topic.
k. writes a response to literature that demonstrates understanding of the text, formulates an opinion, and supports a judgment.
l. writes a persuasive piece that states a clear position.
m. prewrites to generate ideas, develops a rough draft, rereads to revise, and edits to correct.
n. publishes by presenting an edited piece of writing to others.

Name ______________________ Date ______________

English/
Language Arts

ELA3W1

Writing

Understanding Point of View

DIRECTIONS: Read the passages and then answer the questions.

A Sad Tale

A I felt sorry for Jason when I saw him come in this morning. He looked so sad. When it was finally time for recess, I asked him to stay behind. Then he told me his problem. With one quick phone call, the problem was solved.

B I was in such a rush this morning I forgot my lunch. Mom had packed extra cookies today. At recess, Ms. Warner asked me what was wrong. Then she made a phone call and Mom soon brought my lunch.

C As soon as Jason left for the bus, I saw his lunch sitting on the counter. I had planned to bring it to school anyway, but I was glad that Ms. Warner called. Jason was so happy to see those cookies again.

1. Who is the writer of passage A?

____

____

How does this person help?

____

____

2. Who is the writer of passage B?

____

____

What is this person's main problem?

____

____

3. Who is the writer of passage C?

____

____

How does this person help?

____

____

4. What is being described in all three passages?

____

____

____

____

STOP

Name ______________________________ Date ______________

English/
Language Arts

ELA3W1

Writing

Using Writing Structures

DIRECTIONS: Read the paragraph that tells how to make a peanut butter and jelly sandwich. Then think of something you like to make or do. Write a paragraph that tells how to make it. Use the words *first, next, then,* and *last* to show the transition between steps.

These steps tell how to make a peanut butter and jelly sandwich. First, get two pieces of bread, peanut butter, jelly, and a knife. Next, spread peanut butter on one piece of bread. Then, spread jelly on the other piece. Last, press the two pieces of bread together.

1. ______________________________

DIRECTIONS: Read the paragraph below about how to make a peanut butter and jelly sandwich. Notice that the steps are now numbered. In the space below, rewrite your directions for number 1. This time, use numbered steps instead of transitional words.

These steps tell how to make a peanut butter and jelly sandwich.

1. Get two pieces of bread, peanut butter, jelly, and a knife.
2. Spread peanut butter on one piece of bread.
3. Spread jelly on the other piece.
4. Press the two pieces of bread together.

2. ______________________________

Name ________________________________ Date ________________

English/ Language Arts

ELA3W1

Writing

Developing Characters

DIRECTIONS: Read the story, and then answer the questions about the characters on the next page.

From *Through the Looking Glass,* by Lewis Carroll

"She can't do Subtraction," said the White Queen. "Can you do Division? Divide a loaf by a knife—what's the answer to that?"

"I suppose—" Alice was beginning, but the Red Queen answered for her. "Bread-and-Butter, of course. Try another Subtraction sum. Take a bone from a dog: what remains?"

Alice considered. "The bone wouldn't remain, of course, if I took it—and the dog wouldn't remain: it would come to bite me—and I'm sure I shouldn't remain!"

"Then you think nothing would remain?" said the Red Queen.

"I think that's the answer."

"Wrong, as usual," said the Red Queen. "The dog's temper would remain."

"But I don't see how—"

"Why, look here!" the Red Queen cried. "The dog would lose its temper, wouldn't it?"

"Perhaps, it would," Alice replied cautiously.

"Then, if the dog went away, its temper would remain!" the Queen exclaimed triumphantly.

Alice said, as gravely as she could, "They might go different ways." But she couldn't help thinking to herself, "What dreadful nonsense we are talking!"

. . . Here the Red Queen began again. "Can you answer useful questions?" she said. "How is bread made?"

"I know that!" Alice cried eagerly. "You take some flour—"

"Where do you pick the flower?" the White Queen asked. "In a garden or in the hedges?"

"Well, it isn't picked at all," Alice explained: "it's ground—"

"How many acres of ground?" said the White Queen. "You mustn't leave out so many things."

"Fan her head!" the Red Queen anxiously interrupted. "She'll be feverish after so much thinking."

Name ______________________________ Date ______________

1. Which word tells how Alice might be feeling by the end of the passage?

- (A) hopeful
- (B) proud
- (C) frustrated
- (D) excited

2. Which word tells how the Red Queen and the White Queen might be feeling by the end of the passage?

- (F) sorry
- (G) pleased
- (H) sad
- (J) shy

3. Describe each character with two words.

Red Queen ______________________________

____

White Queen ______________________________

____

Alice ______________________________

____

4. Words that sound the same but have different meanings are called *homophones.* Which homophones does the White Queen use at the end of the story?

- (A) whether, weather
- (B) pail, pale
- (C) write, right
- (D) flour, flower

5. Answer the following question with an imaginary dialogue between the Queens and Alice. *How do you make pizza?* Words to consider: dough, flour, ham, cheese.

____

____

____

____

____

____

____

____

____

____

____

____

____

____

____

____

____

____

____

____

____

____

Name ____________________ Date ____________

English/
Language Arts

ELA3W1

Writing

Creating Setting, Character, and Plot

DIRECTIONS: Read the short story about a friend's visit. Then think about a fiction story you would like to write. Write one or two sentences to answer each question below.

Juan looked at the clock. He paced across the floor. His best friend, Bill, was coming to visit for the first time in six months. Bill had moved very far away. Juan wondered if they would still feel like good friends.

The doorbell rang, and Juan raced to answer it. Bill looked a bit unsure. Juan smiled and started talking just as he always had when they had lived near one another. He made Bill feel comfortable. As the day went on, it felt like old times.

1. **Think about the main character. Who is it? What is he or she like? What adjectives would you use to describe this person?**

2. **Where does the story take place? When does the story take place? What adjectives would you use to describe the setting?**

3. **What problem will the main character have? How will he or she try to solve the problem?**

4. **What verbs are used in the passage to describe what Juan is doing? How do the verbs help describe how Juan was feeling about Bill's visit?**

STOP

Name ______________________ Date ______________

English/
Language Arts

ELA3W1

Writing

Using Resources for Research

DIRECTIONS: Choose the best answer

1. **Where would you look to find information about sharks?**
   - Ⓐ in a newspaper
   - Ⓑ in a history book
   - Ⓒ in a dictionary
   - Ⓓ in an encyclopedia

2. **Where would you look to check the pronunciation of to word *accept*?**
   - Ⓕ in a newspaper
   - Ⓖ in an atlas
   - Ⓗ in a dictionary
   - Ⓙ in an encyclopedia

3. **Where would you look to find information about today's weather forecast?**
   - Ⓐ in a newspaper
   - Ⓑ in an atlas
   - Ⓒ in a dictionary
   - Ⓓ in an encyclopedia

4. **Where would you look to find a map of Georgia?**
   - Ⓕ in a newspaper
   - Ⓖ in an atlas
   - Ⓗ in a telephone book
   - Ⓙ in a math textbook

5. **Where would you look to find the president of a company?**
   - Ⓐ in an atlas
   - Ⓑ in a history book
   - Ⓒ on the company's Web site
   - Ⓓ in an encyclopedia

6. **Where would you look to find the date the Gulf War ended?**
   - Ⓕ in a newspaper
   - Ⓖ in an atlas
   - Ⓗ in a dictionary
   - Ⓙ in a history textbook

7. **Raina and Miguel have decided to open a pizza shop. Where should they look to find out how many other pizza shops are in the area?**
   - Ⓐ in an encyclopedia under "business"
   - Ⓑ in a dictionary under "pizza"
   - Ⓒ in the Yellow Pages of the telephone book
   - Ⓓ in an atlas

8. **Where would you look to find information about the fourth president of the United States?**
   - Ⓕ in a newspaper
   - Ⓖ in a magazine
   - Ⓗ in a dictionary
   - Ⓙ in an encyclopedia

9. **Where would you look to find the types of animals in a desert?**
   - Ⓐ in a dictionary
   - Ⓑ in a newspaper
   - Ⓒ in an atlas
   - Ⓓ in an encyclopedia

Name ______________________________ Date ______________

English/
Language Arts

ELA3W1

Writing

Writing to Persuade

DIRECTIONS: Read the letter below. In the letter, a girl explains to her father why she should be allowed to try in-line skating. Think of something you would like to be allowed to do. Write a letter to someone explaining why you should be allowed to do it. Provide at least three reasons to support your position.

Dear Dad,

I would like to try in-line skating. I know that you think it is not safe, but I would be very careful. I would follow every safety rule. I would wear a helmet, elbow pads, and knee pads. I would skate only in safe places. Please give me a chance.

Love,
Bonita

STOP

Name ______________________________ Date ______________

Writing

English/ Language Arts

ELA3W1

Generating Ideas

A *web* is a way to brainstorm ideas by putting them into a drawing. The circle in the middle shows the main topic. The other circles contain ideas about the main topic.

Here is an example of a web about cats.

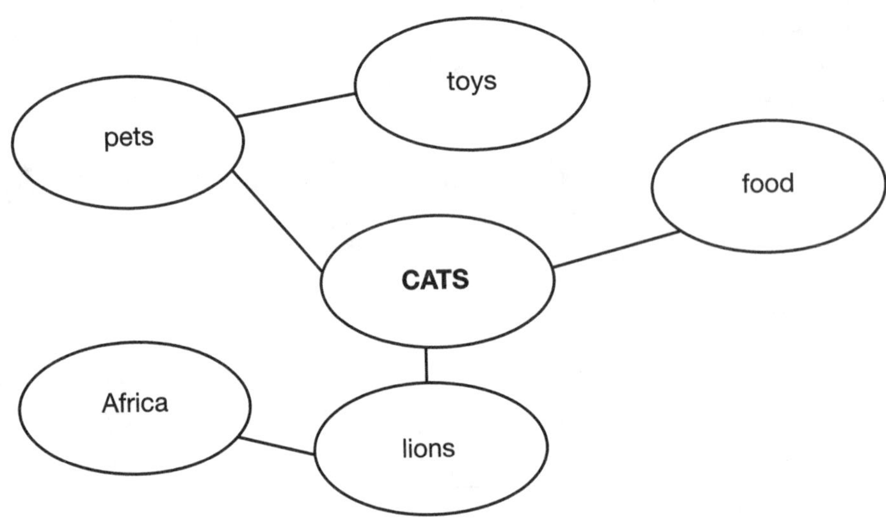

Now pick a topic of your own and brainstorm a web. Draw lines to connect any ideas that are related.

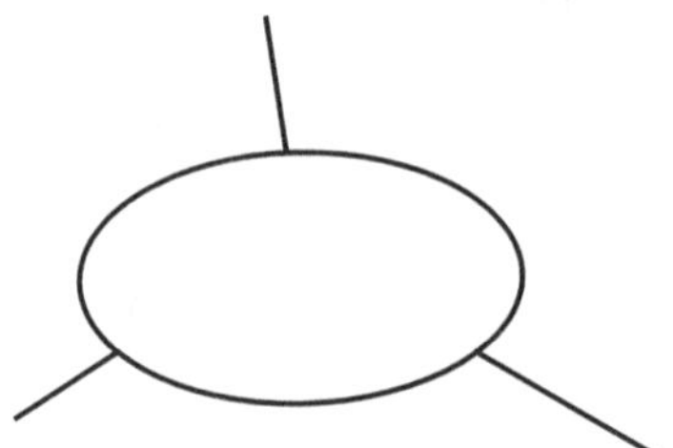

STOP

Name ______________________________ Date ______________

English/
Language Arts
ELA3W1

Writing

Revising and Editing

DIRECTIONS: Read the journal entry. Then answer numbers 1–5. If the sentence needs no changes, choose "correct as it is."

(1) My parents and I, we are flying to Chicago tomorrow. **(2)** My father is attending a business conference. **(3)** While Dad is working, Mom and I am seeing the sights. **(4)** Go to the top of the Hancock Building and the Water Tower. **(5)** We will visiting my Aunt Ruth, too. **(6)** I can hardly wait to go! **(7)** We were leaving at seven o'clock tomorrow morning.

1. Sentence 1 is best written—

Ⓐ My parents and I are flying to Chicago tomorrow.

Ⓑ My parents and I were flying to Chicago tomorrow.

Ⓒ My parents and I, we flew to Chicago tomorrow.

Ⓓ correct as it is

2. Sentence 2 is best written—

Ⓕ My father is attended a business conference.

Ⓖ My father will attending a business conference.

Ⓗ My father attends a business conference.

Ⓙ correct as it is

3. Sentence 5 is best written—

Ⓐ We have visited my Aunt Ruth, too.

Ⓑ We will be visiting my Aunt Ruth, too.

Ⓒ We are visit my Aunt Ruth,

Ⓓ correct as it is

4. Sentence 7 is best written—

Ⓕ We will leaving at seven o'clock tomorrow morning.

Ⓖ We are leaving at seven o'clock tomorrow morning.

Ⓗ We be leaving at seven o'clock tomorrow morning.

Ⓙ correct as it is

5. Which of these is *not* a sentence?

Ⓐ sentence 1

Ⓑ sentence 3

Ⓒ sentence 4

Ⓓ sentence 7

DIRECTIONS: For numbers 6–7, read the topic sentence. Then choose the answer that develops the topic sentence in the best way.

6. Some animals and insects are speedy creatures.

Ⓕ A hummingbird can fly 60 miles an hour, and a duck can fly twice that fast.

Ⓖ Snails move very slowly.

Ⓗ Ducks and hummingbirds are both birds.

Ⓙ There are animals that are fast and some that are slow.

7. The canary is one of the best-liked of all pet birds.

Ⓐ Canaries are not only pretty, but they sing cheerful songs.

Ⓑ Canaries can be yellow, red, or orange.

Ⓒ You have to be careful with a pet bird, or it may escape.

Ⓓ Canaries like to live in the Canary Islands.

STOP

Name ______________________ Date ______________

English/ Language Arts

ELA3W1

For pages 31–39

Mini-Test 2

Writing

DIRECTIONS: Read the following steps to create a report.

1. **Generate ideas for a report on your favorite hobby. Use the space below to organize your ideas. To help you organize your ideas, use a web diagram, list, or chart.**

2. **Create a draft of your report. Be sure to include a topic sentence, supporting details, and a conclusion.**

3. **Edit your draft using appropriate proofreading marks. Revise any sentences that can be improved.**

4. **Write your final report on a separate sheet of paper.**

Conventions Standards

Conventions are essential for reading, writing, and speaking. Instruction in language conventions will, therefore, occur within the context of reading, writing, and speaking, rather than in isolation. The student writes to make connections with the larger world. A student's ideas are more likely to be taken seriously when the words are spelled accurately and the sentences are grammatically correct. Use of Standard English conventions helps readers understand and follow the student's meaning, while errors can be distracting and confusing.

ELA3C1. The student demonstrates understanding and control of the rules of the English language, realizing that usage involves the appropriate application of conventions and grammar in both written and spoken formats. ***(See pages 42–50.)*** **The student:**

- **a.** correctly identifies and uses subject/verb agreement and adjectives.
- **b.** identifies and uses nouns (singular, plural, possessive) correctly.
- **c.** identifies and uses contractions correctly.
- **d.** identifies and uses personal and possessive pronouns.
- **e.** speaks and writes in complete and coherent sentences.
- **f.** identifies and uses increasingly complex sentence structure.
- **g.** distinguishes between complete and incomplete sentences.
- **h.** demonstrates knowledge of when to use formal or informal language exchanges (e.g., slang, colloquialisms, idioms).
- **i.** when appropriate, determines the meaning of a word based on how it is used in an orally presented sentence.
- **j.** uses resources (encyclopedias, Internet, books) to research and share information about a topic.
- **k.** uses the dictionary and thesaurus to support word choices.
- **l.** uses common rules of spelling and corrects words using dictionaries and other resources.
- **m.** uses appropriate capitalization and punctuation (end marks, commas, apostrophes, quotation marks).
- **n.** writes legibly in cursive, leaving space between letters in a word and between words in a sentence.

Name ______________________________ Date ______________

English/ Language Arts

ELA3C1

Conventions

Subject and Verb Agreement

DIRECTIONS: Choose the answer that best completes the sentence.

1. **Chang and Audrey made _________ kites together.**
   - (A) him
   - (B) she
   - (C) they
   - (D) their

2. **Are _________ parents coming to the concert?**
   - (F) she
   - (G) he
   - (H) her
   - (J) it

3. **_________ spoke to my mother on Parents' Night.**
   - (A) Him
   - (B) He
   - (C) Us
   - (D) Them

DIRECTIONS: Choose the answer that could replace the underlined word.

4. **<u>Tyrone</u> has a baseball card collection.**
   - (F) Him
   - (G) He
   - (H) We
   - (J) Them

5. **<u>Jill and Keisha</u> went to soccer practice.**
   - (A) Him
   - (B) Them
   - (C) They
   - (D) She

6. **I thought <u>the play</u> was very good.**
   - (F) him
   - (G) her
   - (H) we
   - (J) it

DIRECTIONS: Choose the answer that uses an incorrect verb.

7.
   - (A) The skipper steering the boat.
   - (B) The wind blew across the lake.
   - (C) The boat stayed on course.
   - (D) The brave skipper brought the boat safely to shore.

8.
   - (F) The dentist cleaned my teeth.
   - (G) I was worried he might have to use the drill.
   - (H) He were very nice.
   - (J) My teeth are shiny now!

9.
   - (A) The pioneer chose his land carefully.
   - (B) He wanted a stream near his cabin.
   - (C) He wanting good land for crops.
   - (D) He knew he could use the trees for building.

STOP

Name ______________________________ Date ______________

English/
Language Arts

ELA3C1

Conventions

Adjectives

DIRECTIONS: Read each item. For numbers 1–4, choose the word or phrase that best completes the sentence.

1. Albert is the _________ person I know.

- (A) funny
- (B) more funny
- (C) funnier
- (D) funniest

2. I think my new dog is the _________ birthday present I've ever had.

- (F) most wonderful
- (G) wonderfullest
- (H) more wonderful
- (J) wonderful

3. I would like the _________ of the two pieces of cake.

- (A) smallest
- (B) small
- (C) smaller
- (D) more small

4. That is the _________ ice cream I've ever had.

- (F) better
- (G) most best
- (H) best
- (J) good

DIRECTIONS: For numbers 5–8, choose the sentence that is written correctly.

5.
- (A) It was the most small elephant.
- (B) First, she climbed onto the tallest platform.
- (C) Then the most short clown climbed up, too.
- (D) These greater circus performers danced together.

6.
- (F) I think camping is the funnest thing to do.
- (G) We take our biggest tent, the one with the little window.
- (H) We find the more quiet campsite we can.
- (J) I think our favoriter place is by a little lake in the woods.

7.
- (A) This is my most better coat.
- (B) This more good coat is my favorite.
- (C) It is also more warmer than my other coats.
- (D) It is the brightest red that I've ever seen.

8.
- (F) The more emptier house is up for sale.
- (G) My most best friend used to live there.
- (H) Her mother is the kindest person I know.
- (J) I was so saddest to see them move away.

STOP

Name ______________________________ Date ______________

English/
Language Arts

ELA3C1

Conventions

Nouns

DIRECTIONS: Read each sentence. Decide if the underlined noun is singular, plural, or possessive. Write **S** for singular, **P** for plural, and **PS** for possessive.

Examples:

A noun is a **singular noun** when it is one person, place, or thing.

Example: The **dog** is running in circles.

A noun is a **plural noun** when it is more than one person, place, or thing.

Example: The **dogs** are chasing each other.

A noun is a **possessive noun** when it shows possession or ownership. To show that a singular noun owns something, add **'s** to the noun.

Example: The **dog's** water bowl is empty.

_________ **1. Kyle and Eric went to the park today.**

_________ **2. The school's library has thousands of books.**

_________ **3. I like to study maps.**

_________ **4. The geese are flying south for the winter.**

_________ **5. The farmer's crops did very well this summer.**

_________ **6. Kathy likes to ride her horse in the pasture.**

_________ **7. Those paintings are beautiful!**

_________ **8. Did you see how fast the pitcher threw that ball?**

_________ **9. My teacher's classroom is bright and colorful.**

_________ **10. Brittany chose to write her report on bears.**

_________ **11. I'd like to be a fireman when I grow up.**

_________ **12. Amanda's computer needs to be repaired.**

_________ **13. She loved to dance and read books.**

STOP

Name ______________________ Date ______________

English/ Language Arts

ELA3C1

Conventions

Contractions

DIRECTIONS: Choose the answer that shows the correct contraction.

1. **We ________ ready for the test.**
   - (A) were'nt
   - (B) weren't
   - (C) we'rent
   - (D) wer'ent

2. **The cake ________ in the oven.**
   - (F) isn't
   - (G) isn't'
   - (H) isnt
   - (J) is'nt

3. **The book ________ on the shelf.**
   - (A) was'nt
   - (B) wasnt
   - (C) wasn't
   - (D) wasn't'

4. **________ forget to bring home your uniform!**
   - (F) Dont
   - (G) Don't
   - (H) Dont'
   - (J) Do'nt

5. **I ________ eaten my lunch yet.**
   - (A) have'nt
   - (B) havent'
   - (C) haven't
   - (D) havent

6. **Dave ________ get his computer to work.**
   - (F) couldn't
   - (G) could'nt
   - (H) cou'ldn't
   - (J) couldnt

7. **________ a great friend.**
   - (A) Youre
   - (B) Your'e
   - (C) Youre'
   - (D) You're

8. **________ great to be going on vacation!**
   - (F) Its
   - (G) I'ts
   - (H) Its'
   - (J) It's

9. **________ going to the park today.**
   - (A) Were
   - (B) W'ere
   - (C) Wer'e
   - (D) We're

10. **The queen ________ wave to the crowd.**
    - (F) didnt
    - (G) didn't'
    - (H) didn't
    - (J) did'nt

NAME BILLY

STOP

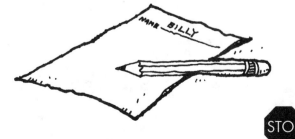

Name ______________________________ Date ______________

English/
Language Arts

ELA3C1

Conventions

Pronouns

DIRECTIONS: For numbers 1–3, choose the pronoun that best completes the sentence.

1. **Fred and Janna gave ________ report today.**
   - Ⓐ him
   - Ⓑ she
   - Ⓒ them
   - Ⓓ their

2. **Please tell ________ to take this note home.**
   - Ⓕ she
   - Ⓖ he
   - Ⓗ her
   - Ⓙ it

3. **________ called my father on Sunday.**
   - Ⓐ Him
   - Ⓑ He
   - Ⓒ Us
   - Ⓓ Them

DIRECTIONS: For numbers 4–6, choose the pronoun that could replace the underlined word(s).

4. **<u>Tim and Lee</u> washed the dishes.**
   - Ⓕ Him
   - Ⓖ Them
   - Ⓗ They
   - Ⓙ She

5. **Did <u>Amanda</u> get her computer repaired?**
   - Ⓐ her
   - Ⓑ she
   - Ⓒ it
   - Ⓓ us

6. **When did you notice <u>the book</u> was missing?**
   - Ⓕ him
   - Ⓖ her
   - Ⓗ we
   - Ⓙ it

DIRECTIONS: For numbers 7–9, choose the answer that has a mistake.

7.
   - Ⓐ The dog followed him home.
   - Ⓑ Him asked if he could keep it.
   - Ⓒ His parents said that they needed to look for the owner first.
   - Ⓓ But he could keep the dog if the owner couldn't be found.

8.
   - Ⓕ They rode through the mud puddles.
   - Ⓖ Jack and Kim were laughing, and they couldn't stop.
   - Ⓗ He was covered with mud.
   - Ⓙ They bikes were muddy, too.

9.
   - Ⓐ On Saturday, she worked on her hobby.
   - Ⓑ Her hobby is photography.
   - Ⓒ Her has taken some good pictures.
   - Ⓓ We have one that we framed and put in our family room.

Name ______________________________ Date ______________

English/ Language Arts

ELA3C1

Conventions

Sentences

DIRECTIONS: Choose the sentence that is correct and complete.

1. Ⓐ Mr. Woo opens his store early.
   Ⓑ Always kind to us.
   Ⓒ Food and other things.
   Ⓓ Like to shop there.

2. Ⓕ We are going on a trip.
   Ⓖ To Japan, China, and Korea.
   Ⓗ Packing our suitcases.
   Ⓙ Can't wait to travel and have fun!

3. Ⓐ Jars of paint are out.
   Ⓑ Painting of trees and flowers.
   Ⓒ I am going to paint for an hour.
   Ⓓ Wonderful to have art class.

DIRECTIONS: Choose the sentence that is incomplete.

4. Ⓕ The train is coming down the tracks.
   Ⓖ I can hear the rumbling of the train.
   Ⓗ A bright headlight and a loud whistle.
   Ⓙ It has fifty cars and a caboose.

5. Ⓐ The birds are smart to do this.
   Ⓑ Using the dust like a bathtub.
   Ⓒ The dust helps them get rid of tiny bugs in their feathers.
   Ⓓ Bird watchers sometimes see birds taking dust baths.

6. Ⓕ Its petals are yellow.
   Ⓖ The sunflower can be up to a foot wide.
   Ⓗ The stem of this flower is very tall.
   Ⓙ Some sunflowers twice as tall as children.

DIRECTIONS: Choose the best combination of the underlined sentences.

7. **Field Day is my favorite day at school. Field Day is May 10.**
   Ⓐ Field Day is my favorite day at school and it is May 10.
   Ⓑ Field Day, my favorite day at school, is May 10.
   Ⓒ Field Day is May 10, my favorite day at school.
   Ⓓ Field Day is my favorite day, May 10, at school.

8. **I like pizza for dinner. I like mushroom pizza.**
   Ⓕ I like mushroom pizza, and I like it for dinner.
   Ⓖ I like pizza, mushroom pizza, for dinner.
   Ⓗ I like mushroom pizza for dinner.
   Ⓙ I like pizza for dinner, and I like mushroom pizza.

9. **Parrots live in the tropics. Parrots are beautiful birds.**
   Ⓐ Parrots are beautiful birds that live in the tropics.
   Ⓑ Parrots, beautiful birds, live in the tropics.
   Ⓒ Parrots live in the tropics and are beautiful birds.
   Ⓓ Parrots, that live in the tropics, are beautiful birds.

Name ______________________________ Date ______________

English/ Language Arts

ELA3C1

Conventions

Spelling

DIRECTIONS: For numbers 1–6, find the underlined word that is not spelled correctly.

1.
- (A) <u>identify</u> a bird
- (B) bottle of <u>juice</u>
- (C) <u>quiet</u> room
- (D) all correct

2.
- (F) easy <u>lesson</u>
- (G) bright <u>lites</u>
- (H) <u>paddle</u> a canoe
- (J) all correct

3.
- (A) good <u>balance</u>
- (B) <u>delicious</u> stew
- (C) <u>private</u> property
- (D) all correct

4.
- (F) great <u>relief</u>
- (G) our <u>mayor</u>
- (H) <u>sunnie</u> day
- (J) all correct

5.
- (A) <u>forty</u> years
- (B) <u>twelve</u> pears
- (C) a <u>thousend</u> questions
- (D) all correct

6.
- (F) my <u>brother</u>
- (G) your <u>friend</u>
- (H) his <u>uncle</u>
- (J) all correct

DIRECTIONS: For numbers 7–11, find the word that is spelled correctly and fits best in the blank.

7. We opened the ________ .
- (A) presence
- (B) presants
- (C) presents
- (D) prasents

8. We picked ________ in our garden.
- (F) berries
- (G) berrys
- (H) berrese
- (J) berreis

9. The ________ helped me.
- (A) nourse
- (B) nurce
- (C) nirse
- (D) nurse

10. The answer to this problem is a ________ .
- (F) frackshun
- (G) fracteon
- (H) fraction
- (J) fracton

11. Did you ________ the page?
- (A) tare
- (B) tair
- (C) tear
- (D) taer

Name ______________________ Date ______________

English/ Language Arts

ELA3C1

Conventions

Capitalization

Clue Remember that sentences and proper nouns start with capital letters.

DIRECTIONS: For numbers 1–5, choose the answer that has a missing capital letter. If no capital letters are missing, choose the answer "none."

1.
- Ⓐ I want
- Ⓑ to read the book,
- Ⓒ *The Light in the window.*
- Ⓓ none

2.
- Ⓕ Oliver knows
- Ⓖ he isn't
- Ⓗ supposed to do that.
- Ⓙ none

3.
- Ⓐ The theater
- Ⓑ is on
- Ⓒ Front street.
- Ⓓ none

4.
- Ⓕ did you
- Ⓖ find your gift
- Ⓗ on the table?
- Ⓙ none

5.
- Ⓐ Tanya lives
- Ⓑ on a quiet street
- Ⓒ in Chicago, illinois.
- Ⓓ none

DIRECTIONS: For numbers 6–9, choose the answer that has the correct capitalization.

6. The ruler of England at that time was _________ .
- Ⓕ king George I
- Ⓖ King George I
- Ⓗ king george I
- Ⓙ King george I

7. The bus arrived at _________ more than three hours late.
- Ⓐ the Station
- Ⓑ The station
- Ⓒ The Station
- Ⓓ the station

8. How was your visit with _________ ?
- Ⓕ aunt alice
- Ⓖ Aunt alice
- Ⓗ Aunt Alice
- Ⓙ aunt Alice

9. My uncle lives in _________ .
- Ⓐ Paris, france
- Ⓑ paris, france
- Ⓒ Paris, France
- Ⓓ paris, France

STOP

Name ______________________________ Date ______________

English/
Language Arts

ELA3C1

Conventions

Punctuation

DIRECTIONS: Choose the answer that shows the correct ending punctuation mark.

1. **Watch out**

   Ⓐ .
   Ⓑ ,
   Ⓒ !
   Ⓓ ?

2. **There were many people at the party**

   Ⓕ .
   Ⓖ ,
   Ⓗ !
   Ⓙ ?

3. **Do you like strawberries**

   Ⓐ .
   Ⓑ ,
   Ⓒ !
   Ⓓ ?

DIRECTIONS: Choose the answer that shows the correct punctuation.

4. **The cake ________ in the oven.**

   Ⓕ wasn't
   Ⓖ wasn't'
   Ⓗ wasnt
   Ⓙ was'nt

5. **Her birthday is ________ .**

   Ⓐ October 16, 1998
   Ⓑ October, 16 1998
   Ⓒ October 16 1998
   Ⓓ October, 16, 1998

6. Ⓕ Lin's family lives in, San Diego California.
   Ⓖ Lin's family lives in San, Diego California.
   Ⓗ Lin's family lives in San, Diego, California.
   Ⓙ Lin's family lives in San Diego, California.

7. Ⓐ Red, blue and, green fireworks lit up the sky.
   Ⓑ Red, blue and green fireworks, lit up the sky.
   Ⓒ Red, blue, and green fireworks lit up the sky.
   Ⓓ Red, blue and green, fireworks lit up the sky.

8. Ⓕ The teacher asked, "Does everyone have a pencil?"
   Ⓖ The teacher asked, "Does everyone have a pencil."
   Ⓗ The teacher asked, "Does everyone have a pencil"?
   Ⓙ The teacher asked, "Does everyone have a pencil".

9. Ⓐ "Let's go to the park." Mary said.
   Ⓑ "Let's go to the park," Mary said.
   Ⓒ "Let's go to the park?" Mary said.
   Ⓓ "Let's go to the park" Mary said.

Name ______________________ Date ______________

English/
Language Arts

ELA3C1

For pages 42–50

Mini-Test 3

Conventions

DIRECTIONS: Choose the answer that shows the correct punctuation mark.

1. How many people were at the party

Ⓐ .
Ⓑ ,
Ⓒ !
Ⓓ ?

2. Mr. Jefferson was mowing his lawn

Ⓕ .
Ⓖ ?
Ⓗ !
Ⓙ ,

3. _________ starting to rain.

Ⓐ Its
Ⓑ I'ts
Ⓒ It's
Ⓓ Its'

DIRECTIONS: Choose the answer that shows the correct punctuation and capitalization.

4. Ⓕ She and i will study now.
Ⓖ the library is closed.
Ⓗ Let's leave now?
Ⓙ May I borrow that book when you're done?

5. Ⓐ What is your favorite team?
Ⓑ my dad likes the yankees.
Ⓒ I always cheer for the red Sox.
Ⓓ I cant believe you like the Tigers!

DIRECTIONS: Choose the word that best completes the sentence.

6. Don't _________ in the hallway.

Ⓕ running
Ⓖ ran
Ⓗ run
Ⓙ had run

7. Please lend _________ your mittens.

Ⓐ her
Ⓑ she
Ⓒ its
Ⓓ they

8. Dr. and Mrs. Brown _________ the school last Monday.

Ⓕ visiting
Ⓖ visit
Ⓗ visits
Ⓙ visited

9. Devon was the _________ person in the relay race.

Ⓐ fastest
Ⓑ fast
Ⓒ most fast
Ⓓ faster

10. The _________ office is open from 9 A.M. to 5 P.M.

Ⓕ doctor
Ⓖ doctor's
Ⓗ doctors
Ⓙ doctor's'

GO

Name ________________________________ Date ________________

DIRECTIONS: Choose the answer that uses an incorrect verb.

11. Ⓐ The cowboy got on his horse.
Ⓑ He rode quickly away from the cattle.
Ⓒ The lost calf was bleating loudly.
Ⓓ The cowboy taken the calf to its mother.

12. Ⓕ The spider spun a beautiful web.
Ⓖ Dew glistened on it in the morning.
Ⓗ The spider wait to catch a fly.
Ⓙ I'm glad the spider is outside.

DIRECTIONS: Find the underlined word that is not spelled correctly.

13. Ⓐ my <u>favorite</u> food
Ⓑ writing <u>journel</u>
Ⓒ best <u>friends</u>
Ⓓ all correct

14. Ⓕ <u>beutiful</u> house
Ⓖ <u>exciting</u> day
Ⓗ <u>write</u> with a pen
Ⓙ all correct

DIRECTIONS: Choose the best answer.

15. Which of the following sentences is incomplete?
Ⓐ The next time I go to the zoo I want to see the elephants.
Ⓑ They are large, gray animals with long trunks.
Ⓒ Also have large ears.
Ⓓ I didn't get to see a baby elephant last year.

16. Which of the following sentences is correct and complete?
Ⓕ John wrote his school report about birds.
Ⓖ Favorite bird is the bald eagle.
Ⓗ It is named for white head.
Ⓙ Symbol of the United States.

17. Which of the following is the best combination of these two sentences?

Independence Day is my favorite holiday.
Independence Day is celebrated on July 4.

Ⓐ Independence Day is my favorite holiday and Independence Day is celebrated on July 4.
Ⓑ Independence Day is celebrated on July 4, my favorite holiday.
Ⓒ Independence Day, my favorite holiday, is celebrated on July 4.
Ⓓ Independence Day is celebrated on my favorite holiday, July 4.

Listening, Speaking, and Viewing Standards

The student demonstrates an understanding of listening, speaking, and viewing skills for a variety of purposes. The student listens critically and responds appropriately to oral communication in a variety of genres and media. The student speaks in a manner that guides the listener to understand important ideas.

ELA3LSV1. The student uses oral and visual strategies to communicate. The student:

a. adapts oral language to fit the situation by following the rules of conversation with peers and adults.
b. recalls, interprets, and summarizes information presented orally.
c. uses oral language for different purposes: to inform, persuade, or entertain.
d. listens to and views a variety of media to acquire information.

How Am I Doing?

Mini-Test 1 Pages 28–29 **Number Correct**	**10–13** answers correct	**Great Job!** Move on to the section test on page 55.
	6–9 answers correct	**You're almost there!** But you still need a little practice. Review practice pages 8–27 before moving on to the section test on page 55.
	0–5 answers correct	**Oops!** Time to review what you have learned and try again. Review the practice section on pages 8–27. Then retake the test on pages 28–29. Now move on to the section test on page 55.
Mini-Test 2 Page 40 **Number Correct**	**4** answers correct	**Awesome!** Move on to the section test on page 55.
	3 answers correct	**You're almost there!** But you still need a little practice. Review practice pages 31–39 before moving on to the section test on page 55.
	0–2 answers correct	**Oops!** Time to review what you have learned and try again. Review the practice section on pages 31–39. Then retake the test on page 40. Now move on to the section test on page 55.
Mini-Test 3 Pages 51–52 **Number Correct**	**14–17** answers correct	**Great Job!** Move on to the section test on page 55.
	9–13 answers correct	**You're almost there!** But you still need a little practice. Review practice pages 42–50 before moving on to the section test on page 55.
	0–8 answers correct	**Oops!** Time to review what you have learned and try again. Review the practice section on pages 42–50. Then retake the test on pages 51–52. Now move on to the section test on page 55.

Name ______________________________ Date ______________

Final English/Language Arts Test
for pages 8–52

DIRECTIONS: Choose the best answer.

1. **Find the answer that means the same or about the same as the underlined word.**

   long <u>tale</u>

   (A) story
   (B) movie
   (C) road
   (D) trip

2. **Find the word that means the opposite of the underlined word.**

   <u>dull</u> ride

   (F) long
   (G) exciting
   (H) boring
   (J) interesting

3. **Read the sentence with the missing word and then read the question. Find the best answer to the question.**

   The weather will ________ tomorrow.

   Which word means the weather will get better?

   (A) improve
   (B) change
   (C) worsen
   (D) vary

4. **Find the word that fits best in the blank.**

   Dogs need ________ to stay healthy.

   (F) treats
   (G) dishes
   (H) exercise
   (J) collars

5. **Choose the word that correctly completes both sentences.**

   Who will ________ this problem?

   The ________ on the shovel is broken.

   (A) solve
   (B) blade
   (C) cause
   (D) handle

6. **Find the word where only the root word is underlined.**

   (F) <u>pret</u>end
   (G) <u>un</u>happy
   (H) wash<u>able</u>
   (J) <u>sew</u>ing

7. **Which word in this sentence has a prefix?**

   The largest bottle of ketchup was unopened.

   (A) largest
   (B) bottle
   (C) ketchup
   (D) unopened

8. **Which word in this sentence has a suffix?**

   Alisha was late and quietly left the party.

   (F) late
   (G) quietly
   (H) left
   (J) party

GO

Name ______________________________ Date ______________

DIRECTIONS: Read the passage and then choose the best answer for each question.

Therapy Dogs

Therapy dogs can help patients get better after illnesses. The dogs' owners bring them into hospital rooms and let patients meet the animals. Dogs sometimes go right up to patients' beds. People in the hospital rooms can pet the dogs, brush them, and talk to them. Studies have shown that being with dogs and other animals is *therapeutic.* It can lower stress, lower blood pressure, and help people heal faster.

Not every dog is a good choice for this important job. To be a therapy dog, a dog must have a calm, friendly *disposition.* Some therapy dog owners feel that their pets were born to help sick people get well again.

9. What is the main idea of this passage?

Ⓐ Therapy dogs like to be brushed.

Ⓑ Therapy dogs are calm and friendly.

Ⓒ Therapy dogs help patients get better after illnesses.

Ⓓ Therapy dogs were born to visit hospitals.

10. The word *disposition* means ________ .

Ⓕ work history

Ⓖ personality

Ⓗ intelligence

Ⓙ breed

11. Which words help you figure out the meaning of *therapeutic*?

Ⓐ "sometimes go right up to patients' beds"

Ⓑ "lower stress, lower blood pressure, and help people heal faster"

Ⓒ "a calm, friendly disposition"

Ⓓ "pet the dogs, brush them, and talk to them"

DIRECTIONS: Read the passage. On the next page, choose the best answer for each question.

Wendy Lost and Found

Wendy was scared. For the second time in her young life, she was lost. When the branch fell on her small house and the fence, she had barely escaped. She had leaped across the fallen fence into the woods. Now, the rain poured down and the wind howled. The little woodchuck shivered under a big oak tree. She did not know what to do.

When Wendy was a baby, her mother died. She had been alone in the woods then, too. She could not find enough food. Then she hurt her paw. All day she scratched at a small hole in the ground, trying to make a burrow. Every night, she was hungry.

One day, Rita found her. Rita had knelt down by Wendy's shallow burrow and set down an apple. Wendy limped slowly out and took the apple. It was the best thing she had ever tasted. Rita took the baby woodchuck to the wildlife center, and Wendy has lived there ever since. Most of the animals at the center were orphans. Rita taught them how to live in the wild, and then let them go when they were ready. But Wendy's paw did not heal well, and Rita knew that Wendy would never be able to go back to the wild. So, Rita made Wendy a house and a pen. Wendy even had a job—she visited schools with Rita so that students could learn all about woodchucks.

Now, the storm had ruined Wendy's house. She did not know how to find Rita. At dawn, the rain ended. Wendy limped down to a big stream and sniffed the air. Maybe the center was across the stream. Wendy jumped onto a rock and then hopped to another one. She landed on her bad paw and fell into the fast-moving water. The little woodchuck struggled to keep her nose above water. The current tossed her against a tangle of branches. Wendy held on with all her might.

"There she is!" Wendy heard Rita's voice. Rita and Ben, another worker from the wildlife center, were across the stream. Rita waded out to the branches, lifted Wendy up, and wrapped her in a blanket. Wendy purred her thanks. By the time Ben and Rita got into the van to go back to the center, Wendy was fast asleep.

Name ______________________________ Date ______________

12. **What genre of literature is this passage?**
    - (F) drama
    - (G) nonfiction
    - (H) fiction
    - (J) poetry

13. **This passage is mostly about __________ .**
    - (A) a wildlife center worker
    - (B) a woodchuck who lives at a wildlife center
    - (C) a woodchuck who can do tricks
    - (D) a woodchuck who learns how to swim

14. **How does the passage start?**
    - (F) with Wendy's life as a baby
    - (G) in the middle of the storm
    - (H) with Wendy's visit to school
    - (J) when Wendy is in the stream

15. **What was the effect of the storm?**
    - (A) Wendy's mother died.
    - (B) Wendy went to live at the wildlife center.
    - (C) Wendy's house was ruined.
    - (D) Wendy hurt her paw.

16. **Why do you think the author wrote about Wendy's life as a baby?**
    - (F) so the reader knows that Wendy has been lost before and knows what to do
    - (G) so the reader knows that Wendy can't live in the wild and is in danger
    - (H) so the reader knows that Wendy trusts people and will be all right
    - (J) so the reader knows that Wendy can find apples to eat

17. **What are the settings for this passage?**
    - (A) the woods and the wildlife center
    - (B) the school and the stream
    - (C) the school and the woods
    - (D) the wildlife center and Rita's house

18. **Which of the following best summarizes the passage?**
    - (F) Wendy is a woodchuck with a job—she visits schools with Rita so that students can learn about woodchucks.
    - (G) Wendy is an orphaned woodchuck who lives at the wildlife center. One night, a storm destroyed her pen and she got lost in the woods. Rita saved her a second time.
    - (H) When Wendy the woodchuck was a baby, she was lost in the woods. Then Rita found her and took her to the wildlife center to live.
    - (J) A storm destroyed Wendy the woodchuck's pen. She was so scared that she ran into the woods and was lost for a second time.

19. **What event from the passage supports the idea that Rita cares about Wendy?**
    - (A) She jumps into the water to save Wendy.
    - (B) She brings Ben to look for Wendy.
    - (C) She takes Rita to schools.
    - (D) She falls asleep.

Name ______________________________ Date ______________

DIRECTIONS: Read the paragraph. Use the information to answer the questions.

(1) Snowflakes look like white stars falling from the sky. **(2)** But there have been times when snow has looked red, green, yellow, and even black. **(3)** Black snow in France one year. **(4)** Another year, gray snow fell in Japan. **(5)** To make this dark snow, snow had mixed with ashes to make it. **(6)** Red snow that fell one year was made of snow mixed with red clay dust. **(7)** Most snow looks white. **(8)** It is really the color of ice. **(9)** Each snowflake begins with a small drop of frozen water. **(10)** When that water is mixed with some other material, the result is strangely colored snow.

20. Sentence 5 is best written—

- Ⓕ Snow had mixed with ashes to make this dark snow.
- Ⓖ Snow mixed with ashes was how this snow was made into dark snow.
- Ⓗ To make this dark snow, it had ashes mixed with it.
- Ⓙ correct as it is

21. Which is not a complete sentence?

- Ⓐ sentence 1
- Ⓑ sentence 2
- Ⓒ sentence 3
- Ⓓ sentence 4

22. How could sentences 7 and 8 best be joined together?

- Ⓕ Really the color of ice, most snow looks white.
- Ⓖ The color of ice, most snow is really white.
- Ⓗ Most snow looks white and it is really the color of ice.
- Ⓙ Most snow looks white, but it is really the color of ice.

DIRECTIONS: Choose the answer that shows the correct punctuation mark.

23. What is your favorite color

- Ⓐ .
- Ⓑ ,
- Ⓒ !
- Ⓓ ?

24. Mr. Jefferson was mowing his lawn

- Ⓕ .
- Ⓖ ?
- Ⓗ !
- Ⓙ ,

25. Look out

- Ⓐ .
- Ⓑ ,
- Ⓒ !
- Ⓓ ?

26. Turn right at the stop sign

- Ⓕ .
- Ⓖ ?
- Ⓗ !
- Ⓙ ,

DIRECTIONS: Choose the answer that shows the correct punctuation and capitalization.

27.
- Ⓐ The bus comes for us at 7:30
- Ⓑ terri likes to ride up front.
- Ⓒ My friends and I like to sit in the back.
- Ⓓ We talk about sports and TV shows?

28.
- Ⓕ the house was dark and still.
- Ⓖ Suddenly, the door creaked open!
- Ⓗ Someone inside the house laughed
- Ⓙ It was my friend, michelle, playing a trick?

GO

Name ______________________________ Date ______________

DIRECTIONS: Choose the word or phrase that best completes the sentence.

29. That was the ________ movie I've ever seen.

- (A) best
- (B) most best
- (C) better
- (D) goodest

30. It is supposed to be ________ tomorrow than it was today.

- (F) warmest
- (G) more warmer
- (H) warmer
- (J) most warm

DIRECTIONS: Choose the best answer.

31. Which of the following words is a singular noun?

- (A) brother's
- (B) computers
- (C) maps
- (D) farm

32. Which of the following words is a possessive noun?

- (F) bike
- (G) lawyer's
- (H) paper
- (J) floods

33. I ________ believe that you are going to the park without me!

- (A) cant
- (B) cant'
- (C) ca'nt
- (D) can't

34. My teacher ________ take us out to recess today.

- (F) didnt
- (G) didn't'
- (H) didn't
- (J) did'nt

35. ________ played basketball until it got dark outside.

- (A) Him
- (B) Us
- (C) They
- (D) Her

36. Why don't you let ________ play with you?

- (F) her
- (G) they
- (H) she
- (J) their

DIRECTIONS: Find the word that is spelled incorrectly.

37.

- (A) load
- (B) October
- (C) therteen
- (D) myself

38.

- (F) weak
- (G) harder
- (H) yestrday
- (J) clown

39.

- (A) earth
- (B) pudle
- (C) broom
- (D) packed

Name ______________________________ Date ____________________

40. (F) sting
(G) heard
(H) messige
(J) pillow

41. **Read the definitions in this dictionary entry. Which definition best fits the word *express* as it is used in the sentence below?**

The <u>express</u> will get us home quickly.

ex · press [ik spres′] *v.* **1.** to put into words **2.** to show or reveal **3.** to send quickly *adj.* **4.** clear or easily understood **5.** quick *n.* **6.** a direct train

(A) 1
(B) 2
(C) 5
(D) 6

DIRECTIONS: Choose the answer that you think is correct.

42. **Where would you look to find the date of Memorial Day this year?**

(F) in a newspaper
(G) in a catalog
(H) in a dictionary
(J) on a calendar

43. **Where would you look to find a biography of Martin Luther King, Jr.?**

(A) in a newspaper
(B) in an atlas
(C) in an encyclopedia
(D) in a math book

44. **Where would you look to find the address of a school?**

(F) in a newspaper
(G) in a telephone book
(H) in a dictionary
(J) in an encyclopedia

DIRECTIONS: Read the Table of Contents. Then answer the questions.

TABLE OF CONTENTS

Chapter 1: Choosing Your Breed of Dog 11
Chapter 2: Selecting the Right Puppy 42
Chapter 3: Care and Feeding of Puppies ... 58
Chapter 4: Training Young Dogs 86
Chapter 5: Medical Care for Dogs 102
Chapter 6: Do You Have a Champion? 116

45. **To learn how to teach your dog to sit, turn to ________ .**

(A) chapter 1
(B) chapter 2
(C) chapter 3
(D) chapter 4

46. **If you can't decide what kind of dog you want, turn to ________ .**

(F) chapter 1
(G) chapter 2
(H) chapter 3
(J) chapter 4

47. **If your puppy seems to have a cold, turn to page ________ .**

(A) 42
(B) 58
(C) 86
(D) 102

Name ______________________________ Date ______________

Final English/Language Arts Test

Answer Sheet

1	Ⓐ	Ⓑ	Ⓒ	Ⓓ	31	Ⓐ	Ⓑ	Ⓒ	Ⓓ
2	Ⓕ	Ⓖ	Ⓗ	Ⓙ	32	Ⓕ	Ⓖ	Ⓗ	Ⓙ
3	Ⓐ	Ⓑ	Ⓒ	Ⓓ	33	Ⓐ	Ⓑ	Ⓒ	Ⓓ
4	Ⓕ	Ⓖ	Ⓗ	Ⓙ	34	Ⓕ	Ⓖ	Ⓗ	Ⓙ
5	Ⓐ	Ⓑ	Ⓒ	Ⓓ	35	Ⓐ	Ⓑ	Ⓒ	Ⓓ
6	Ⓕ	Ⓖ	Ⓗ	Ⓙ	36	Ⓕ	Ⓖ	Ⓗ	Ⓙ
7	Ⓐ	Ⓑ	Ⓒ	Ⓓ	37	Ⓐ	Ⓑ	Ⓒ	Ⓓ
8	Ⓕ	Ⓖ	Ⓗ	Ⓙ	38	Ⓕ	Ⓖ	Ⓗ	Ⓙ
9	Ⓐ	Ⓑ	Ⓒ	Ⓓ	39	Ⓐ	Ⓑ	Ⓒ	Ⓓ
10	Ⓕ	Ⓖ	Ⓗ	Ⓙ					
					40	Ⓕ	Ⓖ	Ⓗ	Ⓙ
11	Ⓐ	Ⓑ	Ⓒ	Ⓓ	41	Ⓐ	Ⓑ	Ⓒ	Ⓓ
12	Ⓕ	Ⓖ	Ⓗ	Ⓙ	42	Ⓕ	Ⓖ	Ⓗ	Ⓙ
13	Ⓐ	Ⓑ	Ⓒ	Ⓓ	43	Ⓐ	Ⓑ	Ⓒ	Ⓓ
14	Ⓕ	Ⓖ	Ⓗ	Ⓙ	44	Ⓕ	Ⓖ	Ⓗ	Ⓙ
15	Ⓐ	Ⓑ	Ⓒ	Ⓓ	45	Ⓐ	Ⓑ	Ⓒ	Ⓓ
16	Ⓕ	Ⓖ	Ⓗ	Ⓙ	46	Ⓕ	Ⓖ	Ⓗ	Ⓙ
17	Ⓐ	Ⓑ	Ⓒ	Ⓓ	47	Ⓐ	Ⓑ	Ⓒ	Ⓓ
18	Ⓕ	Ⓖ	Ⓗ	Ⓙ					
19	Ⓐ	Ⓑ	Ⓒ	Ⓓ					
20	Ⓕ	Ⓖ	Ⓗ	Ⓙ					
21	Ⓐ	Ⓑ	Ⓒ	Ⓓ					
22	Ⓕ	Ⓖ	Ⓗ	Ⓙ					
23	Ⓐ	Ⓑ	Ⓒ	Ⓓ					
24	Ⓕ	Ⓖ	Ⓗ	Ⓙ					
25	Ⓐ	Ⓑ	Ⓒ	Ⓓ					
26	Ⓕ	Ⓖ	Ⓗ	Ⓙ					
27	Ⓐ	Ⓑ	Ⓒ	Ⓓ					
28	Ⓕ	Ⓖ	Ⓗ	Ⓙ					
29	Ⓐ	Ⓑ	Ⓒ	Ⓓ					
30	Ⓕ	Ⓖ	Ⓗ	Ⓙ					

Georgia Mathematics Content Standards

The mathematics section measures knowledge in six different areas:

1) **Number and Operations**
2) **Measurement**
3) **Geometry**
4) **Algebra**
5) **Data Analysis**
6) **Process Skills**

Georgia Mathematics Table of Contents

Number and Operations Standards

M3N. Number and Operations

Students will use decimal fractions and common fractions to represent parts of a whole. They will also understand the four arithmetic operations for whole numbers and use them in basic calculations, and apply them in problem solving situations.

M3N1. Students will further develop their understanding of whole numbers and ways of representing them. ***(See page 65.)***

a. Identify place values from tenths through ten thousands.
b. Understand the relative sizes of digits in place value notation (10 times, 100 times, 1/10 of a single digit whole number) and ways to represent them.

What it means:

- Students should be able to identify **place value** (ones, tens, hundreds, thousands, and ten thousands) of numbers up to 10,000.

M3N2. Students will further develop their skills of addition and subtraction and apply them in problem solving. ***(See pages 66–68.)***

a. Use the properties of addition and subtraction to compute and verify the results of computation.
b. Use mental math and estimation strategies to add and subtract.
c. Solve problems requiring addition and subtraction.

M3N3. Students will further develop their understanding of multiplication of whole numbers and develop the ability to apply it in problem solving. ***(See pages 69–73.)***

a. Describe the relationship between addition and multiplication (i.e., multiplication is defined as repeated addition).
b. Know the multiplication facts with understanding and fluency to 10×10.
c. Use arrays and area models to develop understanding of the distributive property and to determine partial products for multiplication of 2- or 3-digit numbers by a 1-digit number.
d. Understand the effect on the product when multiplying by multiples of 10.
e. Apply the identity, commutative, and associative properties of multiplication and verify the results.
f. Use mental math and estimation strategies to multiply.
g. Solve problems requiring multiplication.

What it means:

- An **array** is an arrangement of items in a number of equal-size rows. For example, an array can be four rows of six, which shows that $4 \times 6 = 24$.
- Students should know the following properties.
  - The **distributive property** means that multiplication can be distributed over addition.
  - The **identity property** means that the product of 1 and any number is that number.
  - The **commutative property** means the order of the numbers can be switched and still yield the same answer.
  - The **associative property** means the grouping of the numbers can be changed and still yield the same answer.

Number and Operations Standards

M3N4. Students will understand the meaning of division and develop the ability to apply it in problem solving. ***(See pages 74–76.)***

a. Understand the relationship between division and multiplication and between division and subtraction.
b. Recognize that division may be two situations: the first is determining how many equal parts of a given size or amount may be taken away from the whole as in repeated subtraction, and the second is determining the size of the parts when the whole is separated into a given number of equal parts as in a sharing model.
c. Recognize problem-solving situations in which division may be applied and write corresponding mathematical expressions.
d. Explain the meaning of a remainder in division in different circumstances.
e. Divide a 2- and 3-digit number by a 1-digit divisor.
f. Solve problems requiring division.

M3N5. Students will understand the meaning of decimal fractions and common fractions in simple cases and apply them in problem-solving situations. ***(See pages 77–80.)***

a. Understand a decimal fraction (i.e., 0.1) and a common fraction (i.e., 1/10) represent parts of a whole.
b. Understand the fraction *a*/*b* represents *a* equal-sized parts of a whole that is divided into *b* equal-sized parts.
c. Understand a one place decimal fraction represents tenths (i.e., 0.3 = 3/10).
d. Know and use decimal fractions and common fractions to represent the size of parts created by equal divisions of a whole.
e. Understand the concept of addition and subtraction of decimal fractions and common fractions with like denominators.
f. Model addition and subtraction of decimal fractions and common fractions.
g. Solve problems involving fractions.

What it means:

- Students should know that fractions are the comparison of two numbers. These numbers can refer to parts of an item and the whole item, such as pieces of a pizza compared to a whole pizza. Or the numbers can be items compared to a whole set of items, such as number of oranges compared to the whole crate of fruit.

Name ____________________ Date ____________

Mathematics

M3N1

Identifying Place Value

Number and Operations

DIRECTIONS: Write the missing number.

1. **2648: _____ is in the tens place**
2. **6397: _____ is in the hundreds place**
3. **73,251: _____ is in the thousands place**
4. **89,251: _____ is in the ten-thousands place**

DIRECTIONS: Choose the value of the underlined number.

5. **65,963**
   - (A) 6 ones
   - (B) 6 tens
   - (C) 6 hundreds
   - (D) 6 thousands

6. **7,907**
   - (F) 7 ones
   - (G) 7 tens
   - (H) 7 hundreds
   - (J) 7 thousands

7. **670,140**
   - (A) 7 tens
   - (B) 7 hundreds
   - (C) 7 thousands
   - (D) 7 ten thousands

DIRECTIONS: Build each number.

8.

   7 ones
   4 thousands
   3 tens
   0 hundreds

9.

   1 tens
   2 thousands
   3 ones
   4 ten thousands
   5 hundreds

DIRECTIONS: Write each of these numbers in decimal form.

10. _________ **sixteen and three tenths**
11. _________ **five and five tenths**
12. _________ **two and one tenth**

DIRECTIONS: Choose the best answer.

13. **How can you write 56,890 in expanded notation?**
   - (F) 5 + 6 + 8 + 9 + 0 =
   - (G) 50,000 + 6,000 + 800 + 90 =
   - (H) 56,000 + 8,900 =
   - (J) 0.5 + 0.06 + 0.008 + 0.0009 =

14. **What is another name for 651?**
   - (A) 6 thousands, 5 tens, and 1 one
   - (B) 6 hundreds, 1 tens, and 5 ones
   - (C) 6 tens and 5 ones
   - (D) 6 hundreds, 5 tens, and 1 one

15. **5 hundreds and 7 thousands equals—**
   - (F) 5,700
   - (G) 7,050
   - (H) 570
   - (J) 7,500

STOP

Name ______________________ Date ______________

Mathematics

M3N2

Opposites Assist

Number and Operations

DIRECTIONS: Solve each story problem. Check answers by using the opposite operations. Show your work.

1. **Yurelli counted 254 vowels on the first page in the book and 578 vowels on the second page. How many vowels in all?**

2. **845 acorns were collected from one tree. 627 acorns were collected from another tree. How many more acorns were collected from the first tree?**

3. **Jade has $3.27 in her lunch account. The lunches she wants to buy this week will cost $5.25. How much money does she need to pay for her lunches?**

4. **Willie wants to watch one movie that is 78 minutes and another that is 120 minutes. How long will the two movies take?**

5. **Mikaela had 158 trading cards. She gave 39 to a friend. How many does she have left?**

6. **The scientists tagged 458 monarch butterflies the first week and 562 monarch butterflies the second week. How many butterflies were tagged during the two weeks?**

Name ______________________________ Date ______________

Mathematics

M3N2

Money Matters

Number and Operations

DIRECTIONS: Solve each part of this story problem. Check answers by using the opposite operations. Show your work for each part.

Thomas is saving up for a new skateboard that costs $60.00. He has saved only $16.25.

1. **How much more does he need?**

2. **Thomas is expecting his allowance. On Friday his mom will pay him $8.00. His little brother will pay back the $0.75 he borrowed. How much does Thomas have now? How much does Thomas still need?**

   Thomas has ________ .

   Thomas needs ________ .

3. **Thomas's grandmother sent him a check for his birthday. The check was equal to half the amount Thomas still needs. How much was the check?**

4. **What is the total amount of money Thomas has saved?**

5. **What is the difference between the amount saved and the cost of the skateboard?**

STOP

Name ______________________________ Date ______________

Mathematics

M3N2

Estimating Strategies

Number and Operations

DIRECTIONS: Choose the best answer.

Example:

Suppose you wanted to estimate how to find 73 + 48 to the nearest 10. Which of these would you use?

(A) 100 + 40
(B) 100 + 50
(C) 70 + 50
(D) 70 + 40

Answer: (C)

1. Which of these is the best way to estimate the answer to this problem?

286 – 109 = ■

(A) 300 – 100 = ■
(B) 200 – 100 = ■
(C) 300 – 200 = ■
(D) 100 – 100 = ■

2. Which number sentence would you use to estimate 97 + 9 to the nearest 10?

(F) 90 + 5
(G) 100 + 10
(H) 90 + 10
(J) 100 + 5

3. Use estimation to find which of these is closest to 1,000.

(A) 591 + 573
(B) 499 + 409
(C) 392 + 589
(D) 913 + 183

4. Which number sentence would you use to estimate 356 – 192 to the nearest 100?

(F) 350 – 190
(G) 300 – 200
(H) 400 – 200
(J) 400 – 190

5. Estimate the answer to this problem by rounding.

12 + 78

(A) 70
(B) 80
(C) 60
(D) 90

6. Use estimation to find which of these is closest to 100?

(F) 498 – 221
(G) 301 – 235
(H) 679 – 448
(J) 399 – 110

STOP

Name ______________________ Date ______________

Mathematics

M3N3

Multiplication Facts

Number and Operations

DIRECTIONS: Fill in the multiplication table. Can you do it in less than three minutes?

x	0	1	2	3	4	5	6	7	8	9	10
0											
1											
2			4								
3											
4											
5						25					
6											
7											
8											
9											
10											

DIRECTIONS: The students at PS 134 are having a book sale. They are arranging the books into categories and stacking them on tables. Read the following problems and write your answers on the lines.

1. **Josh sorted books about sports. When he was finished, he had 8 stacks of 6 books each. How many sports books in all were at the sale?**

   ____

2. **The largest category of books was fiction. Rebecca had 12 stacks with 10 books in each stack. How many fiction books were at the sale?**

   ____

3. **The book sale was in the gym. The students set up tables into 9 rows with 4 tables in each row. What was the total number of tables in the gym?**

   ____

4. **The customers were excited by the sale. They lined up to pay for their books. There were 5 lines with 17 customers in each line. How many customers were waiting to pay?**

   ____

5. **When the sale was over, the students counted the money. Bruno counted the five-dollar bills. He had 14 five-dollar bills. How much money did Bruno have?**

   ____

Name ______________________________ Date ______________

Mathematics

M3N3

Distributive Property

Number and Operations

DIRECTIONS: Use the **distributive property** to rewrite the following expressions. Then use the correct order of operations to solve both sides and check your answers.

Example:

The **distributive property** is used when there is a combination of multiplication over addition or subtraction.

$5(3 + 6) = 5 \times 3 + 5 \times 6$	$16 - 6 = (8 \times 2) - (3 \times 2)$
$5 \times 9 = 15 + 30$	$10 = (8 - 3)2$
$45 = 45$	$10 = 10$

1. $2(6 + 3) =$

2. $12 + 9 =$

3. $4(9 - 1) =$

4. $18 - 6 =$

5. $(15 - 3)2 =$

6. $(7 + 5)8 =$

Name ______________________ Date ______________

Mathematics

M3N3

Number and Operations

Multiplying by One-Digit Numbers

DIRECTIONS: Choose the best answer. Choose "none of these" if the answer is not given.

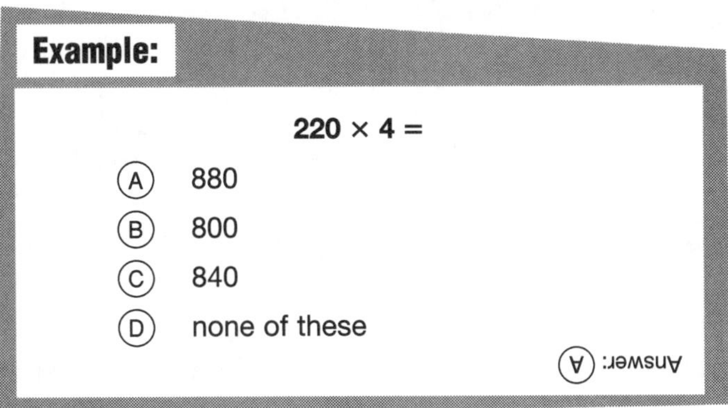

Example:

220 × 4 =

Ⓐ 880
Ⓑ 800
Ⓒ 840
Ⓓ none of these

Answer: Ⓐ

1. 410 × 6 =

Ⓐ 2,466
Ⓑ 2,460
Ⓒ 2,465
Ⓓ none of these

2. 311 × 2 =

Ⓕ 722
Ⓖ 522
Ⓗ 622
Ⓙ none of these

3. 618 × 7 =

Ⓐ 4,326
Ⓑ 4,426
Ⓒ 4,246
Ⓓ none of these

4. 99 × 9 =

Ⓕ 891
Ⓖ 693
Ⓗ 792
Ⓙ none of these

5. 43 × 4 =

Ⓐ 184
Ⓑ 162
Ⓒ 172
Ⓓ none of these

6. 15 × 8 =

Ⓕ 81
Ⓖ 120
Ⓗ 140
Ⓙ none of these

7. 430 × 8 =

Ⓐ 438
Ⓑ 3,440
Ⓒ 3,224
Ⓓ none of these

8. 575 × 3 =

Ⓕ 725
Ⓖ 1,705
Ⓗ 1,575
Ⓙ none of these

STOP

Name ______________________ Date ______________

Mathematics

M3N3

Number and Operations

Multiplying by Multiples of Ten

Example:

Find 20 × 60.

2 × 6 = 12
2 zeros in equation added to above = 1,200

When multiplying by multiples of ten, first multiply the numbers without the zeros. Then count the zeros in the problem and add those to the answer.

1. 5 × 10 = ____________
2. 5 × 100 = ____________
3. 40 × 30 = ____________
4. 70 × 80 = ____________
5. 600 × 90 = ____________
6. 20 × 400 = ____________
7. 3 × 6,000 = ____________
8. 400 × 70 = ____________
9. 20 × 800 = ____________
10. 500 × 30 = ____________
11. 50 × 50 = ____________
12. 10 × 100 = ____________
13. 8 × 500 = ____________
14. 20 × 90 = ____________
15. 250 × 30 = ____________
16. 60 × 80 = ____________
17. 100 × 90 = ____________
18. 8 × 350 = ____________
19. 30 × 200 = ____________
20. 450 × 20 = ____________

STOP

Name ______________________ Date ______________

Mathematics

M3N3

Number and Operations

Identity, Commutative, and Associative Properties

Examples:

The **commutative property** says you can switch the order of the numbers and still get the same answer.

5 + 10 = 10 + 5
15 = 15

5 x 2 = 2 x 5
10 = 10

The **associative property** says you can change the grouping of the numbers and still get the same answer.

(3 + 5) + 6 = 3 + (5 + 6)
8 + 6 = 3 + 11
14 = 14

(3 x 5) x 6 = 3 x (5 x 6)
15 x 6 = 3 x 30
90 = 90

The **identity property** says that when you multiply any number by 1, the answer is that number.

1 x 6 = 6

1 x 22 = 22

DIRECTIONS: Choose the answer that goes in the box.

1. 23 + 16 = 16 + ■

Ⓐ 23
Ⓑ 8
Ⓒ 7
Ⓓ 39

2. 24 × (12 × 12) = (24 × 12) × ■

Ⓕ 24
Ⓖ 12
Ⓗ 36
Ⓙ 21

3. (10 + 5) + 6 = ■ + (5 + 6)

Ⓐ 5
Ⓑ 21
Ⓒ 10
Ⓓ 11

4. (1 × 12) = ■

Ⓕ 1
Ⓖ 12

5. 7.5 × 3.8 = 3.8 × ■

Ⓐ 2.3
Ⓑ 8.3
Ⓒ 7.5
Ⓓ 5.7

6. (6 × 8) × 5 = 6 × (8 × ■)

Ⓕ 45
Ⓖ 53
Ⓗ 5
Ⓙ 48

7. 226 + (835 + 602) = (226 + 835) + ■

Ⓐ 226
Ⓑ 835
Ⓒ 602
Ⓓ 1,663

8. (8 × 1) = ■

Ⓕ 8
Ⓖ 1

STOP

Name ______________________________ Date ______________

Mathematics

M3N4

Number and Operations

Relating Multiplication and Division

DIRECTIONS: Choose the best answer.

1. 32 ÷ 16 = 2; 16 × ■ = 32
   - (A) 32
   - (B) 16
   - (C) 2
   - (D) 8

2. 25 ÷ 5 = ■; 5 × ■ = 25
   - (F) 5
   - (G) 25
   - (H) 50
   - (J) 10

3. 81 ÷ 9 = ■; 9 × ■ = 81
   - (A) 3
   - (B) 81
   - (C) 12
   - (D) 9

4. 144 ÷ 12 = ■; 12 × ■ = 144
   - (F) 48
   - (G) 14
   - (H) 24
   - (J) 12

5. 56 ÷ 14 = ■; 14 × ■ = 56
   - (A) 6
   - (B) 4
   - (C) 8
   - (D) 9

6. 64 ÷ 8 = ■; 8 × ■ = 64
   - (F) 9
   - (G) 8
   - (H) 12
   - (J) 56

7. 3 × ■ = 27; 27 ÷ ■ = 3
   - (A) 3
   - (B) 27
   - (C) 9
   - (D) 8

8. 7 × ■ = 56; 56 ÷ 7 = ■
   - (F) 8
   - (G) 9
   - (H) 14
   - (J) 28

9. 13 × 3 = ■; ■ ÷ 3 = 13
   - (A) 16
   - (B) 26
   - (C) 39
   - (D) 52

10. 11 × ■ = 121; 121 ÷ ■ = 11
    - (F) 10
    - (G) 11
    - (H) 12
    - (J) 13

STOP

Name ______________________ Date ______________

Mathematics

M3N4

Division with Remainders

Number and Operations

DIRECTIONS: Solve each problem using division.

Example:

$4\overline{)22}$ quotient 6: $6 \times 4 = 24$, so 6 is too many.

$4\overline{)22}$ quotient 5 R2; -20; 2 Remainder

1. $5\overline{)28}$ ___ R ___
2. $4\overline{)19}$ ___ R ___
3. $8\overline{)26}$ ___ R ___
4. $7\overline{)45}$ ___ R ___
5. $3\overline{)26}$ ___ R ___
6. $2\overline{)19}$ ___ R ___
7. $6\overline{)51}$ ___ R ___
8. $9\overline{)65}$ ___ R ___

DIRECTIONS: The five members of the Porter family decided to visit Denali National Park for their summer vacation. Read each problem. Write the answer on the line.

9. **The Porter family will eat 30 meals while they are in the park. To be fair, each of the five family members will choose the place to eat an equal number of times. How many times will each person choose?**

____

10. **Mr. Porter bought a set of 24 postcards for everyone in the family to share. How many postcards will each person get to send to friends back home, and how many will be left to put in the scrapbook?**

____

11. **The family went to a ranger talk. They learned that there had been one large moose herd with 91 moose in it. The herd had been divided into 6 smaller herds; however, the herds could not be divided evenly. The extra moose were placed in the first herd. How many moose were in each herd? How many extra moose were placed in the first herd?**

____

12. **A maximum of 72 tourists can go on the Horseshoe Lake walk. If the walk is full and there are 8 rangers leading groups, how many tourists will be in each group?**

____

STOP

Name ______________________ Date ______________

Mathematics

M3N4

Number and Operations

Dividing by One-Digit Numbers

DIRECTIONS: Use division to solve each problem.

Examples:

15 ÷ 3 = 5 sets
in all, in each set

3 ⟌ 15 in all = 5 sets
3 in each set

1. 81 ÷ 3 = ________ 3 ⟌ 81

2. 219 ÷ 3 = ________ 3 ⟌ 219

3. 20 ÷ 5 = ________ 5 ⟌ 20

4. 147 ÷ 7 = ________ 7 ⟌ 147

5. 18 ÷ 2 = ________ 2 ⟌ 18

6. 12 ÷ 4 = ________ 4 ⟌ 12

7. 48 ÷ 3 = ________ 3 ⟌ 48

8. 168 ÷ 4 = ________ 4 ⟌ 168

9. 12 ÷ 2 = ________ 2 ⟌ 12

10. 240 ÷ 6 = ________ 6 ⟌ 240

STOP

Name ______________________________ Date ______________

Mathematics

M3N5

Using Decimal Fractions

Number and Operations

DIRECTIONS: Express the shaded parts as a decimal.

Example:

A **decimal point** is a period placed between the ones place and the tenths place.

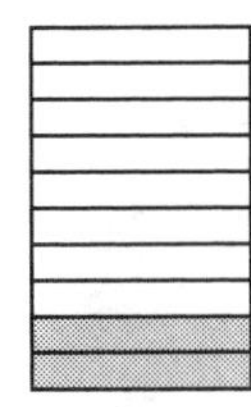

0.2 is read as two tenths.

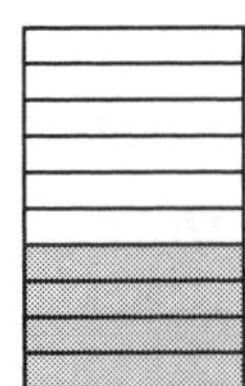

0.4 is read as four tenths.

1.

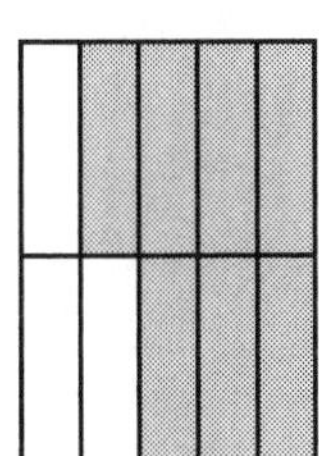

____

2.

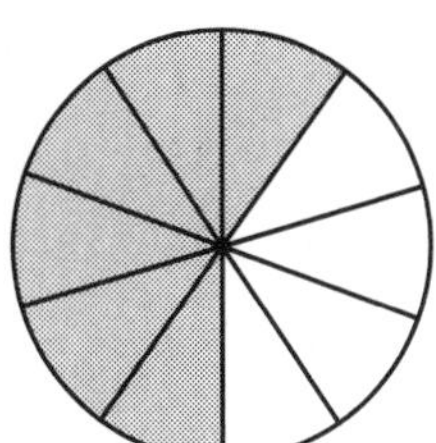

____

3.

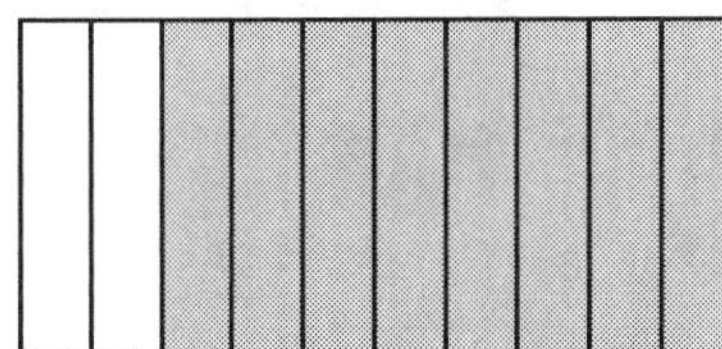

____

4.

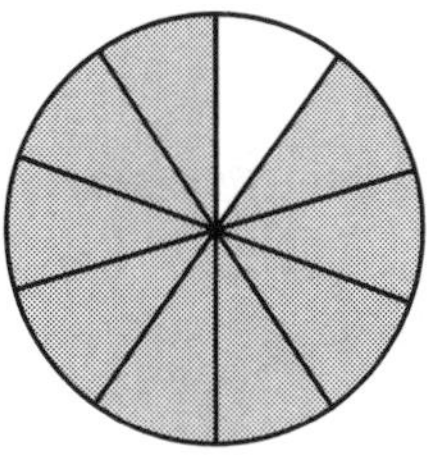

____

5.

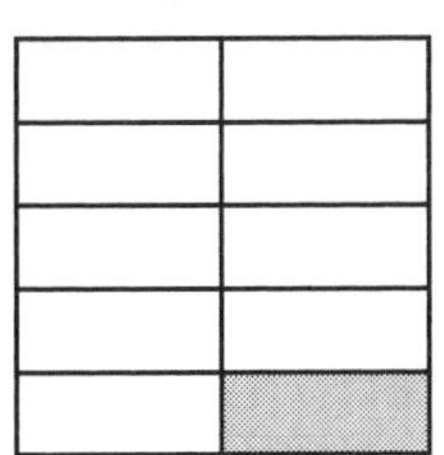

____

6.

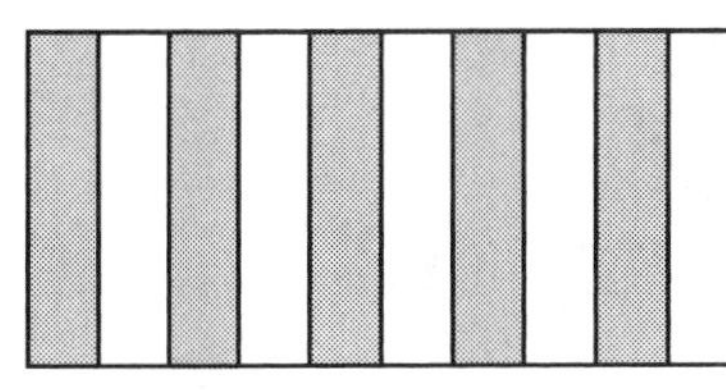

____

DIRECTIONS: Color parts to match the decimals below each figure.

7.

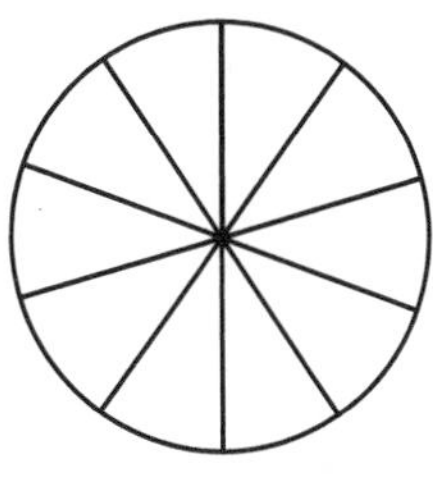

0.4

8.

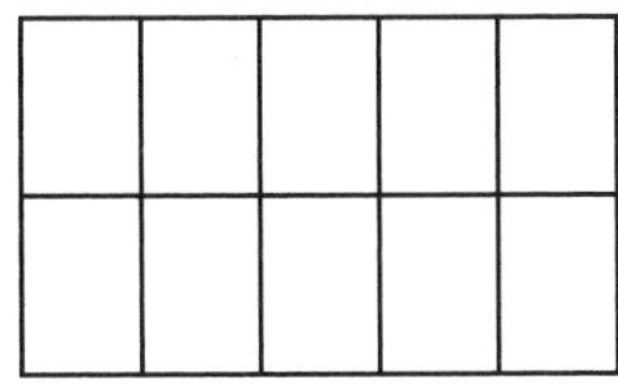

0.3

9.

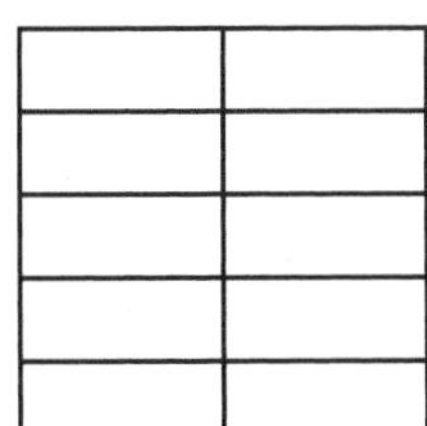

0.2

STOP

Name ______________________ Date ______________

Mathematics

M3N5

Using Fractions

Number and Operations

DIRECTIONS: Choose the best answer.

Example:

A fraction is made up of two numbers separated by a line. Danny and Brian ate 5 slices of a pizza. The pizza had a total of 8 slices, so they ate $\frac{5}{8}$ of the pizza.

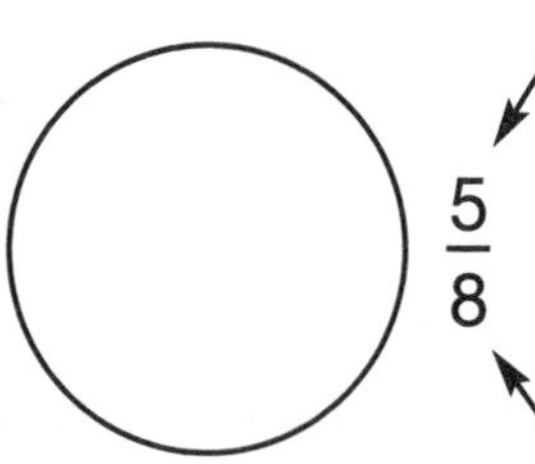

$\frac{5}{8}$

The top number of the fraction tells how many slices of pizza they ate. The fraction $\frac{5}{8}$ tells us they ate 5 slices.

The bottom number tells how many slices the pizza was divided into. The fraction $\frac{5}{8}$ tells us the whole pizza was divided into 8 slices.

1. How much of this figure is shaded?

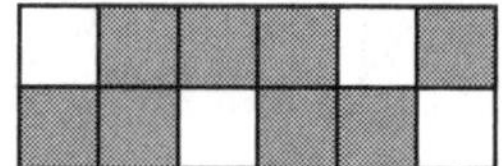

Ⓐ $\frac{8}{12}$

Ⓑ $\frac{4}{8}$

Ⓒ $\frac{10}{12}$

Ⓓ $\frac{3}{10}$

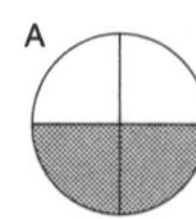

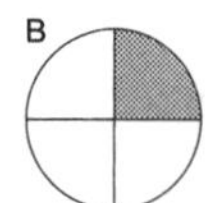

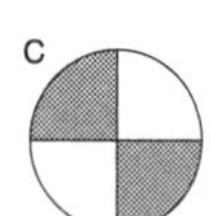

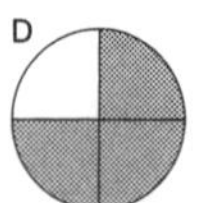

2. Which figure above equals $\frac{3}{4}$?

Ⓕ A

Ⓖ B

Ⓗ C

Ⓙ D

3. In which figure are $\frac{5}{8}$ of the boxes shaded?

Ⓐ 

Ⓑ 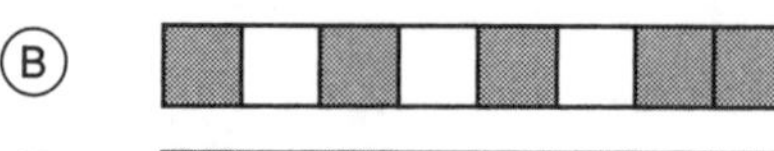

Ⓒ 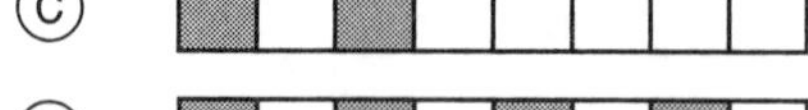

Ⓓ

4. In which figure are $\frac{3}{6}$ of the stars shaded?

Ⓕ 

Ⓖ 

Ⓗ 

Ⓙ 

STOP

Name ______________________ Date ______________

Mathematics

M3N5

Number and Operations

Adding and Subtracting Fractions

DIRECTIONS: Choose the best answer.

1. $\frac{6}{7} - \frac{3}{7} =$
   - Ⓐ $\frac{3}{14}$
   - Ⓑ $\frac{9}{14}$
   - Ⓒ $\frac{1}{14}$
   - Ⓓ $\frac{3}{7}$

2. $\frac{2}{8} + \frac{1}{8} =$
   - Ⓕ $\frac{1}{12}$
   - Ⓖ $\frac{1}{4}$
   - Ⓗ $\frac{3}{8}$
   - Ⓙ $\frac{3}{16}$

3. $\frac{1}{6} + \frac{4}{6} =$
   - Ⓐ $\frac{5}{12}$
   - Ⓑ $\frac{1}{12}$
   - Ⓒ $\frac{5}{6}$
   - Ⓓ $\frac{2}{3}$

4. $\frac{7}{9} - \frac{4}{9} =$
   - Ⓕ $\frac{3}{9}$
   - Ⓖ $\frac{3}{18}$
   - Ⓗ $\frac{11}{9}$
   - Ⓙ $\frac{11}{18}$

5. $\frac{5}{6} - \frac{4}{6} =$
   - Ⓐ $\frac{9}{16}$
   - Ⓑ $\frac{1}{6}$
   - Ⓒ $\frac{1}{12}$
   - Ⓓ $\frac{9}{12}$

6. $\frac{4}{5} + \frac{1}{5} =$
   - Ⓕ $1\frac{1}{5}$
   - Ⓖ $\frac{5}{10}$
   - Ⓗ 1
   - Ⓙ $1\frac{4}{5}$

DIRECTIONS: Work the following problems. When adding or subtracting decimals, remember to include the decimal in the answer.

7. $\begin{array}{r} 4.2 \\ +\ 5.2 \\ \hline \end{array}$

8. $\begin{array}{r} 6.4 \\ +\ 1.4 \\ \hline \end{array}$

9. $\begin{array}{r} 3.1 \\ +\ 7.8 \\ \hline \end{array}$

10. $\begin{array}{r} 4.7 \\ +\ 3.2 \\ \hline \end{array}$

Name ______________________________ Date ______________

11.

$$\begin{array}{r} 4.9 \\ +\ 2.0 \\ \hline \end{array}$$

12.

$$\begin{array}{r} 5.9 \\ -\ 3.2 \\ \hline \end{array}$$

13.

$$\begin{array}{r} 6.7 \\ -\ 5.6 \\ \hline \end{array}$$

14.

$$\begin{array}{r} 7.8 \\ -\ 2.5 \\ \hline \end{array}$$

15.

$$\begin{array}{r} 5.8 \\ -\ 3.3 \\ \hline \end{array}$$

16.

$$\begin{array}{r} 3.9 \\ -\ 1.5 \\ \hline \end{array}$$

17.

$$\begin{array}{r} 2.3 \\ +\ 2.5 \\ \hline \end{array}$$

18.

$$\begin{array}{r} 4.6 \\ -\ 1.3 \\ \hline \end{array}$$

DIRECTIONS: Read each word problem and then choose the correct answer.

19. Debbie's cookie recipe calls for $\frac{3}{4}$ cup of sugar. She has $\frac{1}{4}$ cup of sugar in the bowl now. How much more sugar does she need to add?

- Ⓐ $\frac{1}{4}$ cup
- Ⓑ $\frac{2}{4}$ cup
- Ⓒ $\frac{3}{4}$ cup
- Ⓓ 1 cup

20. Debbie's cookie recipe calls for $1\frac{1}{2}$ cups of flour. She has decided to double her recipe, so how much flour will she need?

- Ⓕ 2 cups
- Ⓖ $2\frac{1}{4}$ cups
- Ⓗ $2\frac{1}{2}$ cups
- Ⓙ 3 cups

21. Kyle, Tanner, and Devon ordered a pizza for dinner. Kyle ate $\frac{3}{12}$ of the pizza, Tanner ate $\frac{2}{12}$ of the pizza, and Devon ate $\frac{4}{12}$ of the pizza. How much pizza did they eat altogether?

- Ⓐ $\frac{6}{12}$
- Ⓑ $\frac{9}{12}$
- Ⓒ $\frac{8}{12}$
- Ⓓ $\frac{10}{12}$

22. Using your answer to question 21, how much of the pizza was left over?

- Ⓕ $\frac{1}{12}$
- Ⓖ $\frac{2}{12}$
- Ⓗ $\frac{3}{12}$
- Ⓙ $\frac{4}{12}$

Name ______________________________ Date ______________

Mathematics

M3N1–M3N5

For pages 65–80

Mini-Test 1

Number and Operations

DIRECTIONS: Choose the best answer.

1. **What is the value of the underlined number?**

   48,723 (the 8 is underlined)

   (A) 8 tens
   (B) 8 hundreds
   (C) 8 thousands
   (D) 8 ten thousands

2. **What is another name for 9 thousands, 5 hundreds, 8 tens, and 8 ones?**

   (F) 1,416
   (G) 956
   (H) 9,580
   (J) 9,588

3. **How can you write 43,776 in expanded notation?**

   (A) 40,000 + 3,000 + 700 + 70 + 6
   (B) 43,000 + 3,700 + 76
   (C) 4 + 3 + 7 + 7 + 6
   (D) 43,000 + 776

4. **How would you estimate 73 + 48 to the nearest 10?**

   (F) 100 + 40
   (G) 100 + 50
   (H) 70 + 50
   (J) 70 + 40

5. **75 − 39 =**

   (A) 41
   (B) 26
   (C) 36
   (D) 114

6. **26 + 6 =**

   (F) 30
   (G) 32
   (H) 31
   (J) 20

7. **21 ÷ 7 =**

   (A) 14
   (B) 28
   (C) 2
   (D) 3

8. $\begin{array}{r} \mathbf{44} \\ \underline{\times\ \mathbf{4}} \end{array}$

   (F) 48
   (G) 166
   (H) 176
   (J) 256

9. **400 × 10 =**

   (A) 400
   (B) 4,000
   (C) 40,000
   (D) 400,000

10. $\begin{array}{r} \mathbf{6.9} \\ \underline{+\ \mathbf{8.6}} \end{array}$

    (F) 14.3
    (G) 15.3
    (H) 14.5
    (J) 15.5

GO

Name ______________________ Date ______________

11. $\frac{1}{8} + \frac{5}{8} =$

- (A) $\frac{6}{8}$
- (B) $\frac{4}{8}$
- (C) $\frac{3}{8}$
- (D) $\frac{2}{4}$

12. $\frac{7}{16} - \frac{4}{16} =$

- (F) $\frac{1}{2}$
- (G) $\frac{11}{16}$
- (H) $\frac{3}{16}$
- (J) $\frac{4}{16}$

13. 32 ÷ 16 = 2; 16 × ■ = 32

- (A) 32
- (B) 16
- (C) 2
- (D) 8

14. 12 × 10 = ■ × 12

- (F) 10
- (G) 12
- (H) 120
- (J) 2

15. Which number is the same as $\frac{22}{100}$?

- (A) 2.2
- (B) 22
- (C) 0.022
- (D) 0.22

16. Which fraction is the same as 0.7?

- (F) $\frac{1}{7}$
- (G) $\frac{7}{100}$
- (H) $\frac{700}{100}$
- (J) $\frac{7}{10}$

17. What fraction of this figure is shaded?

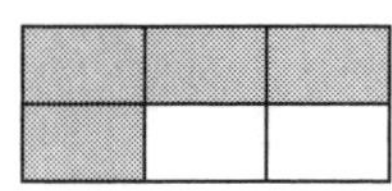

- (A) $\frac{4}{3}$
- (B) $\frac{2}{8}$
- (C) $\frac{2}{6}$
- (D) $\frac{4}{6}$

18. Reagan's birthday cake was cut into 24 pieces. There were 8 people at the party. How many pieces did each person get?

- (F) 2 pieces
- (G) 3 pieces
- (H) 4 pieces
- (J) 5 pieces

19. Jason's book had 6 chapters. There were 8 pages in each chapter. How many pages were in the book?

- (A) 48 pages
- (B) 32 pages
- (C) 36 pages
- (D) 14 pages

STOP

Measurement Standards

M3M. Measurement

Students will understand and measure time and length. They will also model and calculate perimeter and area of simple geometric figures.

M3M1. Students will further develop their understanding of the concept of time by determining elapsed time of a full, half, and quarter hour. ***(See page 84.)***

M3M2. Students will measure length choosing appropriate units and tools. ***(See pages 85–87.)***

a. Use the units kilometer (km) and mile (mi.) to discuss the measure of long distances.
b. Measure to the nearest 1/4 inch, 1/2 inch, and millimeter (mm) in addition to the previously learned inch, foot, yard, centimeter, and meter.
c. Estimate length and represent it using appropriate units.
d. Compare one unit to another within a single system of measurement.

M3M3. Students will understand and measure the perimeter of simple geometric figures (squares and rectangles). ***(See page 88.)***

a. Understand the meaning of the linear unit and measurement in perimeter.
b. Understand the concept of perimeter as being the boundary of a simple geometric figure.
c. Determine the perimeter of a simple geometric figure by measuring and summing the lengths of the sides.

What it means:

- Students should know that the **perimeter** is the distance around an area.

M3M4. Students will understand and measure the area of simple geometric figures (squares and rectangles). ***(See page 89.)***

a. Understand the meaning of the square unit and measurement in area.
b. Model (by tiling) the area of a simple geometric figure using square units (square inch, square foot, etc.).
c. Determine the area of squares and rectangles by counting, adding, and multiplying using models.

What it means:

- Students should know that the **area** is the amount of space inside a closed figure.

Name ______________________ Date ______________

Mathematics

M3M1

Measurement

Determining Elapsed Time

The size of an angle is measured in many ways. One method is to use degrees. The degrees tell you how far you rotated to make the angle. Think of the minute hand on a clock. In one hour, the hand sweeps around in one full circle, ending back where it started. It has made one full turn, which equals 360 degrees, or 360°. This chart shows angles measured by the rotation of a circle, the minutes on a clock, and degrees. Use it to help you with the questions below.

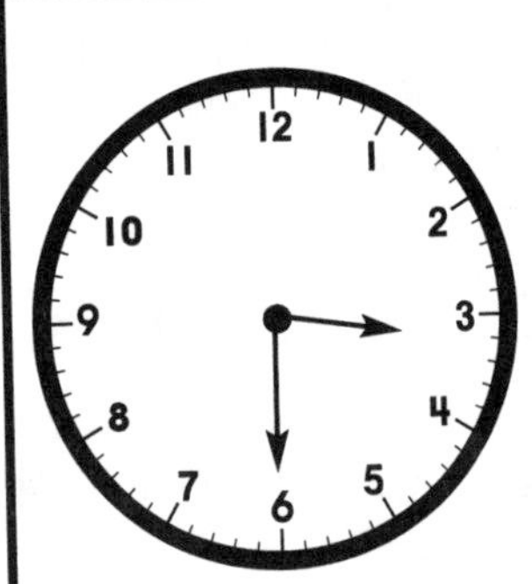

Rotation	Minutes	Degrees
$\frac{1}{4}$ turn	15	90
$\frac{1}{2}$ turn	30	180
$\frac{3}{4}$ turn	45	270
full turn	60	360

DIRECTIONS: For numbers 1–9, write the degree measure of the angle made when the minute hand on a clock travels from the first time to the second time. The first one is done for you.

1. **3:15 to 3:30** 90 degrees
2. **7:45 to 8:15** ________
3. **4:15 to 5:15** ________
4. **2:00 to 2:45** ________
5. **6:30 to 7:00** ________
6. **11:15 to 11:45** ________
7. **9:30 to 9:45** ________
8. **5:45 to 6:30** ________
9. **4:15 to 5:15** ________

DIRECTIONS: For numbers 10–18, write the number of minutes that have passed when the minute hand on a clock travels from the first time to the second time.

10. **8:45 to 9:00** ________
11. **4:25 to 4:40** ________
12. **9:30 to 10:30** ________
13. **3:30 to 4:00** ________
14. **4:20 to 4:50** ________
15. **7:03 to 7:48** ________
16. **5:10 to 5:25** ________
17. **2:15 to 3:15** ________
18. **6:04 to 6:49** ________

Name ______________________________ Date ______________

Mathematics

M3M2

Measurement

Measuring Long Distances

DIRECTIONS: Miles and kilometers are used to measure long distances. Below is a chart of length conversions. Use the chart to help you answer the questions.

1 yard = 3 feet	**1 meter (m) = 100 centimeters (cm)**
1 mile = 5,280 feet	**1 kilometer (km) = 1,000 meters (m)**
1 mile = 1.609 kilometers	**1 kilometer (km) = 0.621 miles (mi.)**

1. Tanner ran 2 miles during gym class. How many kilometers is this? ________

2. During that same gym class, Matt ran 1.6 kilometers. Who ran farther—Tanner or Matt?

____

3. Micah went for a bike ride. He measured the distance using an odometer on his bike. When he started, his odometer was at 36 miles. When he returned home, his odometer was at 48 miles. How many miles did he ride?

____

4. Josie and her mom walked to the store to pick up some groceries. Their round trip measured 2,640 feet. How many miles did they walk? ________

5. On Friday, Jordan traveled 263 miles to his grandmother's house. He returned home on Monday. How many total miles did he travel?

____

6. Jordan wants to figure out how far he traveled in kilometers. Using your answer to question 5, how many kilometers did Jordan travel? Round to the nearest whole number. ________

7. Tisha flew 1,150 kilometers from Atlanta to Chicago. Rounded to the nearest whole number, how many miles did she fly?

____

8. Anna is walking in a 5-kilometer charity event. How many meters will she walk by the time she reaches the finish line? ________

9. Jonathan is running in the 10,000-meter race. How many kilometers is the race? ________

STOP

Name ______________________ Date ______________

Mathematics **Measurement**

M3M2

Measuring Lines

DIRECTIONS: For items 1–4, use a ruler to measure the following lines to the nearest $\frac{1}{4}$ inch.

1. ____________________

2. ________________________________

3. ____

4. ______________

DIRECTIONS: For items 5–8, measure each line to the nearest $\frac{1}{2}$ inch.

5. _____________________________

6. ____

7. _________________

8. _______________________

DIRECTIONS: For items 9–12, measure each line to the nearest millimeter.

9. ________

10. ________________________________

11. ________________________

12. ______________________________

STOP

Name ______________________________ Date ______________

M3M2

Comparing Units of Length

DIRECTIONS: Fill in the blanks with the equivalent measurement. Below is a chart of customary length conversions. Use the chart to help you answer the questions.

1 foot = 12 inches

1 yard = 3 feet

1 mile = 5,280 feet

1. 7 yards = _____ feet

2. 24 inches = _____ feet

3. 6 feet = _____ yard(s)

4. 10 miles = _____ feet

5. 60 inches = _____ feet

6. 30 feet = _____ yard(s)

7. 5 feet + 2 inches = _____ inches

8. 3 feet = _____ inches

DIRECTIONS: The metric measuring system is based on multiples of 10. Below is a chart of metric conversions. Use the chart to help you answer the questions.

1 centimeter (cm) = 10 millimeters (mm)

1 meter (m) = 100 centimeters (cm)

1 kilometer (km) = 1,000 meters (m)

9. Jodi measured her tomato plant. It is 34 centimeters. How many millimeters is this?
____

10. Meg has a plastic case that is 4 centimeters long. She found a shell that is 34 millimeters long. Will it fit in her case? __________

11. Kifa jumped 3 meters. How many centimeters is this? __________

12. Jordan's desk is 1 meter by 1 meter. He would like to put his science project inside his desk. The science project is on poster board that is 95 centimeters by 110 centimeters. Will it fit inside his desk without sticking out?
____

13. Amar's room measures 10 meters by 12 meters. What is the room's measurement in centimeters? __________

STOP

Name ______________________________ Date ____________________

Mathematics

M3M3

Finding the Perimeter

Measurement

Perimeter is the distance around an area. To find the perimeter, add the lengths of sides together.

DIRECTIONS: Find the perimeter of each figure below. Include the correct units in your answers.

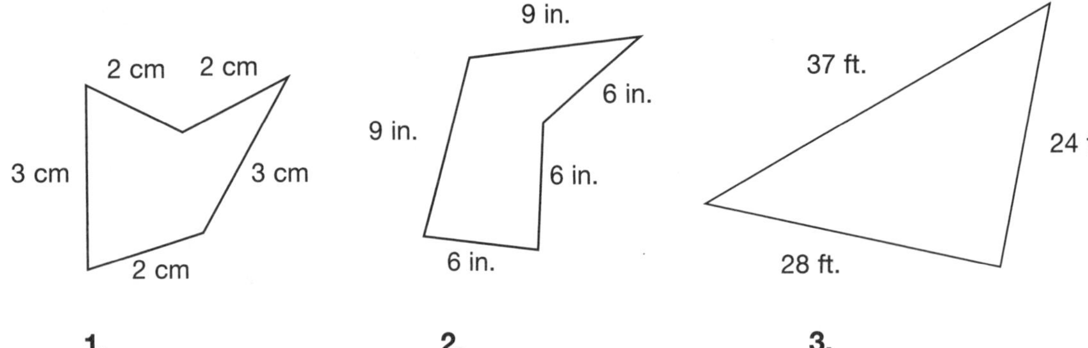

1. __________ **2.** __________ **3.** __________

DIRECTIONS: Choose the best answer.

4. What is the perimeter of this triangle?

Ⓐ 13 centimeters

Ⓑ 12 centimeters

Ⓒ 17 centimeters

Ⓓ 18 centimeters

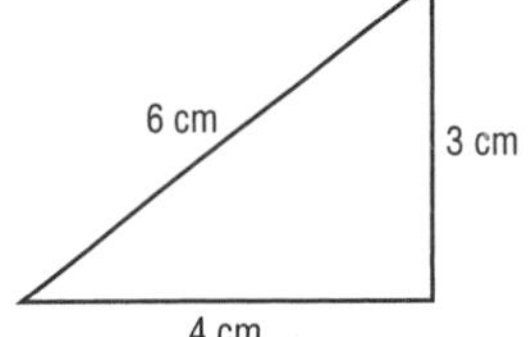

5. If the perimeter of this figure is 50 inches, the missing side is __________ .

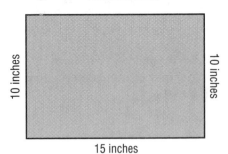

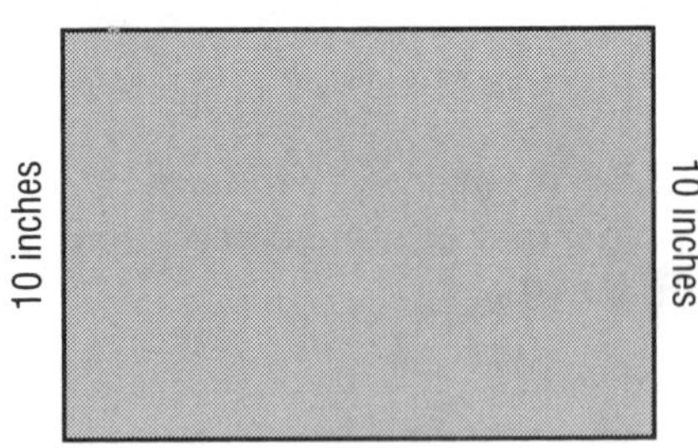

Ⓕ 15 inches long

Ⓖ 20 inches long

Ⓗ 10 inches long

Ⓙ 25 inches long

6. The perimeter of this figure is __________ .

Ⓐ 14 units

Ⓑ 20 units

Ⓒ 12 units

Ⓓ 4 units

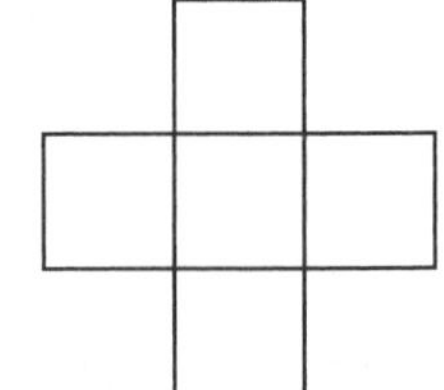

7. What is the perimeter of this figure?

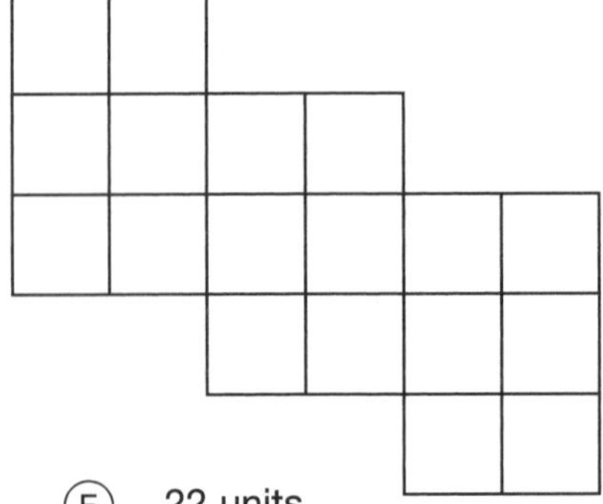

Ⓕ 22 units

Ⓖ 14 units

Ⓗ 18 units

Ⓙ 24 units

Name ______________________ Date ______________

Mathematics

M3M4

Measurement

Finding Area

Area is the amount of space inside a closed figure. To find the area of a square or rectangle, multiply the length times the height.

DIRECTIONS: Find the area of each figure below by counting the square units. Each square measures 1 unit by 1 unit.

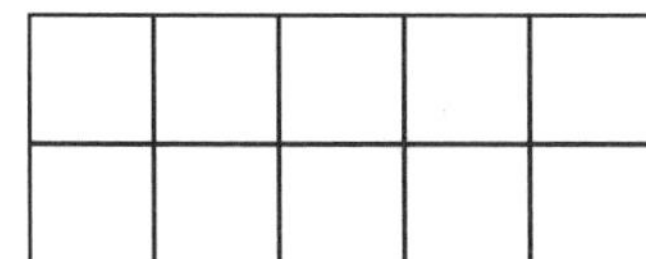

1. ____________

2. ____________

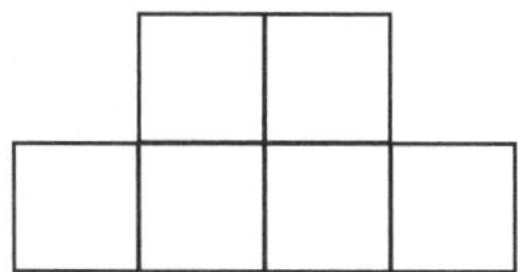

3. ____________

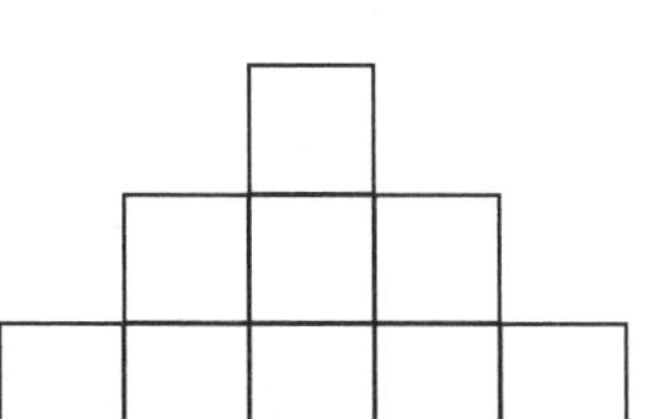

4. ____________

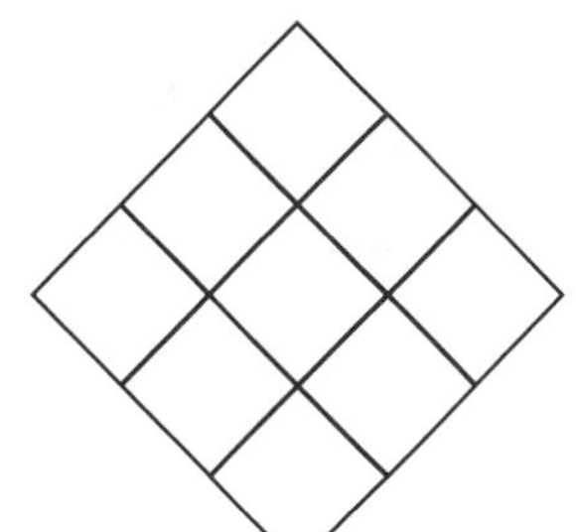

5. ____________

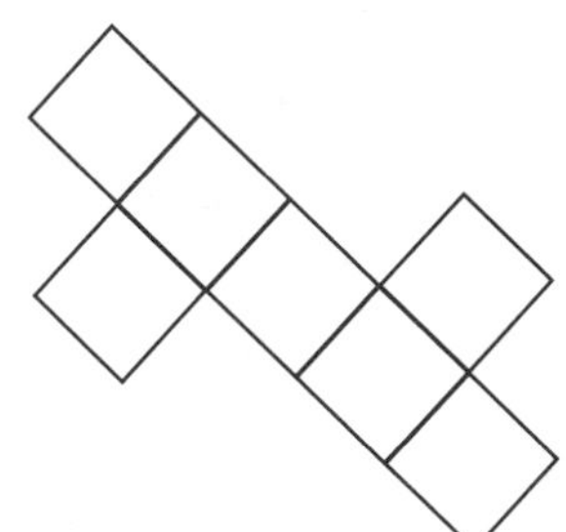

6. ____________

DIRECTIONS: Choose the best answer.

7. Find the area of the following square.

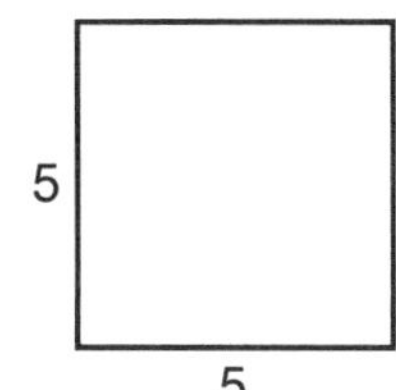

Ⓐ 50 square units
Ⓑ 25 square units
Ⓒ 30 square units
Ⓓ 15 square units

8. Find the area of the following rectangle.

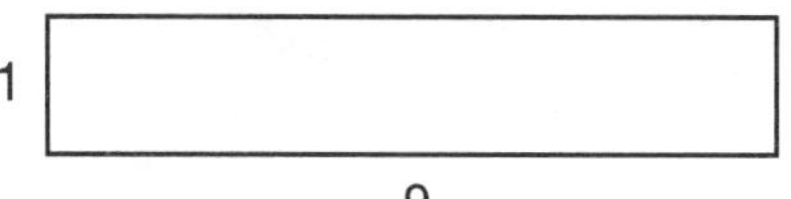

Ⓕ 10 square units
Ⓖ 20 square units
Ⓗ 5 square units
Ⓙ 9 square units

STOP

Name ______________________________ Date ____________________

Mathematics

M3M1–M3M4

For pages 84–89

Mini-Test 2

Measurement

DIRECTIONS: Choose the best answer.

1. **Rita left dance class at 3:32 P.M. She arrived home at 4:17 P.M. How long did it take Rita to get home?**

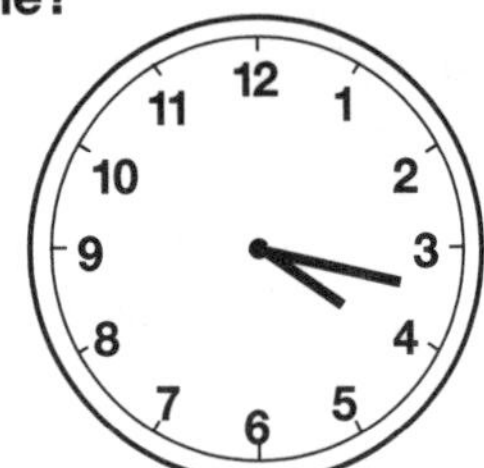

   Ⓐ 1 hour, 15 minutes
   Ⓑ 45 minutes
   Ⓒ 35 minutes
   Ⓓ 15 minutes

2. **What metric unit is best to use to measure the distance between two cities?**
   Ⓕ kilometer
   Ⓖ meter
   Ⓗ centimeter
   Ⓙ millimeter

3. **A sheet of writing paper is $8\frac{1}{2}$ inches by 11 inches. If you wanted to measure a sheet of writing paper using the metric system, which unit would you use?**
   Ⓐ meters
   Ⓑ centimeters
   Ⓒ grams
   Ⓓ kilometers

4. **How many inches are in two feet?**
   Ⓕ 18 inches
   Ⓖ 36 inches
   Ⓗ 24 inches
   Ⓙ 12 inches

5. **If the perimeter of this figure is 88 inches, the missing side is _________ .**

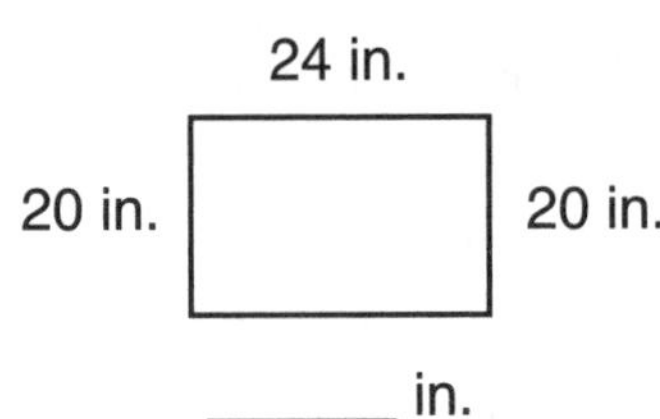

   Ⓐ 12 inches long
   Ⓑ 20 inches long
   Ⓒ 24 inches long
   Ⓓ 22 inches long

6. **What is the area of this square?**

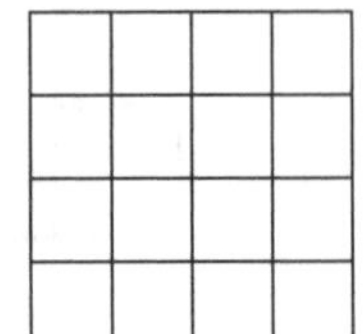

   Ⓕ 289 square inches
   Ⓖ 40 square inches
   Ⓗ 19 square inches
   Ⓙ 16 square inches

7. **Elana wants to put a fence around her flower garden. How many feet of fencing will she need?**

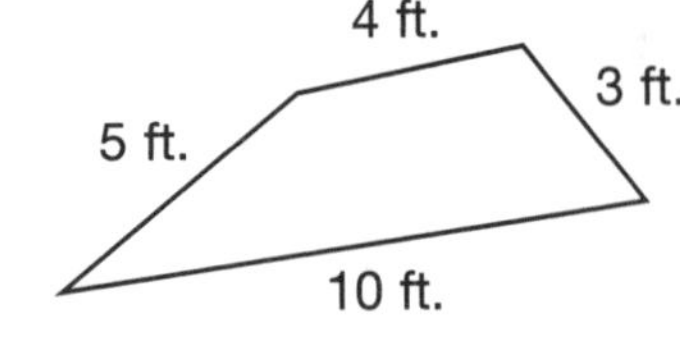

   Ⓐ 22 ft.

   Ⓑ 50 ft.
   Ⓒ 62 ft.
   Ⓓ 33 ft.

8. **What is the area of the figure?**

3 ft.

6 ft.

   Ⓕ 9 square ft.
   Ⓖ 18 square ft.
   Ⓗ 36 square ft.
   Ⓙ 360 square ft.

STOP

Geometry Standards

M3G. Geometry

Students will further develop their understanding of characteristics of previously studied geometric figures.

M3G1. Students will further develop their understanding of geometric figures by drawing them. They will also state and explain their properties. ***(See pages 92–95.)***

- **a.** Draw and classify previously learned fundamental geometric figures and scalene, isosceles, and equilateral triangles.
- **b.** Identify and explain the properties of fundamental geometric figures.
- **c.** Examine and compare angles of fundamental geometric figures.
- **d.** Identify the center, diameter, and radius of a circle.

What it means:

- Students should know that a **scalene triangle** has no sides that are equal, an **isosceles triangle** has two sides that are equal, and an **equilateral triangle** has all three sides that are equal.
- Students should know the following terms.
  - The **center point** of a circle is the same distance from all the points on a circle.
  - The **radius** of a circle is the distance from the center point of the circle to any other point on the circle.
  - The **diameter** of a circle is the distance from one point of the circle through the center point to the other side of the circle. The diameter is twice the length of the radius.

Name ______________________ Date ______________

Mathematics **Geometry**

M3G1

Identifying Geometric Figures

DIRECTIONS: Choose the best answer.

Example:

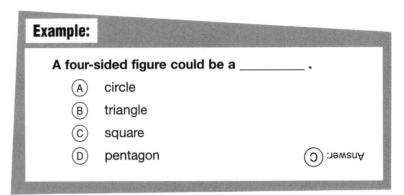

A four-sided figure could be a _________ .

Ⓐ circle
Ⓑ triangle
Ⓒ square
Ⓓ pentagon

Answer: Ⓒ

Think of objects, such as stop signs, to help you remember the different shapes.

1. This shape is called a(n) _________ .

Ⓐ pentagon
Ⓑ hexagon
Ⓒ octagon
Ⓓ triangle

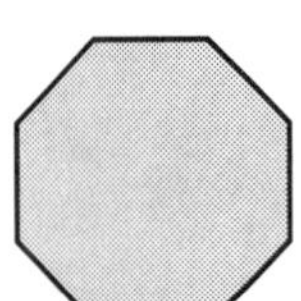

2. A polygon that has 6 sides and 6 angles is a(n) _________ .

Ⓕ pentagon
Ⓖ hexagon
Ⓗ octagon
Ⓙ trapezoid

3. Which polygon has more sides than a hexagon?

Ⓐ pentagon
Ⓑ triangle
Ⓒ octagon
Ⓓ square

4. How many sides does a quadrilateral have?

Ⓕ 3 sides
Ⓖ 4 sides
Ⓗ 5 sides
Ⓙ 6 sides

5. A polygon that only has one pair of parallel sides is a _________ .

Ⓐ parallelogram
Ⓑ quadrilateral
Ⓒ hexagon
Ⓓ trapezoid

6. A four-sided figure that has opposite sides that are parallel is called a _________ .

Ⓕ pentagon
Ⓖ parallelogram
Ⓗ triangle
Ⓙ hexagon

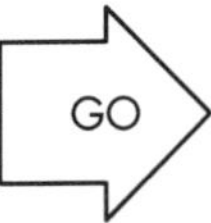

Name ______________________________ Date ______________

7. **Which shape is a rectangle?**

Ⓐ 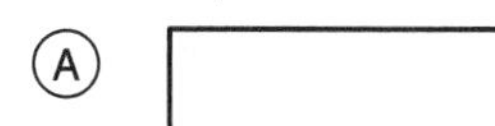

Ⓑ

Ⓒ

Ⓓ

8. **How is a square different from a rectangle?**

Ⓕ A square has four equal sides.

Ⓖ A square has two equal sides.

Ⓗ A square has right angles.

Ⓙ A square has parallel sides.

9. **A shape with 5 sides is known as what?**

Ⓐ a rectangle

Ⓑ a hexagon

Ⓒ a pentagon

Ⓓ an octagon

10. **If you were to draw a figure with no sides and no angles, what would it look like?**

Ⓕ 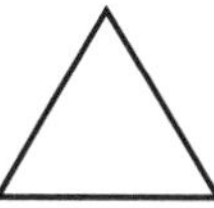

Ⓖ 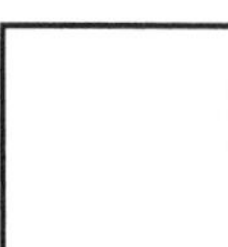

Ⓗ 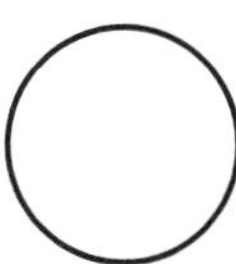

Ⓙ 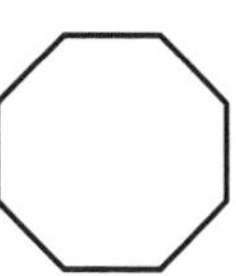

11. **If you were to draw a polygon with 4 equal sides and 4 square corners, what would it look like?**

Ⓐ 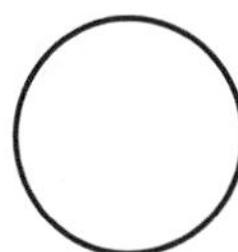

Ⓑ 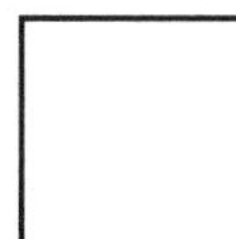

Ⓒ 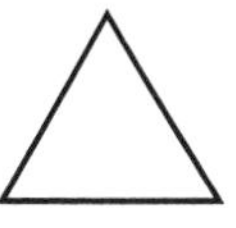

Ⓓ 

12. **If you were to draw a polygon with 3 sides and 3 angles, what might it look like?**

Ⓕ 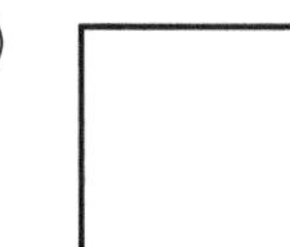

Ⓖ 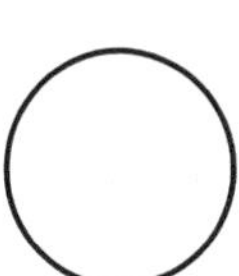

Ⓗ 

Ⓙ 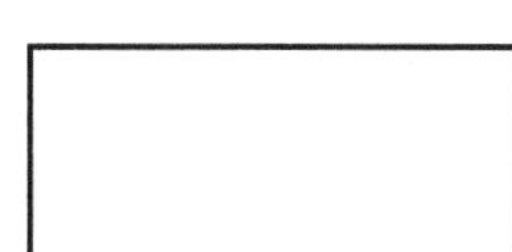

STOP

Name ______________________________ Date ______________

Mathematics

M3G1

Identifying Triangles

Geometry

DIRECTIONS: Choose the best answer.

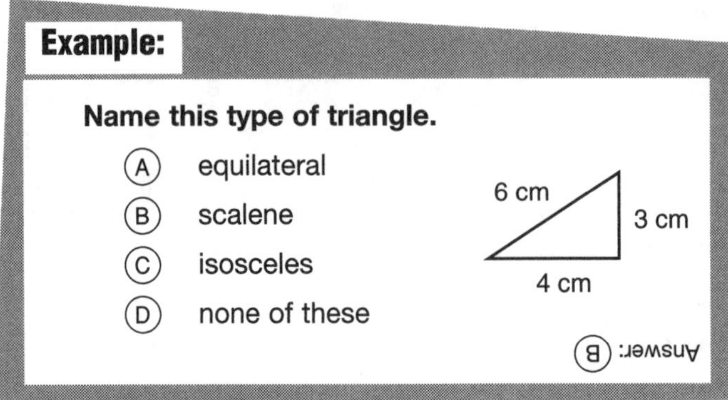

Example:
Name this type of triangle.
(A) equilateral
(B) scalene
(C) isosceles
(D) none of these
6 cm
3 cm
4 cm
Answer: (B)

If you don't know the meaning of a word, sometimes the answers will give you hints.

1. A polygon with three sides and three angles is a _________ .

- (A) square
- (B) triangle
- (C) rectangular prism
- (D) octagon

2. A triangle with two sides of equal length is _________ .

- (F) an isosceles triangle
- (G) an equilateral triangle
- (H) a scalene triangle
- (J) none of these

3. A triangle with three sides of equal length is _________ .

- (A) an isosceles triangle
- (B) an equilateral triangle
- (C) a scalene triangle
- (D) none of these

4. A triangle that has no sides of equal length is _________ .

- (F) an isosceles triangle
- (G) an equilateral triangle
- (H) a scalene triangle
- (J) none of these

5. Name this type of triangle.

- (A) equilateral
- (B) scalene
- (C) right
- (D) isosceles

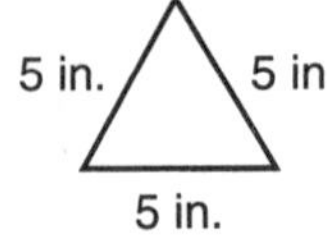

6. Name this type of triangle.

- (F) equilateral
- (G) scalene
- (H) right
- (J) isosceles

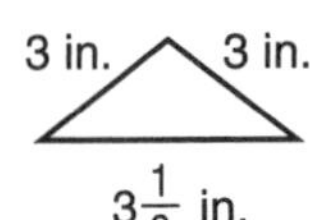

STOP

Name ______________________ Date ______________

Mathematics | Geometry

M3G1

Identifying the Radius and Diameter

DIRECTIONS: Choose the best answer.

Example:

- The **center point** of a circle is the same distance from all the points on a circle.
- The **radius** of a circle is the distance from the center point of the circle to any other point on the circle.
- The **diameter** of a circle is the distance from one point of the circle through the center point to the other side of the circle. The diameter is twice the length of the radius.

The radius of Circle A is 3 cm.

The diameter of Circle A is 6 cm.

Circle A

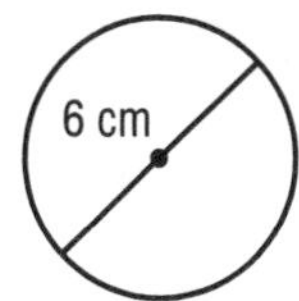

1. What is the radius of Circle B?

Ⓐ 5 in.
Ⓑ 10 in.
Ⓒ 20 in.
Ⓓ 15 in.

Circle B

2. What is the diameter of Circle B?

Ⓕ 5 in.
Ⓖ 10 in.
Ⓗ 20 in.
Ⓙ 15 in.

3. What is the radius of Circle C?

Ⓐ 12 yd.
Ⓑ 16 yd.
Ⓒ 8 yd.
Ⓓ 4 yd.

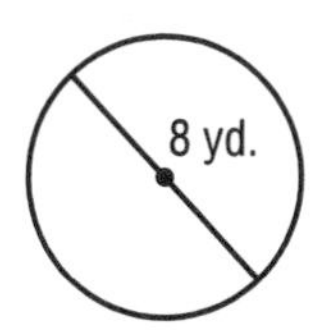

Circle C

4. What is the diameter of Circle C?

Ⓕ 12 yd.
Ⓖ 16 yd.
Ⓗ 8 yd.
Ⓙ 4 yd.

5. What is the radius of Circle D?

Ⓐ 6 mi.
Ⓑ 12 mi.
Ⓒ 18 mi.
Ⓓ 24 mi.

Circle D

6. What is the diameter of Circle D?

Ⓕ 6 mi.
Ⓖ 12 mi.
Ⓗ 18 mi.
Ⓙ 24 mi.

7. What is the radius of Circle E?

Ⓐ 2 m
Ⓑ 4 m
Ⓒ 8 m
Ⓓ 12 m

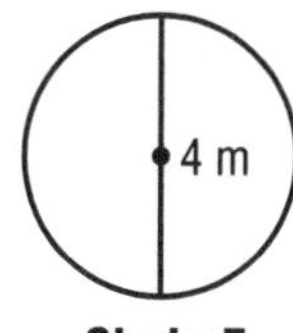

Circle E

8. What is the diameter of Circle E?

Ⓕ 2 m
Ⓖ 4 m
Ⓗ 8 m
Ⓙ 12 m

STOP

Name ______________________ Date ______________

Mathematics

M3G1

For pages 92–95

Geometry

Mini-Test 3

DIRECTIONS: Choose the best answer.

1. This shape is called a(n) ________ .

Ⓐ circle
Ⓑ pentagon
Ⓒ octagon
Ⓓ hexagon

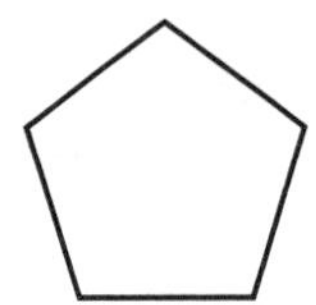

2. Which polygon has fewer sides than a square?

Ⓕ pentagon
Ⓖ triangle
Ⓗ octagon
Ⓙ square

3. A polygon that has 4 sides and 4 angles is a ________ .

Ⓐ pentagon
Ⓑ hexagon
Ⓒ octagon
Ⓓ trapezoid

4. A octagon has ________ .

Ⓕ 5 sides
Ⓖ 6 sides
Ⓗ 7 sides
Ⓙ 8 sides

5. What type of triangle is shown?

Ⓐ isosceles
Ⓑ equilateral
Ⓒ right
Ⓓ hexagon

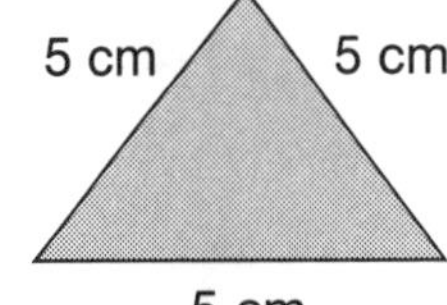

6. Name this type of triangle.

Ⓕ equilateral
Ⓖ scalene
Ⓗ right
Ⓙ isosceles

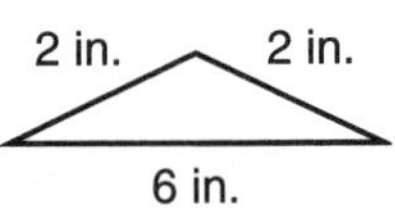

7. Name this type of triangle.

Ⓐ equilateral
Ⓑ scalene
Ⓒ right
Ⓓ isosceles

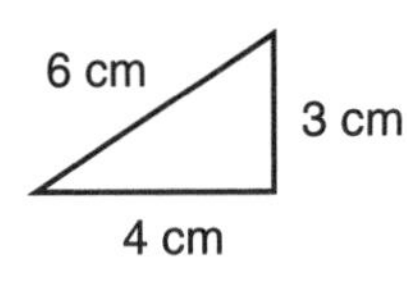

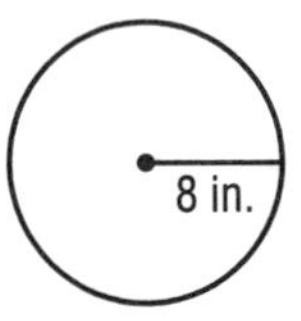

Circle A

8. What is the radius of Circle A?

Ⓕ 2 inches
Ⓖ 4 inches
Ⓗ 8 inches
Ⓙ 16 inches

9. What is the diameter of Circle A?

Ⓐ 2 inches
Ⓑ 4 inches
Ⓒ 8 inches
Ⓓ 16 inches

STOP

Algebra Standards

M3A. Algebra

Students will understand how to express relationships as mathematical expressions.

M3A1. Students will use mathematical expressions to represent relationships between quantities and interpret given expressions. ***(See pages 98–100.)***

a. Describe and extend numeric and geometric patterns.

b. Describe and explain a quantitative relationship represented by a formula (such as the perimeter of a geometric figure).

c. Use a symbol, such as ■ or ▲, to represent an unknown and find the value of the unknown in a number sentence.

Name ______________________ Date ______________

Mathematics

M3A1

Algebra

Extending Patterns

DIRECTIONS: Choose the best answer.

1. **What number is missing from the sequence?**

3	6		12	15

Ⓐ 8
Ⓑ 9
Ⓒ 10
Ⓓ 11

2. **What number is missing from the sequence?**

11	22		44	55

Ⓕ 33
Ⓖ 23
Ⓗ 66
Ⓙ 42

3. **What number is missing from the sequence?**

6	12	18		30

Ⓐ 20
Ⓑ 24
Ⓒ 22
Ⓓ 26

4. **What number is missing from the sequence?**

429	433	437	441	

Ⓕ 443
Ⓖ 444
Ⓗ 445
Ⓙ 446

5. **Look at the pattern below. Which grouping is missing from the pattern?**

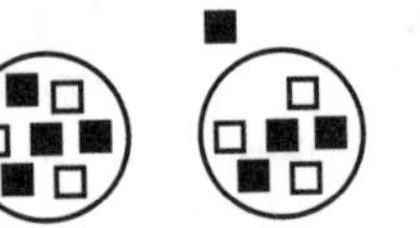 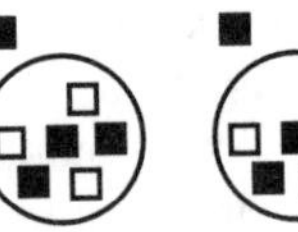 ______ 

Ⓐ 

Ⓑ 

Ⓒ 

Ⓓ 

6. **Look at the pattern. Which shape below should come next in the pattern?**

Ⓕ 

Ⓖ 

Ⓗ 

Ⓙ 

STOP

Name ______________________ Date ______________

Mathematics

M3A1

Algebra

Using Formulas

DIRECTIONS: Choose the best answer.

Use this shape for numbers 1–2.

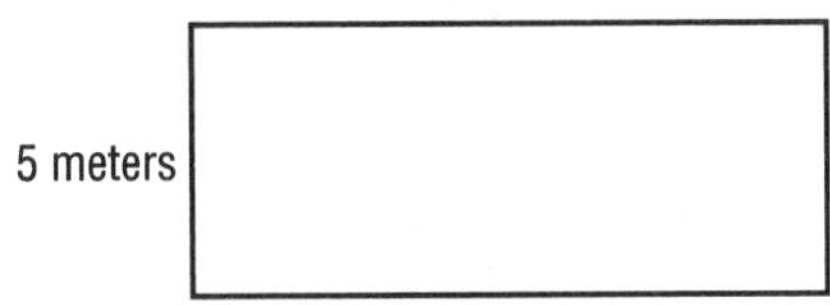

1. What is the area of this shape? (Area = length × width)

Ⓐ 60 square meters

Ⓑ 34 square meters

Ⓒ 17 square meters

Ⓓ 65 square meters

2. What is the perimeter of this shape? (Perimeter = 2 × length + 2 × width)

Ⓕ 60 meters

Ⓖ 34 meters

Ⓗ 17 meters

Ⓙ 64 meters

3. What is the area of a square room if each side is 11 feet? (Area = length × width)

Ⓐ 22 square feet

Ⓑ 110 square feet

Ⓒ 44 square feet

Ⓓ 121 square feet

Use this shape for numbers 4–5.

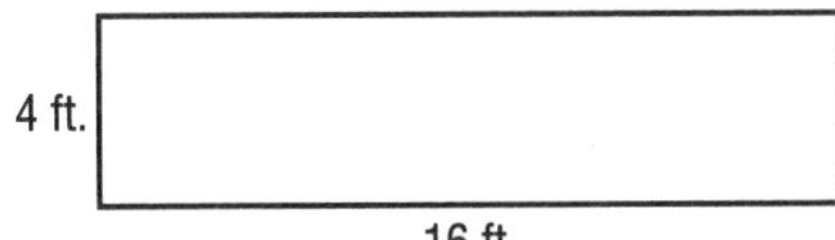

4. What is the perimeter of the shape? (Perimeter = 2 × length + 2 × width)

Ⓕ 40 feet

Ⓖ 20 feet

Ⓗ 64 feet

Ⓙ 24 feet

5. What is the area of the shape? (Area = length × width)

Ⓐ 40 square feet

Ⓑ 20 square feet

Ⓒ 64 square feet

Ⓓ 24 square feet

6. Cara charges 25 cents for a glass of lemonade at her lemonade stand. Which of these number sentences should be used to find how much money she made on a day when she sold 24 glasses?

Ⓕ 24 + $0.25 =

Ⓖ 24 – $0.25 =

Ⓗ 24 × $0.25 =

Ⓙ 24 ÷ $0.25 =

7. If 1 pound of potatoes costs $2.60 and Miko needs to buy 8 pounds to make potato salad, what formula would she use to find the total cost?

Ⓐ $2.60 + 8 =

Ⓑ 8 – $2.60 =

Ⓒ $2.60 × 8 =

Ⓓ 8 ÷ $2.60 =

STOP

Name ______________________________ Date ______________

Mathematics

M3A1

Algebra

Using Variables

DIRECTIONS: Choose the best answer.

1. **What number makes this number sentence true? ■ × 4 = 8**
   (A) 1
   (B) 2
   (C) 0
   (D) 4

2. **What number makes this number sentence true? ■ × ■ = 9**
   (F) 0
   (G) 2
   (H) 3
   (J) 4

3. **What number makes this number sentence true? ■ ÷ 2 = 7**
   (A) 9
   (B) 5
   (C) 3
   (D) 14

4. **What number makes this number sentence true? ■ − 37 = 53**
   (F) 100
   (G) 110
   (H) 90
   (J) 89

5. **What number makes this number sentence true? ■ ÷ 4 = 51**
   (A) 204
   (B) 240
   (C) 47
   (D) 55

6. **What number makes this number sentence true? 9 − ■ = 1**
   (F) 7
   (G) 8
   (H) 6
   (J) 4

7. **What number makes this number sentence true? 22 − ■ = 8**
   (A) 12
   (B) 13
   (C) 14
   (D) 31

8. **What number makes this number sentence true? ■ + 9 = 389**
   (F) 38
   (G) 398
   (H) 12
   (J) 380

9. **The ■ stands for what number? ■ × 12 = 36**
   (A) 6
   (B) 48
   (C) 24
   (D) 3

10. **The ■ stands for what number? 3 × 3 × ■ = 72**
    (F) 7
    (G) 12
    (H) 8
    (J) 4

STOP

Name ______________________________ Date ____________

Mathematics

M3A1

For pages 98–100

Mini-Test 4

Algebra

DIRECTIONS: Choose the best answer.

1. **What shape is missing from this pattern?**

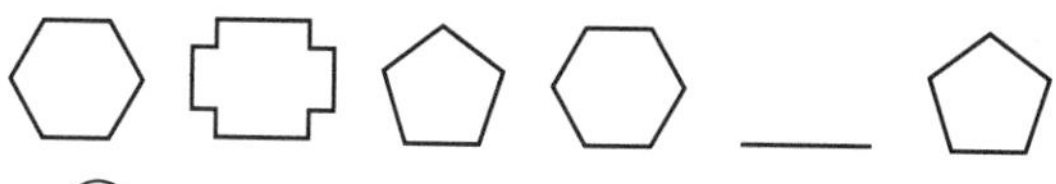

Ⓐ

Ⓑ

Ⓒ

Ⓓ none of these

2. **What number is missing from the sequence?**

4	7		13	16

Ⓕ 8
Ⓖ 9
Ⓗ 10
Ⓙ 11

3. **What number is missing from the sequence?**

128	122	116		104

Ⓐ 112
Ⓑ 110
Ⓒ 108
Ⓓ 106

4. **Which of the following is the formula for finding the area of a shape?**

Ⓕ length + width
Ⓖ length × width
Ⓗ 2 × length + 2 × width
Ⓙ 2 × length + width

5. **Which of the following is the formula for finding the perimeter of a shape?**

Ⓐ length + width
Ⓑ length × width
Ⓒ 2 × length + 2 × width
Ⓓ 2 × length + width

6. **What number makes this number sentence true? 7 × ■ = 56?**

Ⓕ 7
Ⓖ 8
Ⓗ 9
Ⓙ 10

7. **What number makes this number sentence true? ■ ÷ 2 = 68?**

Ⓐ 136
Ⓑ 66
Ⓒ 34
Ⓓ 70

STOP

Data Analysis Standards

M3D. Data Analysis

Students will gather, organize, and display data and interpret graphs.

M3D1. Students will create and interpret simple tables and graphs.
(See pages 103–104.)

a. Solve problems by organizing and displaying data in bar graphs and tables.
b. Construct and interpret bar graphs using scale increments of 1, 2, 5, and 10.

Name ______________________________ Date ____________

Mathematics

M3D1

Data Analysis

Displaying Data

DIRECTIONS: A student rolled a 6-sided number cube 20 times. The results are shown in the table below. Read the table and use the information to fill in the bar graph. Then answer the questions.

Roll	1	2	3	4	5	6	7	8	9	10	11	12	13	14	15	16	17	18	19	20
Number Rolled	3	6	1	4	6	1	5	3	3	6	4	2	6	5	3	1	4	4	3	6

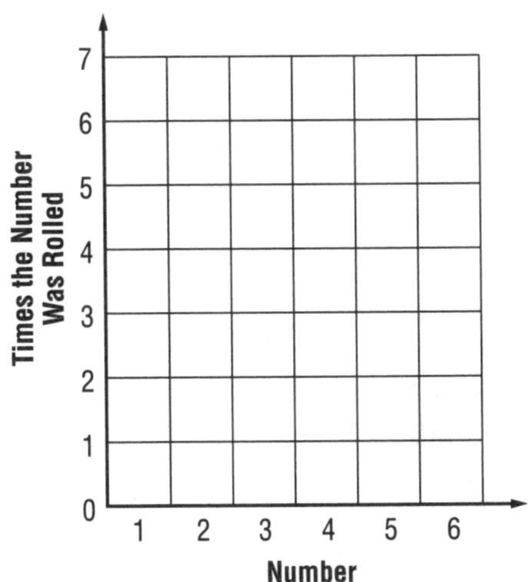

1. How many times did the student roll a 4?

Ⓐ 2 times

Ⓑ 3 times

Ⓒ 4 times

Ⓓ 5 times

2. How many times did the student roll a 1?

Ⓕ 2 times

Ⓖ 3 times

Ⓗ 4 times

Ⓙ 5 times

3. How many times did the student roll a 5?

Ⓐ 2 times

Ⓑ 3 times

Ⓒ 4 times

Ⓓ 5 times

4. What number did he roll the least?

Ⓕ 1

Ⓖ 2

Ⓗ 3

Ⓙ 6

5. How many times did he roll an even number?

Ⓐ 10 times

Ⓑ 12 times

Ⓒ 13 times

Ⓓ 14 times

6. How many times did he roll an odd number?

Ⓕ 13 times

Ⓖ 14 times

Ⓗ 10 times

Ⓙ 16 times

7. What two numbers came up the most?

Ⓐ 2, 5

Ⓑ 1, 2

Ⓒ 1, 5

Ⓓ 3, 6

STOP

Name ______________________________ Date ________________

Mathematics **Data Analysis**

M3D1

Interpreting a Bar Graph

DIRECTIONS: The third-grade students at Millbrook School made a graph about where they wanted to go on vacation. Study the graph, and then answer the questions.

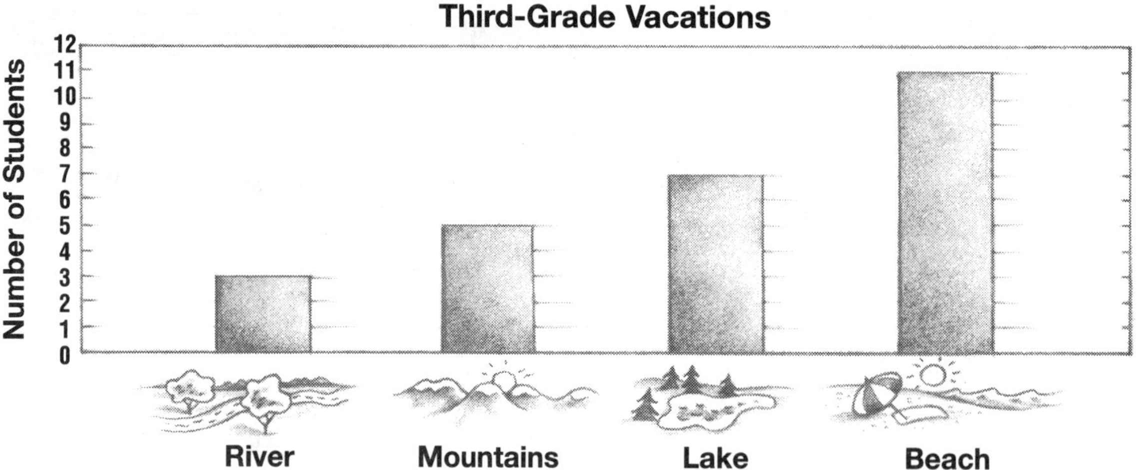

1. **Which of these is another way to show how many students wanted to go to the beach?**

   (A)

   (B)

   (C)

   (D)

2. **Two of the students changed their minds and decided to go to a lake instead of the beach. How many students then wanted to go to a lake?**

   (F) 7 students

   (G) 8 students

   (H) 5 students

   (J) 9 students

3. **How many students wanted to go to a river for vacation?**

   (A) 11 students

   (B) 3 students

   (C) 8 students

   (D) 5 students

4. **What was the third graders' favorite vacation spot?**

   (F) river

   (G) mountains

   (H) lake

   (J) beach

STOP

Name ______________________ Date ______________

Mathematics

M3D1

For pages 103–104

Mini-Test 5

Data Analysis

DIRECTIONS: Look at the graph and then choose the best answer.

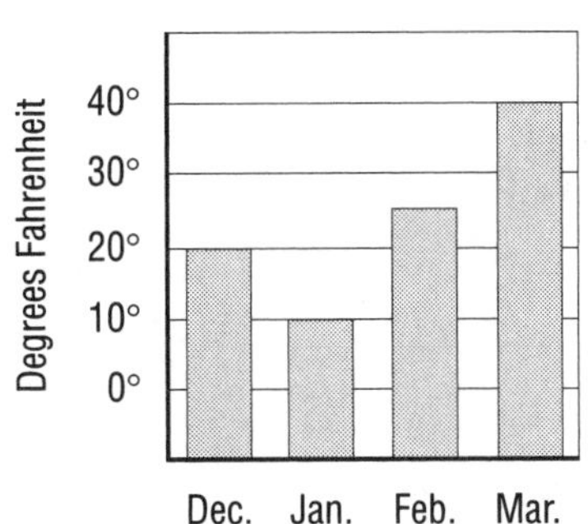

1. In which month was the average daily temperature the lowest?

Ⓐ January
Ⓑ December
Ⓒ March
Ⓓ February

2. What was the average daily temperature in March?

Ⓕ 10°
Ⓖ 20°
Ⓗ 30°
Ⓙ 40°

3. How much did the average daily temperature change from February to March?

Ⓐ 25°
Ⓑ 15°
Ⓒ 10°
Ⓓ 5°

DIRECTIONS: Choose the best answer.

4. Look at the graph below that gives the number of coins in Willie's change jar. How many dimes does Willie have in the change jar?

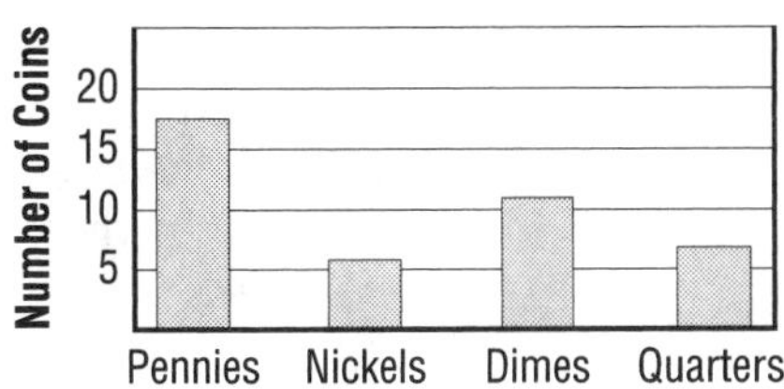

Ⓕ 7 dimes
Ⓖ 11 dimes
Ⓗ 18 dimes
Ⓙ 6 dimes

5. Which animal is between 15 and 40 feet long?

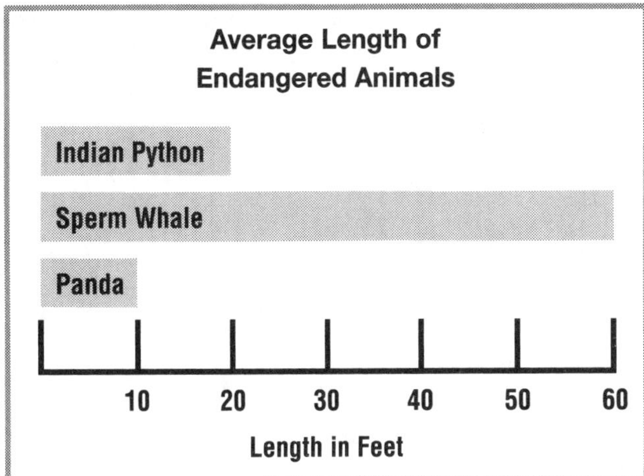

Ⓐ panda
Ⓑ sperm whale
Ⓒ Indian python
Ⓓ none of these

STOP

Process Skills Standards

M3P. Process Skills

Students will apply mathematical concepts and skills in the context of authentic problems and will understand concepts rather than merely following a sequence of procedures. The students will use the process standards as a way of acquiring and using content knowledge.

M3P1. Students will solve problems that arise in mathematics and in other contexts. ***(See pages 107–108.)***

a. Solve nonroutine word problems using the strategy of logical reasoning as well as all strategies learned in previous grades.

b. Solve single- and multi-step routine word problems related to all appropriate third-grade math standards.

c. Determine the operation(s) needed to solve a problem.

d. Determine the most efficient way to solve a problem (mental math, paper/pencil, or calculator).

M3P2. Students will investigate, develop, and evaluate mathematical arguments. ***(See page 109.)***

M3P3. Students will use the language of mathematics to express ideas precisely. ***(See pages 110–111.)***

M3P4. Students will understand how mathematical ideas interconnect and build on one another and apply mathematics in other content areas. ***(See page 112.)***

M3P5. Students will create and use pictures, manipulatives, models, and symbols to organize, record, and communicate mathematical ideas. ***(See pages 113–114.)***

Name ______________________________ Date ______________

Mathematics

M3P1

Solving Word Problems

Process Skills

DIRECTIONS: Choose the best answer.

1. **The music store had 757 customers last month and 662 customers this month. How many customers did the store have altogether in those two months?**
   - (A) 1,409 customers
   - (B) 1,419 customers
   - (C) 1,429 customers
   - (D) 1,439 customers

2. **Janna has invited 5 girls and 3 boys to her birthday party. She plans to give each of her guests two balloons and keep one for herself. How many balloons will she need in all?**
   - (F) 17 balloons
   - (G) 9 balloons
   - (H) 8 balloons
   - (J) 18 balloons

3. **Cody played in 3 basketball games. In the first game, he scored 17 points. In the second game, he scored 22 points. In the third game, he scored twice as many points as in his first game. How many points did he score in the third game?**
   - (A) 44 points
   - (B) 36 points
   - (C) 34 points
   - (D) 42 points

4. **Amir has $3.00 to buy lunch. He chooses a sandwich that costs $1.50 and an orange that costs $0.45. How much money does he have left?**
   - (F) $0.05
   - (G) $1.05
   - (H) $1.15
   - (J) $1.60

5. **The trip from Homeville to Lincoln usually takes 25 minutes by car. While making the trip, a driver spent 12 minutes getting gas and 5 minutes waiting for a road crew. How long did it take the driver to make the trip?**
   - (A) 32 minutes
   - (B) 37 minutes
   - (C) 48 minutes
   - (D) 42 minutes

6. **The price of bread was $1.29, but it increased by 8 cents. The price of a gallon of milk is $2.49. What was the new price of the bread?**
   - (F) $1.21
   - (G) $1.36
   - (H) $1.37
   - (J) $1.39

7. **Arnell wants to buy 3 books. Arnell has $15.00 to spend on the books. Each book costs $3.95. How much will it cost to pay for all the books?**
   - (A) $11.85
   - (B) $12.55
   - (C) $7.90
   - (D) $9.50

8. **Michael has 4 quarters and 2 dimes for bus fare. The bus ride will take 25 minutes. If the bus ride costs $0.75, how much money will he have left?**
   - (F) $0.25
   - (G) $0.35
   - (H) $0.45
   - (J) $0.50

STOP

Name ______________________ Date ______________

Mathematics **Process Skills**

M3P1

Determining the Operations to Solve Problems

DIRECTIONS: Choose the best answer.

1. 10 ▩ 2 = 20

   Which operation sign belongs in the box?

   Ⓐ +
   Ⓑ −
   Ⓒ ×
   Ⓓ ÷

2. 25 ▩ 5 = 5

   Which operation sign belongs in the box?

   Ⓕ +
   Ⓖ −
   Ⓗ ×
   Ⓙ ÷

3. 18 ▩ 9 = 9

   Which operation sign belongs in the box?

   Ⓐ +
   Ⓑ −
   Ⓒ ×
   Ⓓ ÷

4. **Sue buys a coat that costs $75. To find her change for $80, which operation would you use?**

   Ⓕ addition
   Ⓖ subtraction
   Ⓗ multiplication
   Ⓙ division

5. **There are 762 CD titles listed in the computer. Macy enters 292 new titles into the computer. To find the total number of CD titles listed now, which operation would you use?**

   Ⓐ addition
   Ⓑ subtraction
   Ⓒ multiplication
   Ⓓ division

6. **The store sells 5 cans of peas for $1.25. Which operation helps you find out how much each can costs?**

   Ⓕ addition
   Ⓖ subtraction
   Ⓗ multiplication
   Ⓙ division

7. **Brandon has a new fish tank. In his tank there are 4 guppies, 2 neon tetras, and 1 goldfish. Brandon uses __________ to find out how many fish he has in his tank.**

   Ⓐ addition
   Ⓑ subtraction
   Ⓒ multiplication
   Ⓓ division

Name ______________________ Date ______________

Mathematics **Process Skills**

M3P2

Evaluating Mathematical Arguments

DIRECTIONS: Choose the best answer.

1. **Michael has five pieces of candy. Estimate the number of pieces he would have if he adds five additional pieces each minute for three minutes.**
   - (A) 15
   - (B) 20
   - (C) 25
   - (D) none of these

2. **Which number sentence shows how to verify the estimation in question 1?**
   - (F) $5 + 10 = 15$
   - (G) $5 \times 3 + 5 = 20$
   - (H) $5 \times 5 = 25$
   - (J) none of these

3. **Tai carried four boxes of tiles into the kitchen. Each box held 12 tiles. How would you best estimate the total number of tiles he carried into the kitchen?**
   - (A) multiply
   - (B) subtract
   - (C) divide
   - (D) none of these

4. **Which number sentence proves the total number of tiles Tai carried into the kitchen?**
   - (F) $4 \times 12 = 48$
   - (G) $12 - 4 = 8$
   - (H) $48 \div 8 = 6$
   - (J) none of these

5. **This map shows Janelle's yard. She came in through the gate and walked three yards in one direction, then turned and went two yards in a different direction. She ended up closest to the steps. In which directions can you predict that she traveled?**

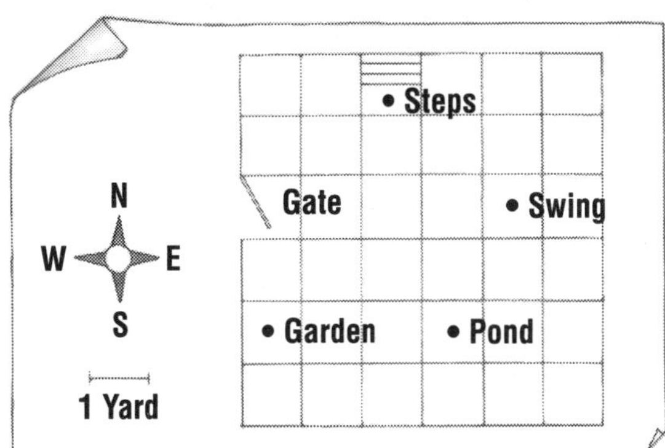

   - (A) east and north
   - (B) south and east
   - (C) west and south
   - (D) north and west

STOP

Name ______________________ Date ______________

Mathematics **Process Skills**

M3P3

Using Mathematical Language

DIRECTIONS: Choose the best answer.

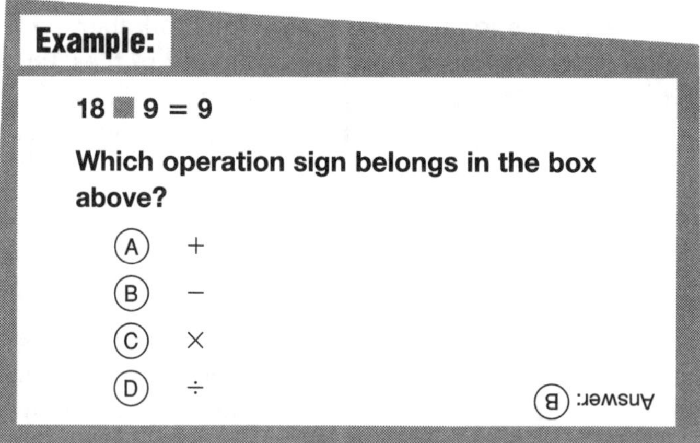
Example:

18 ■ 9 = 9

Which operation sign belongs in the box above?

Ⓐ +
Ⓑ −
Ⓒ ×
Ⓓ ÷

Answer: Ⓑ

When you are not sure of an answer, make your best guess and move on to the next problem.

1. Which operation sign belongs in both boxes?

27 ■ 8 = 19   10 ■ 2 = 8

Ⓐ +
Ⓑ −
Ⓒ ×
Ⓓ ÷

2. You have a bag of candy to share with your class. There are 25 students in your class. You want each student to get 7 pieces. What operation will you need to use to figure out how many candies you need?

Ⓕ addition
Ⓖ subtraction
Ⓗ multiplication
Ⓙ division

3. Look at the figure. What is its perimeter?

Ⓐ 20 inches
Ⓑ 15 inches
Ⓒ 12 inches
Ⓓ 38 inches

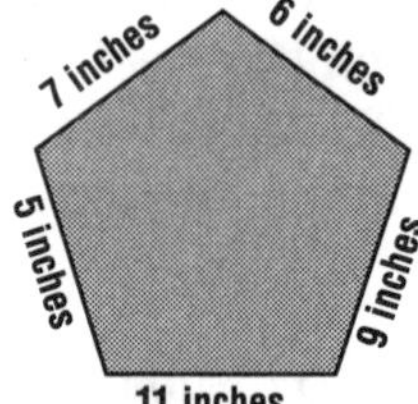

4. Tad wants to find the weight of a box of cereal. What unit of measurement will he probably find on the side of the box?

Ⓕ millimeters
Ⓖ pounds
Ⓗ hectoliters
Ⓙ ounces

GO

Name ______________________________ Date ______________

5. Which of these numbers shows 587 rounded to the nearest hundred?

Ⓐ 580

Ⓑ 600

Ⓒ 690

Ⓓ 500

6. How can you write 9,876 in expanded notation?

Ⓕ 9,800 + 76 + 0

Ⓖ 9,800 + 70 + 60

Ⓗ 9,000 + 870 + 60

Ⓙ 9,000 + 800 + 70 + 6

7. Which of these numbers has a 1 in the tens place and a 7 in the ones place?

Ⓐ 710

Ⓑ 701

Ⓒ 517

Ⓓ 471

8. What sign correctly completes the number sentence?

24 ■ 6 = 4

Ⓕ ÷

Ⓖ −

Ⓗ +

Ⓙ ×

9. What sign correctly completes the number sentence?

72 ■ 9 = 63

Ⓐ ÷

Ⓑ −

Ⓒ +

Ⓓ ×

10. Which decimal is equal to $\frac{1}{4}$?

Ⓕ 0.25

Ⓖ 0.025

Ⓗ 0.75

Ⓙ 0.033

11.

■	■	■
■		

The fraction for the shaded boxes is ________ .

Ⓐ $\frac{4}{3}$

Ⓑ $\frac{2}{8}$

Ⓒ $\frac{2}{6}$

Ⓓ $\frac{4}{6}$

12. Which amount is the same as 25 cents?

Ⓕ $\frac{1}{4}$ dollar

Ⓖ $\frac{1}{2}$ dollar

Ⓗ $\frac{2}{3}$ dollar

Ⓙ $\frac{3}{4}$ dollar

STOP

Name ______________________________ Date ______________

Mathematics **Process Skills**

M3P4

Math in Other Content Areas

DIRECTIONS: The fourth-grade students at Zinser Elementary were asked to do reports on one of the following five birds: hummingbird, hawk, owl, blue jay, or California condor. Use the graph below to answer questions 1–3.

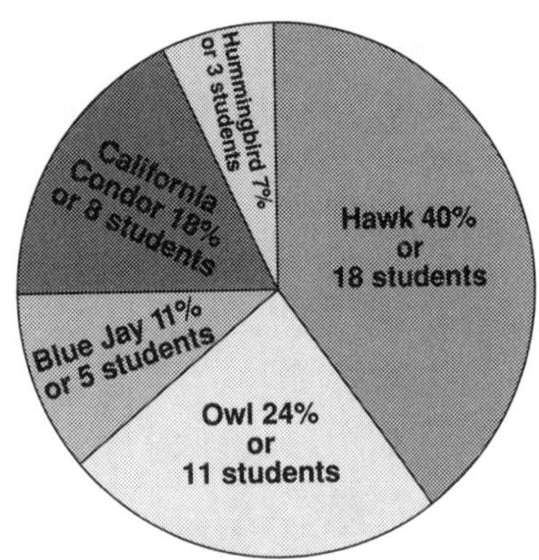

1. Which of the following lists the birds from least to most favorite?

Ⓐ hawk, owl, California condor, blue jay, hummingbird
Ⓑ blue jay, hummingbird, California condor, owl, hawk
Ⓒ hummingbird, blue jay, California condor, owl, hawk
Ⓓ California condor, hawk, owl, blue jay, hummingbird

2. Which two kinds of birds combined below get more than 50 percent of the vote?

Ⓕ hawk and owl
Ⓖ hummingbird and California condor
Ⓗ hummingbird and blue jay
Ⓙ hawk and hummingbird

3. What percent of the vote do the hummingbird, California condor, and blue jay make up together?

Ⓐ 40%
Ⓑ 25%
Ⓒ 30%
Ⓓ 36%

DIRECTIONS: Use the graph for questions 4–5.

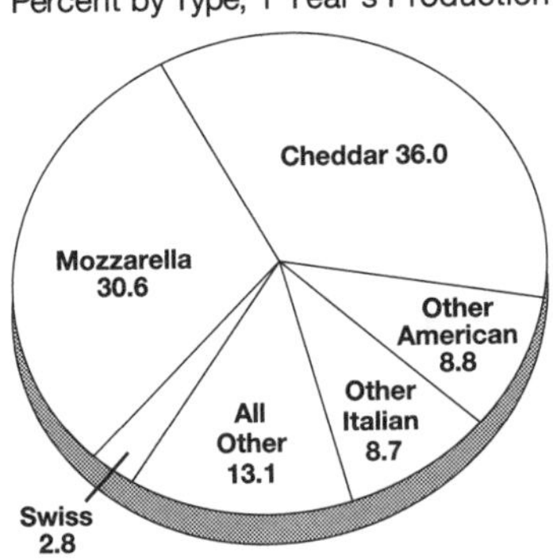

4. Which cheese is made the least?

Ⓕ Other Italian Ⓗ Cheddar
Ⓖ Mozzarella Ⓙ Swiss

5. Which two cheeses together make up 66.6% of the year's production?

Ⓐ Other American and Other Italian
Ⓑ Cheddar and Mozzarella
Ⓒ Mozzarella and Swiss
Ⓓ Cheddar and Swiss

DIRECTIONS: Choose the best answer.

Saturday

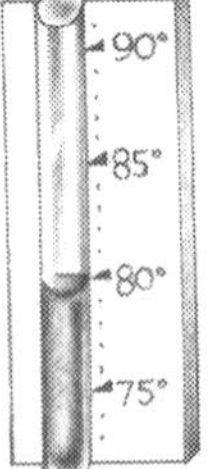

Sunday

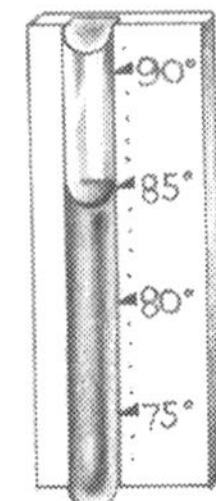

6. How did the temperature change between Saturday and Sunday? On Sunday it was __________.

Ⓕ 5 degrees cooler than Saturday
Ⓖ 10 degrees cooler than Saturday
Ⓗ 5 degrees warmer than Saturday
Ⓙ 10 degrees warmer than Saturday

Name ______________________ Date ______________

M3P5

Using Pictures to Communicate Mathematical Ideas

DIRECTIONS: Choose the best answer.

Decide what useful information you can get from a picture, chart, or graph before you read the question.

1. Sarah just read that her town has the highest population in the county. Based on the chart below, in which city does Sarah live?

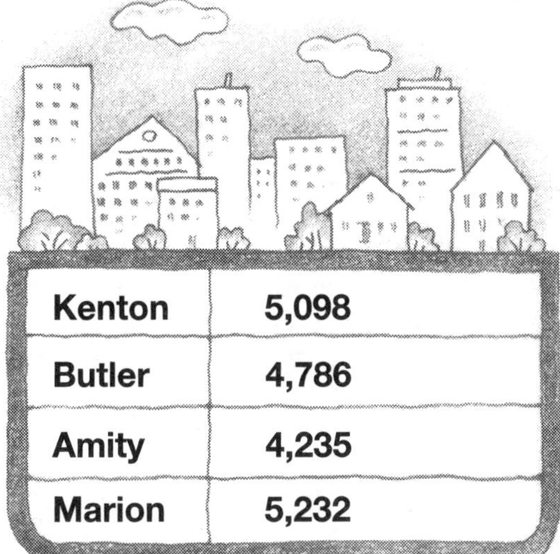

Kenton	5,098
Butler	4,786
Amity	4,235
Marion	5,232

Ⓐ Kenton
Ⓑ Butler
Ⓒ Amity
Ⓓ Marion

2. Which number sentence shows the total number of beans?

Ⓕ 18 + 2
Ⓖ 30 ÷ 2
Ⓗ 10 − 2
Ⓙ 3 × 4

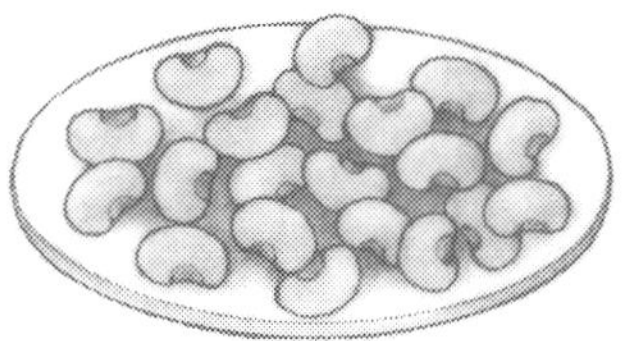

3. Which two things together would cost $30.00?

Ⓐ hat and shirt
Ⓑ belt and socks
Ⓒ shirt and socks
Ⓓ hat and belt

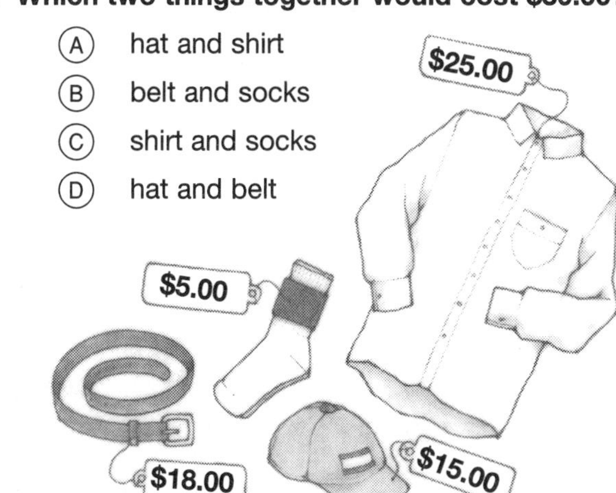

4. Look at the pattern of fruit. Which of these is the missing piece of fruit?

Ⓕ orange
Ⓖ banana
Ⓗ pear
Ⓙ apple

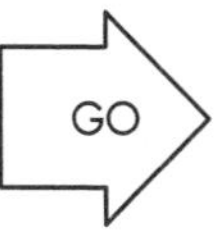

Name ________________________________ Date ________________

DIRECTIONS: Solve these problems using paper and pencil. Write directions or show the steps for solving the problem in the space provided.

5. **There are 8 classrooms at Tanglewood Elementary School that have 17 students in them. There are 7 classrooms that have 18 students in them. How many students are there in all 15 classrooms?**

   Ⓐ 126 students
   Ⓑ 262 students
   Ⓒ 136 students
   Ⓓ 321 students

6. **At the county fair, there are 2 dunking booths, 16 rides, 4 shows, 21 games, and 1 hall of mirrors. How many attractions are at the county fair altogether?**

   Ⓕ 44 attractions
   Ⓖ 23 attractions
   Ⓗ 43 attractions
   Ⓙ 32 attractions

7. **Taina had a rectangle made out of paper. She drew a line down the middle of the rectangle, and then she drew a line diagonal through the rectangle. She had drawn 4 shapes. What is one shape she made?**

   Ⓐ square
   Ⓑ circle
   Ⓒ triangle
   Ⓓ oval

8. **Julie bought a model robot building kit for $135 and a model rocket building kit for $128. She started with $350. How much money does she have left?**

   Ⓕ $215
   Ⓖ $222
   Ⓗ $87
   Ⓙ $78

Name ______________________ Date ______________

Mathematics

M3P1–M3P5

For pages 107–114

Mini-Test 6

Process Skills

DIRECTIONS: Use the following price information to answer questions 1–4.

Family Tent: $90.00
Two Person Tent: ______
Sleeping Bags: $16.00
Cooking Stove: $25.00
Cooking Sets: $23.00
(dishes, pots)
Cutlery: $15.00

1. How much would 1 family tent and 4 sleeping bags cost?

Ⓐ $154.00
Ⓑ $152.00
Ⓒ $90.00
Ⓓ $64.00

2. The two-person tent costs $\frac{1}{3}$ the price of the family tent. It costs ________ .

Ⓕ $20.00
Ⓖ $30.00
Ⓗ $60.00
Ⓙ $70.00

3. Which is the cheapest to buy?

Ⓐ 1 family tent and 2 sleeping bags
Ⓑ 2 two-person tents and 2 sleeping bags
Ⓒ 4 sleeping bags and 1 cooking stove
Ⓓ 1 family tent and 1 cooking stove

4. If someone bought 1 cooking stove, 1 cooking set, and 1 pair of hiking boots, he would pay ________ .

Ⓕ $60.00
Ⓖ $62.00
Ⓗ $63.00
Ⓙ not enough information

DIRECTIONS: Diagram a solution to numbers 5–6.

5. A waiter put 9 napkins on each table. There were 4 tables total. The waiter used ________ napkins.

Ⓐ 18
Ⓑ 27
Ⓒ 36
Ⓓ 42

6. There are 24 students in Tony's class at school. Sixteen of the students are girls. How many boys are in his class?

Ⓕ 8 boys
Ⓖ 9 boys
Ⓗ 10 boys
Ⓙ 12 boys

GO

Name ______________________________ Date ______________

DIRECTIONS: Choose the best answer. Use a calculator if needed to find the solution.

7. **There were 488 balloons decorating the gymnasium for a party. There were 97 students at the party. If each student brought home an equal number of balloons after the party, how many balloons were left over?**
   - (A) 3 balloons
   - (B) 46 balloons
   - (C) 12 balloons
   - (D) none of these

8. **If you burn 318 calories in 60 minutes of playing tennis, how many calories would you burn in 30 minutes?**
   - (F) 159 calories
   - (G) 636 calories
   - (H) 258 calories
   - (J) 288 calories

9. **There are 62 students on a class trip. They are taking a bus to the nature park. Lunch at the park costs $3.25 per child. How much will it cost for all of the students to have lunch at the park?**
   - (A) $201.50
   - (B) $50.00
   - (C) $120.25
   - (D) not enough information

10. **The school play sold out every night. The play ran for 3 nights, and 345 people attended each night. Tickets cost $4.25 each. How much money did the school play make?**
    - (F) $1,239.50
    - (G) $1,466.25
    - (H) $1,035.00
    - (J) $4,398.75

DIRECTIONS: Study the graph. Use the information to answer questions 11–13.

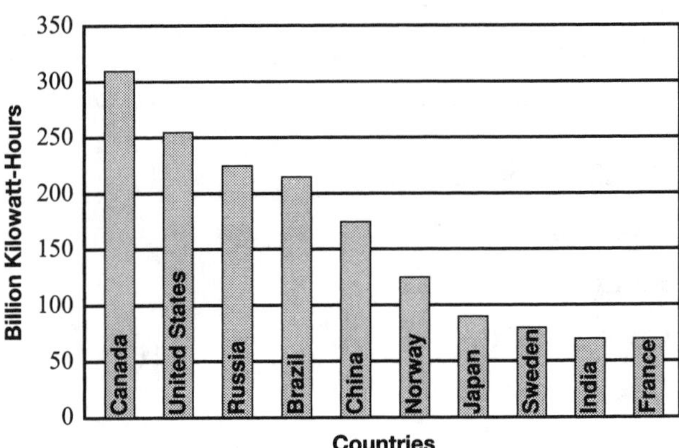

11. **Which country below produces the least amount of hydroelectricity?**
    - (A) Brazil
    - (B) China
    - (C) India
    - (D) Canada

12. **Which country produces more hydroelectricity than Brazil and less than the United States?**
    - (F) Russia
    - (G) China
    - (H) Canada
    - (J) Brazil

13. **In which class would a graph like this most likely be used?**
    - (A) geography
    - (B) music
    - (C) English
    - (D) gym

How Am I Doing?

Mini-Test 1 Pages 81–82 **Number Correct**	**15–19** answers correct	**Great Job!** Move on to the section test on page 119.
	11–14 answers correct	**You're almost there!** But you still need a little practice. Review practice pages 65–80 before moving on to the section test on page 119.
	0–10 answers correct	**Oops!** Time to review what you have learned and try again. Review the practice section on pages 65–80. Then retake the test on pages 81–82. Now move on to the section test on page 119.
Mini-Test 2 Page 90 **Number Correct**	**8** answers correct	**Awesome!** Move on to the section test on page 119.
	4–7 answers correct	**You're almost there!** But you still need a little practice. Review practice pages 84–89 before moving on to the section test on page 119.
	0–3 answers correct	**Oops!** Time to review what you have learned and try again. Review the practice section on pages 84–89. Then retake the test on page 90. Now move on to the section test on page 119.
Mini-Test 3 Page 96 **Number Correct**	**9** answers correct	**Great Job!** Move on to the section test on page 119.
	5–8 answers correct	**You're almost there!** But you still need a little practice. Review practice pages 92–95 before moving on to the section test on page 119.
	0–4 answers correct	**Oops!** Time to review what you have learned and try again. Review the practice section on pages 92–95. Then retake the test on page 96. Now move on to the section test on page 119.

How Am I Doing?

Mini-Test 4 Page 101 **Number Correct**	**7** answers correct	**Great Job!** Move on to the section test on page 119.
	5–6 answers correct	**You're almost there!** But you still need a little practice. Review practice pages 98–100 before moving on to the section test on page 119.
	0–4 answers correct	**Oops!** Time to review what you have learned and try again. Review the practice section on pages 98–100. Then retake the test on page 101. Now move on to the section test on page 119.
Mini-Test 5 Page 105 **Number Correct**	**5** answers correct	**Awesome!** Move on to the section test on page 119.
	4 answers correct	**You're almost there!** But you still need a little practice. Review practice pages 103–104 before moving on to the section test on page 119.
	0–3 answers correct	**Oops!** Time to review what you have learned and try again. Review the practice section on pages 103–104. Then retake the test on page 105. Now move on to the section test on page 119.
Mini-Test 6 Pages 115–116 **Number Correct**	**10–13** answers correct	**Great Job!** Move on to the section test on page 119.
	6–9 answers correct	**You're almost there!** But you still need a little practice. Review practice pages 107–114 before moving on to the section test on page 119.
	0–5 answers correct	**Oops!** Time to review what you have learned and try again. Review the practice section on pages 107–114. Then retake the test on pages 115–116. Now move on to the section test on page 119.

Name ______________________________ Date ______________

Final Mathematics Test

for pages 65–116

DIRECTIONS: Choose the best answer.

1. Which of these numbers is eight thousand, six hundred twenty-two?

- Ⓐ 8,622
- Ⓑ 8,602
- Ⓒ 862
- Ⓓ 88,622

2. How can you write 26,345 in expanded notation?

- Ⓕ 26 + 34 + 5
- Ⓖ 2,600 + 3,400 + 5
- Ⓗ 26,000 + 6,000 + 300 + 45 + 1
- Ⓙ 20,000 + 6,000 + 300 + 40 + 5

3. 12 + 17 + 25 =

- Ⓐ 45
- Ⓑ 55
- Ⓒ 54
- Ⓓ none of these

4.
$$\begin{array}{r} 373 \\ -369 \\ \hline \end{array}$$

- Ⓕ 2
- Ⓖ 3
- Ⓗ 4
- Ⓙ none of these

5. 212 × 5 =

- Ⓐ 1,050
- Ⓑ 1,024
- Ⓒ 1,060
- Ⓓ none of these

6. 48 ÷ 6 =

- Ⓕ 8
- Ⓖ 7
- Ⓗ 9
- Ⓙ none of these

7. Which of these is the best way to estimate the answer to this problem?

394 + 219 = ■

- Ⓐ 300 + 200 = ■
- Ⓑ 400 − 200 = ■
- Ⓒ 400 + 200 = ■
- Ⓓ 300 − 200 = ■

8. 6 × 3 =

- Ⓕ 6 + 6 + 6
- Ⓖ 6 + 3
- Ⓗ 3 + 3 + 3 + 6
- Ⓙ 6 ÷ 3

9. 4 × (2 + 5) =

- Ⓐ (4 × 2) + (2 + 5)
- Ⓑ 4 + 2 + 5
- Ⓒ (4 × 2) + (4 × 5)
- Ⓓ 4 × 5 + 2

10. 7 × 300 =

- Ⓕ 210
- Ⓖ 2,100
- Ⓗ 1,000
- Ⓙ 21,000

GO

Name ______________________________ Date ______________

11. 65 + 12 = ■ + 65

Ⓐ 77

Ⓑ 65

Ⓒ 12

Ⓓ 43

12. 2 × (4 × 5) = (2 × 4) × ■

Ⓕ 2

Ⓖ 20

Ⓗ 4

Ⓙ 5

13. 121 ÷ 11 = ■; 11 × ■ = 121

Ⓐ 12

Ⓑ 11

Ⓒ 132

Ⓓ 10

14. 48 ÷ 7 =

Ⓕ 7

Ⓖ 6 R1

Ⓗ 6 R3

Ⓙ 6 R6

15. Which fraction is the same as 0.9?

Ⓐ $\frac{9}{10}$

Ⓑ $\frac{9}{100}$

Ⓒ $\frac{1}{9}$

Ⓓ $\frac{90}{1,000}$

16. Which is the same as $\frac{14}{100}$?

Ⓕ 14.00

Ⓖ 0.014

Ⓗ 0.14

Ⓙ 1.4

17. Which of these figures shows $\frac{3}{4}$?

Ⓐ 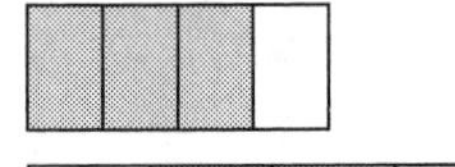

Ⓑ

Ⓒ 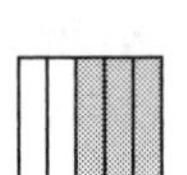

Ⓓ

18. $\frac{2}{5} + \frac{1}{5} =$

Ⓕ $\frac{3}{5}$

Ⓖ $\frac{4}{5}$

Ⓗ $\frac{5}{5}$

Ⓙ none of these

19. $\frac{7}{8} - \frac{6}{8} =$

Ⓐ $\frac{2}{8}$

Ⓑ $\frac{1}{4}$

Ⓒ $\frac{1}{8}$

Ⓓ none of these

20. $\begin{array}{r} 8.2 \\ +\ 3.6 \\ \hline \end{array}$

Ⓕ 10.9

Ⓖ 12.8

Ⓗ 12.4

Ⓙ 11.8

GO

Name ______________________________ Date ______________

21. **How many minutes have passed when the minute hand on a clock travels from 2:10 to 2:55?**

Ⓐ 25 minutes
Ⓑ 35 minutes
Ⓒ 45 minutes
Ⓓ 60 minutes

22. **If you wanted to measure the distance from your house to your school, what unit would you most likely use?**

Ⓕ inches
Ⓖ centimeters
Ⓗ yards
Ⓙ miles

23. **Which of these statements is not true?**

Ⓐ 1 kilometer = 1,000 meters
Ⓑ 1 mile = 1 kilometer
Ⓒ 1 mile = 5,280 feet
Ⓓ 1 yard = 3 feet

24. **5 feet = _____ inches**

Ⓕ 24
Ⓖ 36
Ⓗ 48
Ⓙ 60

25. **3 meters = _____ centimeters**

Ⓐ 30
Ⓑ 300
Ⓒ 3,000
Ⓓ 36

26. **Which of these paper clips is approximately 2 inches long?**

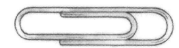

Ⓕ 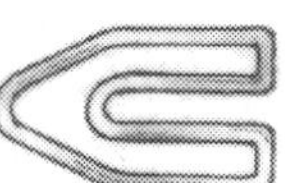

Ⓖ 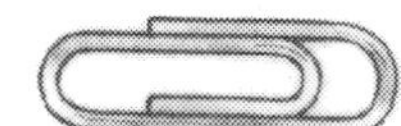

Ⓗ 

Ⓙ 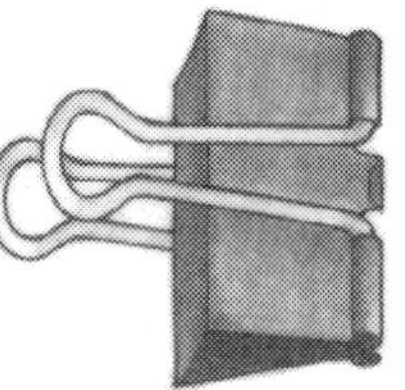

27. **What is the perimeter of the rectangle?**

4 meters
7 meters

Ⓐ 22 meters
Ⓑ 18 meters
Ⓒ 11 meters
Ⓓ 3 meters

28. **What is the area of the shaded region?**

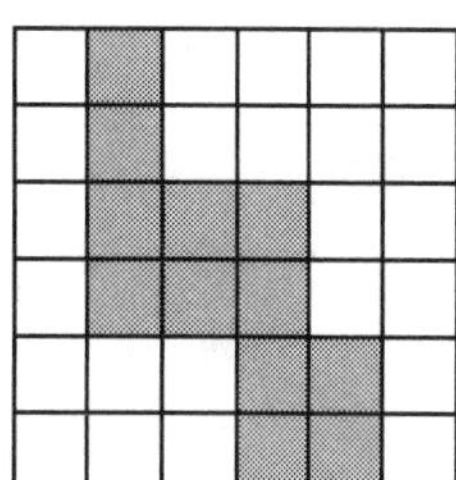

Ⓕ 36 square units
Ⓖ 20 square units
Ⓗ 12 square units
Ⓙ 24 square units

GO

Name ______________________ Date ______________

29. A square garden is 7 feet long on each side. What is the perimeter of the garden?

- Ⓐ 14 feet
- Ⓑ 21 feet
- Ⓒ 24 feet
- Ⓓ 28 feet

30. What is the area of the garden in question 29?

- Ⓕ 14 square feet
- Ⓖ 28 square feet
- Ⓗ 49 square feet
- Ⓙ 21 square feet

31. A polygon that has 5 sides and 5 angles is __________ .

- Ⓐ a square
- Ⓑ a hexagon
- Ⓒ an octagon
- Ⓓ a pentagon

32. This shape is a __________ .

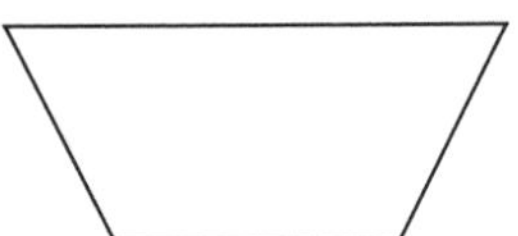

- Ⓕ hexagon
- Ⓖ trapezoid
- Ⓗ square
- Ⓙ rectangle

33 Which triangle is an equilateral triangle?

- Ⓐ 
- Ⓑ
- Ⓒ
- Ⓓ

34. Which triangle is an isosceles triangle?

- Ⓕ
- Ⓖ
- Ⓗ
- Ⓙ

35. If a circle has a radius of 3 inches, what is its diameter?

- Ⓐ 30 inches
- Ⓑ 6 inches
- Ⓒ 9 inches
- Ⓓ none of these

GO

Name ______________________ Date ______________

DIRECTIONS: Choose the best answer.

36. What is the next number after 3, 6, 9, 12?

- (F) 13
- (G) 11
- (H) 15
- (J) 14

37. What is the next number after 4, 8, 12, 16?

- (A) 14
- (B) 20
- (C) 15
- (D) 19

38. Steph ran 2 miles each day for a week. Which number sentence describes how far she ran?

- (F) $2 \times 4 = \blacksquare$
- (G) $7 \times 4 = \blacksquare$
- (H) $2 \times 7 = \blacksquare$
- (J) $2 \times 2 = \blacksquare$

39. What number makes this number sequence true? $6 \times \blacksquare = 42$

- (A) 7
- (B) 9
- (C) 8
- (D) 5

40. Which picture should come next to complete the pattern in the model below?

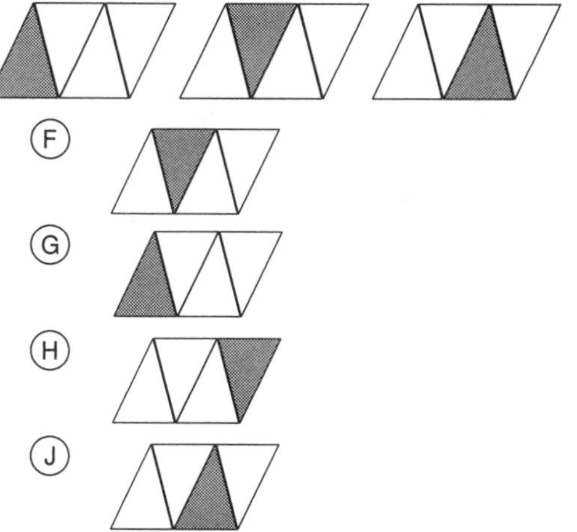

DIRECTIONS: Use the bar graph below to answer questions 41–43. The information in the graph is about Mrs. Coleson's students and their favorite cafeteria lunches. All the students are represented in the graph.

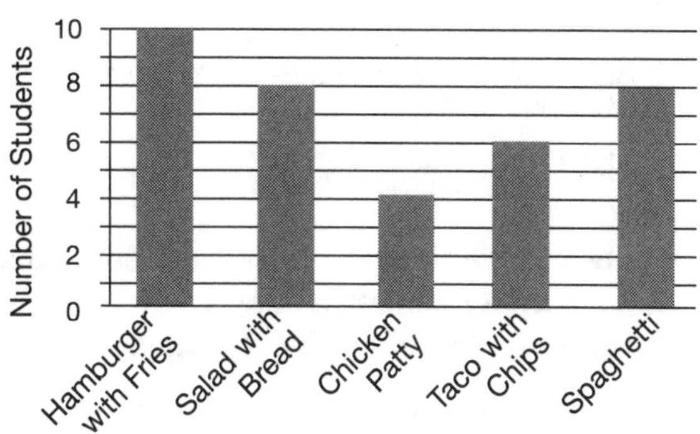

41. Which lunch did the students like the most?

- (A) hamburger with fries
- (B) spaghetti
- (C) chicken patty
- (D) taco with chips

42. Which lunches did the same number of students like?

- (F) chicken patty and spaghetti
- (G) hamburger with fries and spaghetti
- (H) taco with chips and chicken patty
- (J) salad with bread and spaghetti

43. How many students chose taco with chips as their favorite lunch?

- (A) 5 students
- (B) 6 students
- (C) 3 students
- (D) 4 students

GO

Name ______________________________ Date ______________

DIRECTIONS: Choose the best answer.

44. A plane has 124 passengers. There are 3 members of the flying crew and 9 cabin attendants. How many people are on the plane?

- (F) 136 people
- (G) 135 people
- (H) 133 people
- (J) 112 people

45. A babysitter works for 4 hours and earns $20. Which number sentence shows how to find the amount of money the babysitter earns in one hour?

- (A) 4 × $20 = ■
- (B) $5 + ■ = $20
- (C) $20 ÷ $4 = ■
- (D) 4 × ■ = $20

46. Jackie has 20 yards of rope. She wants to cut it into 5 pieces. How long will each piece of rope be?

- (F) 25 yards
- (G) 7 yards
- (H) 5 yards
- (J) 4 yards

47. The forest service in Red Park planted 25 new trees every year for 4 years. How many trees were planted in all?

- (A) 125 trees
- (B) 100 trees
- (C) 50 trees
- (D) 75 trees

48. Look at the clock. How long will it take the minute hand to reach the 6?

- (F) 3 minutes
- (G) 5 minutes
- (H) 12 minutes
- (J) 15 minutes

49. There are 10 centimeters in a decimeter and 100 centimeters in a meter. How many decimeters are in a meter?

- (A) 5 decimeters
- (B) 10 decimeters
- (C) 100 decimeters
- (D) 1,000 decimeters

50. If each of these nails is 1.5 centimeters long, how long would they be altogether if you laid them end-to-end?

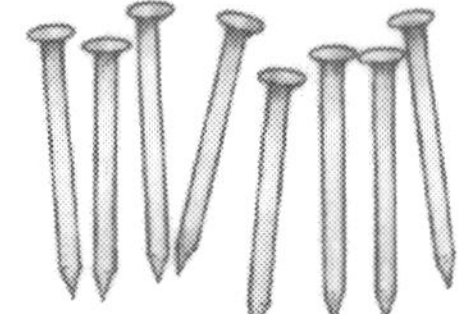

- (F) 10 centimeters
- (G) 11 centimeters
- (H) 12 centimeters
- (J) 13 centimeters

51. Jimmy wants to buy baseball cards for his collection. At a sale, the cards are being sold in packs.

Number of Packs	Number of Cards
2	16
4	32
5	40
6	?
7	56

What is the missing number in the chart?

- (A) 38
- (B) 42
- (C) 48
- (D) none of these

STOP

Name ____________________ Date ____________

Final Mathematics Test

Answer Sheet

1 Ⓐ Ⓑ Ⓒ Ⓓ
2 Ⓕ Ⓖ Ⓗ Ⓙ
3 Ⓐ Ⓑ Ⓒ Ⓓ
4 Ⓕ Ⓖ Ⓗ Ⓙ
5 Ⓐ Ⓑ Ⓒ Ⓓ
6 Ⓕ Ⓖ Ⓗ Ⓙ
7 Ⓐ Ⓑ Ⓒ Ⓓ
8 Ⓕ Ⓖ Ⓗ Ⓙ
9 Ⓐ Ⓑ Ⓒ Ⓓ
10 Ⓕ Ⓖ Ⓗ Ⓙ

11 Ⓐ Ⓑ Ⓒ Ⓓ
12 Ⓕ Ⓖ Ⓗ Ⓙ
13 Ⓐ Ⓑ Ⓒ Ⓓ
14 Ⓕ Ⓖ Ⓗ Ⓙ
15 Ⓐ Ⓑ Ⓒ Ⓓ
16 Ⓕ Ⓖ Ⓗ Ⓙ
17 Ⓐ Ⓑ Ⓒ Ⓓ
18 Ⓕ Ⓖ Ⓗ Ⓙ
19 Ⓐ Ⓑ Ⓒ Ⓓ
20 Ⓕ Ⓖ Ⓗ Ⓙ

21 Ⓐ Ⓑ Ⓒ Ⓓ
22 Ⓕ Ⓖ Ⓗ Ⓙ
23 Ⓐ Ⓑ Ⓒ Ⓓ
24 Ⓕ Ⓖ Ⓗ Ⓙ
25 Ⓐ Ⓑ Ⓒ Ⓓ
26 Ⓕ Ⓖ Ⓗ Ⓙ
27 Ⓐ Ⓑ Ⓒ Ⓓ
28 Ⓕ Ⓖ Ⓗ Ⓙ
29 Ⓐ Ⓑ Ⓒ Ⓓ
30 Ⓕ Ⓖ Ⓗ Ⓙ

31 Ⓐ Ⓑ Ⓒ Ⓓ
32 Ⓕ Ⓖ Ⓗ Ⓙ
33 Ⓐ Ⓑ Ⓒ Ⓓ
34 Ⓕ Ⓖ Ⓗ Ⓙ
35 Ⓐ Ⓑ Ⓒ Ⓓ
36 Ⓕ Ⓖ Ⓗ Ⓙ
37 Ⓐ Ⓑ Ⓒ Ⓓ
38 Ⓕ Ⓖ Ⓗ Ⓙ
39 Ⓐ Ⓑ Ⓒ Ⓓ
40 Ⓕ Ⓖ Ⓗ Ⓙ

41 Ⓐ Ⓑ Ⓒ Ⓓ
42 Ⓕ Ⓖ Ⓗ Ⓙ
43 Ⓐ Ⓑ Ⓒ Ⓓ
44 Ⓕ Ⓖ Ⓗ Ⓙ
45 Ⓐ Ⓑ Ⓒ Ⓓ
46 Ⓕ Ⓖ Ⓗ Ⓙ
47 Ⓐ Ⓑ Ⓒ Ⓓ
48 Ⓕ Ⓖ Ⓗ Ⓙ
49 Ⓐ Ⓑ Ⓒ Ⓓ
50 Ⓕ Ⓖ Ⓗ Ⓙ
51 Ⓐ Ⓑ Ⓒ Ⓓ

Georgia Social Studies Content Standards

The social studies section measures knowledge in four different areas:

1) **History**

2) **Geography**

3) **Government/Civics**

4) **Economics**

Georgia Social Studies Table of Contents

History Standards

SS3H1. The student will explain the political roots of our modern democracy in the United States of America. ***(See page 128.)***

a. Identify the influence of Greek architecture (Parthenon, U.S. Supreme Court Building), law, and the Olympic Games on the present.

b. Explain the ancient Athenians' idea that a community should choose its own leaders.

c. Compare and contrast Athens as a direct democracy and the United States as a representative democracy.

What it means:

- Students should know that a **direct democracy** is a form of democracy in which all citizens can directly participate in the decision-making process. A **representative democracy** is a form of democracy in which voters choose representatives to act in their interests.

SS3H2. The student will discuss the lives of Americans who expanded people's rights and freedoms in a democracy. ***(See pages 129–130.)***

a. Paul Revere (independence), Frederick Douglass (civil rights), Susan B. Anthony (women's rights), Mary McLeod Bethune (education), Franklin D. Roosevelt (New Deal and World War II), Eleanor Roosevelt (United Nations and human rights), Thurgood Marshall (civil rights), Lyndon B. Johnson (Great Society and voting rights), and Cesar Chavez (worker's rights).

b. Explain social barriers, restrictions, and obstacles that these historical figures had to overcome, and describe how they overcame them.

Name ______________________________ Date ______________

Social Studies

History

SS3H1

Democracy

DIRECTIONS: Choose the best answer.

1. **The word *democracy* means _________ .**
   - Ⓐ rule of one
   - Ⓑ rule by a few
   - Ⓒ rule by the people
   - Ⓓ rule by the wealthy

2. **Democracy originated, or started, in _________ .**
   - Ⓕ Athens, Greece
   - Ⓖ Sparta, Greece
   - Ⓗ Rome, Italy
   - Ⓙ London, England

3. **The possibility of attack was always present in ancient Greece. In Athens, the middle-class citizens made up the largest part of the army. The purpose of democracy was to assure the middle class that they had a voice in government. Based on this information, which of the following is a reason Athenians wanted democracy for their city?**
   - Ⓐ The aristocracy was tired of leading the city.
   - Ⓑ Athenians did not want to lose their army in case of war.
   - Ⓒ Soldiers were considered to be the best leaders.
   - Ⓓ Athens wanted to bring peace to Greece.

4. **In a direct democracy, decisions are voted on by _________ .**
   - Ⓕ elected representatives
   - Ⓖ eligible citizens
   - Ⓗ the president
   - Ⓙ appointed judges

5. **The form of democracy in which voters choose representatives to act in their interests is known as _________ .**
   - Ⓐ an oligarchy
   - Ⓑ an aristocracy
   - Ⓒ a free democracy
   - Ⓓ a representative democracy

6. **Who was given the right to vote in ancient Athens?**
   - Ⓕ adult males
   - Ⓖ adult females
   - Ⓗ foreigners living in Athens
   - Ⓙ all of the above

7. **What type of democracy was practiced in ancient Athens?**
   - Ⓐ free
   - Ⓑ direct
   - Ⓒ political
   - Ⓓ representative

8. **What type of democracy is practiced in the United States today?**
   - Ⓕ free
   - Ⓖ direct
   - Ⓗ political
   - Ⓙ representative

9. **Which of the following structures in Washington, D.C., most shows the influence of Greek architecture as seen in the Parthenon?**
   - Ⓐ Washington Monument
   - Ⓑ Vietnam Veterans Memorial Wall
   - Ⓒ U.S. Supreme Court Building
   - Ⓓ White House

Name ______________________________ Date ______________

Social Studies **History**

SS3H2

Americans Who Expanded Rights and Freedoms

DIRECTIONS: Study the table below and use it to help you answer the questions.

Name	Accomplishment
Susan B. Anthony	Fought to get women the right to vote
Mary McLeod Bethune	Established a school for young African-American women
Cesar Chavez	Labor union leader who fought for the rights of Mexican farm workers
Frederick Douglass	Fought to end slavery; started a newspaper that supported the end of slavery
Lyndon B. Johnson	Signed laws that did not allow most segregation, did not allow discrimination in the workplace, and protected the voting rights of African Americans
Thurgood Marshall	Fought to end segregation in schools
Paul Revere	Fought for independence from Great Britain
Eleanor Roosevelt	Head of a commission that lobbied, or tried to influence, Congress for equal pay for women
Franklin D. Roosevelt	Developed the New Deal programs to help end the Great Depression, signed laws that ended child labor, created a 40-hour workweek for many workers, and provided more protection for workers

Segregation is a term describing the separation of a group of people, such as a race, from another group.

1. Cesar Chavez is best known for ________ .

- (A) establishing a school
- (B) helping farm workers live better lives
- (C) helping to end slavery
- (D) helping to end segregation

2. Which of the following people did *not* affect the rights of workers?

- (F) Eleanor Roosevelt
- (G) Franklin D. Roosevelt
- (H) Susan B. Anthony
- (J) Cesar Chavez

3. Which of the following people helped American women gain the right to vote?

- (A) Susan B. Anthony
- (B) Lyndon B. Johnson
- (C) Eleanor Roosevelt
- (D) Thurgood Marshall

4. Which of the following people helped to protect the civil rights of African Americans?

- (F) Eleanor Roosevelt
- (G) Cesar Chavez
- (H) Paul Revere
- (J) Lyndon B. Johnson

Name ______________________ Date ______________

Social Studies

History

SS3H2

Historic Figures Who Faced Obstacles

DIRECTIONS: Choose the best answer.

1. **Who escaped from slavery before publishing an antislavery newspaper?**
   - (A) Paul Revere
   - (B) Mary McLeod Bethune
   - (C) Frederick Douglass
   - (D) Thurgood Marshall

2. **Which of the following people was born into a poor South Carolina family but was determined to get an education?**
   - (F) Eleanor Roosevelt
   - (G) Cesar Chavez
   - (H) Thurgood Marshall
   - (J) Mary McLeod Bethune

3. **What disease did President Franklin D. Roosevelt become infected with in 1921?**
   - (A) tuberculosis
   - (B) polio
   - (C) multiple sclerosis
   - (D) scarlet fever

4. **How did Franklin D. Roosevelt keep his political career alive while recovering from his disease?**
   - (F) by organizing a large letter-writing campaign
   - (G) by having his wife, Eleanor, speak for him
   - (H) by having his cousin Theodore speak for him
   - (J) none of the above

5. **When southern Senators attempted to prevent the Civil Rights Act of 1957 from passing, who put together a compromise that helped the act to pass?**
   - (A) Lyndon B. Johnson
   - (B) Thurgood Marshall
   - (C) Franklin D. Roosevelt
   - (D) Paul Revere

6. **Who was not allowed to attend the University of Maryland Law School because he or she was an African American?**
   - (F) Paul Revere
   - (G) Cesar Chavez
   - (H) Thurgood Marshall
   - (J) Susan B. Anthony

7. **Cesar Chavez helped start the United Farm Workers Union. As a union leader, he worked to improve the rights of farm workers in California. In spite of his efforts, the grape growers did not listen to the demands of their workers for higher wages and better working conditions. Chavez organized a strike by the workers, but the employers still did not listen to their demands. How did Chavez respond?**
   - (A) He decided to give up the fight.
   - (B) He organized a national boycott of grapes to force the employers to meet the workers' demands.
   - (C) He agreed with the employers that the workers' demands were not reasonable.
   - (D) He tried to persuade workers to work for lower wages.

Name ______________________________ Date ______________

Social Studies

SS3H1–SS3H2

For pages 128–130

Mini-Test 1

History

DIRECTIONS: Choose the best answer.

1. A government in which the leaders are elected is called __________ .

- Ⓐ a monarchy
- Ⓑ a dictatorship
- Ⓒ a democracy
- Ⓓ an empire

2. With which of the following did democracy most likely begin?

- Ⓕ the Revolutionary War
- Ⓖ the U.S. Constitution
- Ⓗ Greek political ideas
- Ⓙ the Roman Empire

3. In ancient Athens, jury members were chosen by lottery from among the citizens. How are jurors in the United States selected today?

- Ⓐ Citizens volunteer for jury duty.
- Ⓑ Citizens are elected to juries.
- Ⓒ Citizens are selected by lottery from a juror list, for example, of registered voters.
- Ⓓ Citizens are hired for the job of juror.

4. In a representative democracy, __________ .

- Ⓕ people elect others to represent them
- Ⓖ only a representative percentage of the population is allowed to vote
- Ⓗ leaders are appointed to represent the people
- Ⓙ the upper class rules

5. Which of the following people helped in the United States's fight for independence?

- Ⓐ Paul Revere
- Ⓑ Frederick Douglass
- Ⓒ Cesar Chavez
- Ⓓ Lyndon B. Johnson

6. Mary McLeod Bethune __________ .

- Ⓕ helped slaves on the Underground Railroad
- Ⓖ established a school for young African American women
- Ⓗ fought for women's voting rights
- Ⓙ fought for equal pay for women

7. Which of the following people is known for producing an antislavery newspaper?

- Ⓐ Thurgood Marshall
- Ⓑ Frederick Douglass
- Ⓒ Paul Revere
- Ⓓ Cesar Chavez

8. As a response to __________ , Franklin D. Roosevelt developed his New Deal programs.

- Ⓕ World War I
- Ⓖ World War II
- Ⓗ the Great Depression
- Ⓙ the issue of segregation

STOP

Geography Standards

SS3G1. The student will locate major topographical features of the United States of America. ***(See pages 133–134.)***

a. Identify major rivers of the United States of America: Mississippi, Ohio, Rio Grande, Colorado, Hudson.

b. Identify major mountains of the United States of America: Appalachian, Rocky.

c. Locate the Equator, Prime Meridian, and lines of latitude and longitude on a globe.

d. Locate Greece on a world map.

SS3G2. The student will describe the cultural and geographic systems associated with the historical figures in SS3H2a. ***(See pages 135–136.)***

a. Identify specific locations significant to the life and times of these historic figures on a political map.

b. Describe how place (physical and human characteristics) affected the lives of these historic figures.

c. Describe how each of these historic figures adapted to and was influenced by his or her environment.

d. Trace examples of travel and movement of these historic figures and their ideas across time.

e. Describe how the region in which these historic figures lived affected their lives and had an impact on their cultural identification.

Name ______________________________ Date ______________

Social Studies

SS3G1

Geography

Identifying Major U.S. Rivers and Mountains

DIRECTIONS: Each of the following rivers and mountains is identified with a number on the map below. Match the names of the rivers and mountains with the numbers on the map.

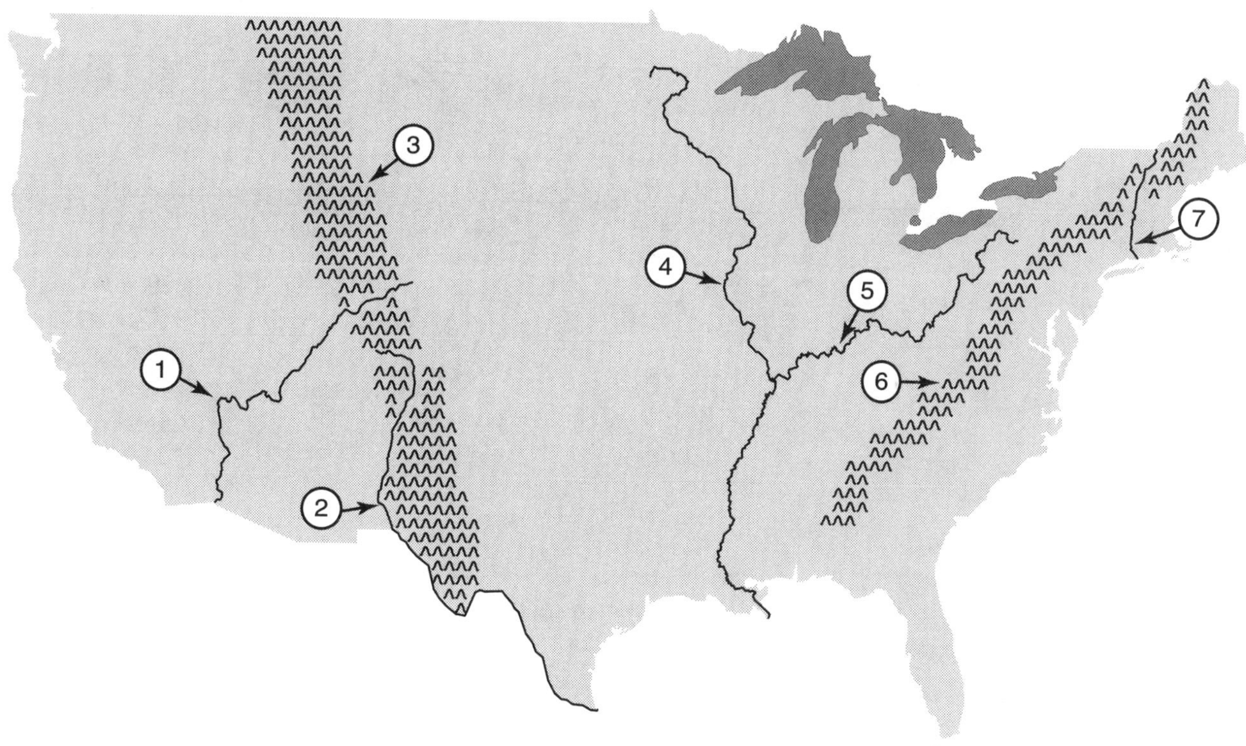

_____ 1. **A. Mississippi River**

_____ 2. **B. Rocky Mountains**

_____ 3. **C. Appalachian Mountains**

_____ 4. **D. Hudson River**

_____ 5. **E. Rio Grande River**

_____ 6. **F. Ohio River**

_____ 7. **G. Colorado River**

STOP

Name ______________________________ Date ______________

Social Studies

SS3G1

Geography

Lines of Latitude and Longitude

DIRECTIONS: Use the maps below to answer the questions.

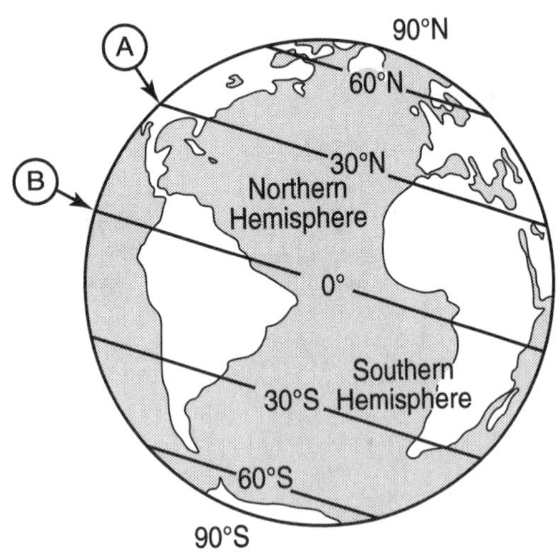

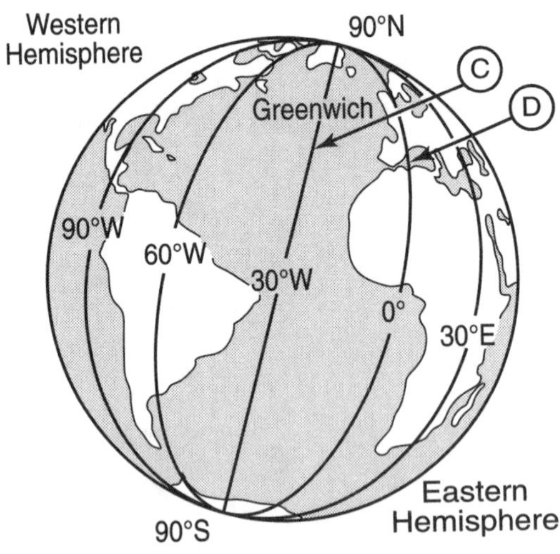

Lines of latitude on a map run from east to west. *Lines of longitude* run from north to south.

1. Which letter on the map represents the Prime Meridian?

Ⓐ A
Ⓑ B
Ⓒ C
Ⓓ D

2. Which letter on the map represents a line of longitude other than the Prime Meridian?

Ⓕ A
Ⓖ B
Ⓗ C
Ⓙ D

3. Which letter on the map represents the Equator?

Ⓐ A
Ⓑ B
Ⓒ C
Ⓓ D

4. Which letter on the map represents a line of latitude other than the Equator?

Ⓕ A
Ⓖ B
Ⓗ C
Ⓙ D

STOP

Name ______________________ Date ______________

Social Studies

SS3G2

Geography

Identifying Historic Locations

DIRECTIONS: Choose the name of the state where each event took place. Then write the names of each of the states in the correct location on the map.

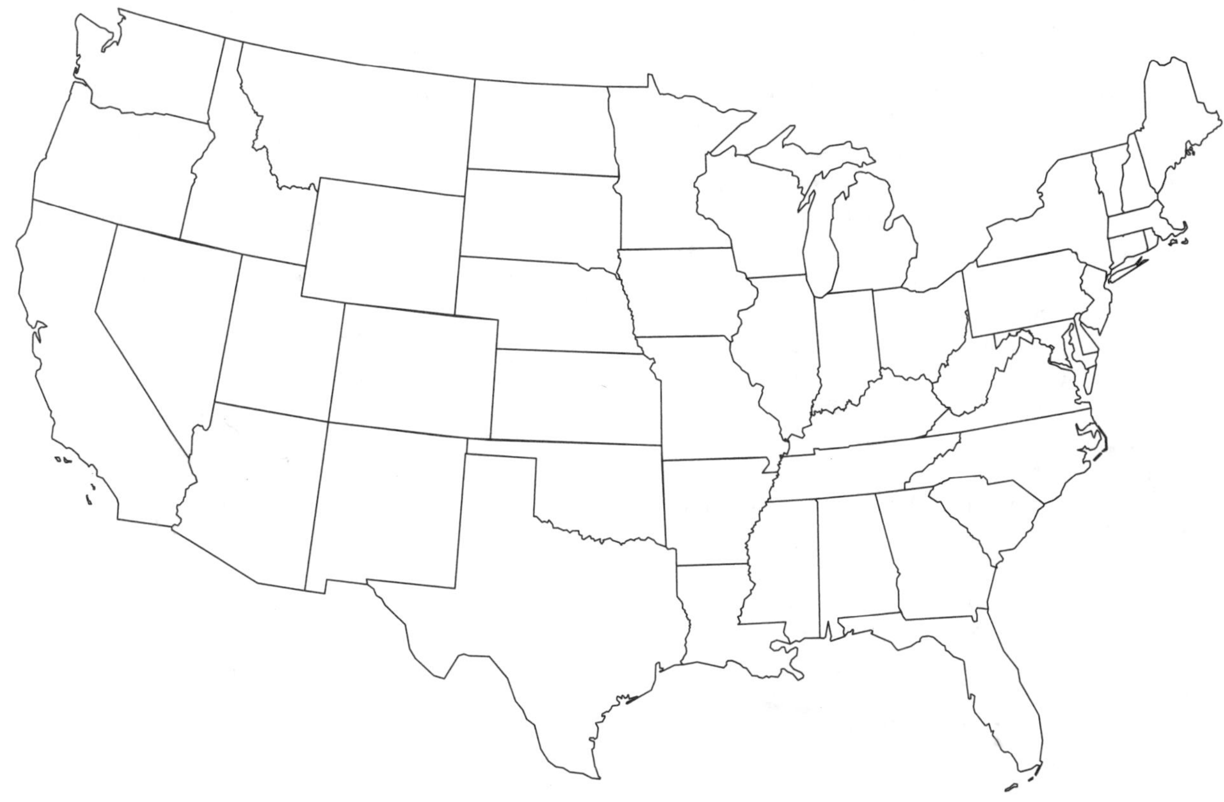

1. In which state did Paul Revere's "Midnight Ride" take place?

Ⓐ Massachusetts
Ⓑ Maryland
Ⓒ Florida
Ⓓ California

2. Frederick Douglass was born a slave in which state?

Ⓕ Massachusetts
Ⓖ Maryland
Ⓗ Florida
Ⓙ California

3. Mary McLeod Bethune founded a school for African American women in which state?

Ⓐ Massachusetts
Ⓑ Maryland
Ⓒ Florida
Ⓓ California

4. Cesar Chavez led a strike to demand higher wages for grape pickers in which state?

Ⓕ Massachusetts
Ⓖ Maryland
Ⓗ Florida
Ⓙ California

Name ________________________________ Date ________________

Social Studies **Geography**

SS3G2

Impact of Location on Historic Figures

DIRECTIONS: Read the passage and then answer the questions.

Cesar Chavez was a Mexican American born in 1927. He grew up on his family's farm in Arizona, but his father lost the ranch in 1937. This was during the Great Depression. The Southwest was also experiencing severe droughts during this time.

Chavez's family moved to California to become migrant farm workers. This was one of the few job opportunities open to Mexican Americans. Many workers were needed to harvest the crops grown in California, such as potatoes, peas, lettuce, lemons, and grapes. Migrant workers moved from farm to farm as each crop became ready to harvest. They would help harvest a crop, and then move to another farm to begin another harvest. Both working and living conditions were poor. Migrant workers had no permanent homes and had to live in dingy, overcrowded quarters. There were often no sanitation features, such as bathrooms. They received little pay and benefits for their work, and they had no job security.

Chavez managed to graduate from the eighth grade. This was unusual because the families of migrant workers moved frequently to follow the crops. Teachers often felt they were wasting their time on these students because they were only there for a short period of time. Also, many of the children spoke only Spanish. Chavez had to leave school after finishing eighth grade to work on the farms. Many children of migrant farm workers also worked to help support their families.

As an adult, Chavez joined and eventually led the movement to improve the conditions of migrant farm workers, particularly Mexican Americans, who continued to make up the bulk of this workforce.

1. Why did Chavez's family move to California?

- (A) They wanted their children to get a good education.
- (B) They became migrant farm workers.
- (C) The working conditions were better in California.
- (D) They wanted to have a permanent home.

2. Which of the following describes the working conditions of migrant farm workers?

- (F) dingy and overcrowded
- (G) no job security
- (H) little pay and benefits
- (J) both G and H

3. Why was it difficult for children of farm workers to get an education?

- (A) Their families moved a lot.
- (B) They spoke only Spanish.
- (C) They had to work to help support their families.
- (D) all of the above

4. How did the area Chavez was born and grew up in influence his adult life?

____

____

____

____

____

STOP

Name ______________________________ Date ______________

Social Studies

SS3G1–SS3G2

For pages 133–136

Mini-Test 2

Geography

DIRECTIONS: Choose the best answer.

1. Which of the following rivers is the longest in the United States?

Ⓐ Rio Grande
Ⓑ Colorado
Ⓒ Ohio
Ⓓ Mississippi

2. Which of the following rivers is found in the state of New York?

Ⓕ Red
Ⓖ Hudson
Ⓗ Rio Grande
Ⓙ Ohio

3. You are visiting the Blue Ridge Mountains in Virginia. These mountains are part of what larger mountain chain?

Ⓐ Rocky Mountains
Ⓑ Cascades
Ⓒ Sierra Nevada
Ⓓ Appalachian Mountains

4. What is the longest mountain range in the United States?

Ⓕ Rocky Mountains
Ⓖ Appalachian Mountains
Ⓗ Cascades
Ⓙ Sierra Nevada

5. What would you find at 0° longitude on a globe?

Ⓐ the North Pole
Ⓑ the South Pole
Ⓒ the Equator
Ⓓ the Prime Meridian

6. The lines that go from north to south on a globe are called ________ .

Ⓕ longitude lines
Ⓖ latitude lines
Ⓗ poles
Ⓙ equators

7. What would you find at 0° latitude on a globe?

Ⓐ the North Pole
Ⓑ the South Pole
Ⓒ the Equator
Ⓓ the Prime Meridian

8. You are trying to locate Greece on a world map. On which continent would you look to find this country?

Ⓕ Europe
Ⓖ Asia
Ⓗ Africa
Ⓙ South America

9. Cesar Chavez led a movement to improve the conditions for ________ .

Ⓐ farmers
Ⓑ Mexican Americans
Ⓒ students
Ⓓ migrant farm workers

10. Which of the following describes the living conditions of the people Chavez helped?

Ⓕ dingy
Ⓖ overcrowded
Ⓗ no sanitation features
Ⓙ all of the above

STOP

Government/Civics Standards

SS3CG1. The student will explain the importance of the basic principles that provide the foundation of a republican form of government. ***(See page 139.)***

a. Explain why the United States has separation of powers between branches of government and levels of government.

b. Name the three levels of government (national, state, local) and the three branches in each (executive, legislative, judicial), including the names of the legislative branch (Congress, General Assembly, city commission or city council).

c. State an example of the responsibilities of each level and branch of government.

SS3CG2. The student will describe how these historic figures display positive character traits of cooperation, diligence, liberty, justice, tolerance, freedom of conscience and expression, and respect for and acceptance of authority. ***(See page 140.)***

Name ______________________________ Date ______________

Social Studies

Government/Civics

SS3CG1

Levels and Branches of Government

DIRECTIONS: Choose the best answer.

1. **Which of the following is *not* one of the three levels of government in the United States?**
   - (A) national
   - (B) local
   - (C) state
   - (D) judicial

2. **Which of the following is *not* one of the three branches of government that can be found in each level of government?**
   - (F) executive
   - (G) legislative
   - (H) state
   - (J) judicial

3. **The powers and duties of the government are divided into different branches. This system is known as _________ .**
   - (A) divide and conquer
   - (B) the separation of powers
   - (C) republicanism
   - (D) federalism

4. **Which document divided the government into branches?**
   - (F) Articles of Confederation
   - (G) Constitution
   - (H) Declaration of Independence
   - (J) Emancipation Proclamation

5. **The legislative branch is responsible for _________ .**
   - (A) making laws
   - (B) interpreting and explaining laws
   - (C) making sure laws are obeyed
   - (D) changing laws

6. **The judicial branch is responsible for _________ .**
   - (F) making laws
   - (G) interpreting and explaining laws
   - (H) making sure laws are followed
   - (J) changing laws

7. **In state government, the name of the legislative branch is _________ .**
   - (A) Congress
   - (B) the General Assembly
   - (C) the city commission
   - (D) the city council

8. **In the national government, the name of the legislative branch is _________ .**
   - (F) Congress
   - (G) the Supreme Court
   - (H) the Senate
   - (J) none of the above

9. **Issuing driver's licenses is the responsibility of which level of government?**
   - (A) national
   - (B) local
   - (C) state
   - (D) none of the above

STOP

Name ______________________ Date ______________

Social Studies | Government/Civics

SS3CG2

Traits of Historic Figures

DIRECTIONS: Read the passage and then answer the questions.

Paul Revere was born in Boston, Massachusetts, in 1735. Like his father, he became a silversmith, which means he worked with gold and silver. He made items such as spoons and tea sets, and eventually became a dentist, cleaning teeth and making false teeth.

In 1765, the British placed a direct tax on colonists, which became known as the Stamp Act. This angered many of the colonists. Following the passage of the Stamp Act, Revere joined the secret patriot organization called the Sons of Liberty. A *patriot* is someone who proudly supports and defends his country. The Sons of Liberty was an anti-British group that protested such actions as the Stamp Act. Revere was also a member of other secret patriot organizations.

Because Revere was an excellent rider, he was often used to carry messages between the different patriot groups in Boston, New York, and Philadelphia. In 1773, Revere joined with others in the Boston Tea Party, throwing tea into the Boston Harbor to protest high British taxes. He rode to New York and Philadelphia to spread the word of the Boston Tea Party to patriots in those cities.

At 10 P.M. on April 18, 1775, Revere was given instructions to ride to Lexington, Massachusetts, to warn John Hancock and Samuel Adams that British troops were coming to arrest them and that the British were planning to attack. Revere rode his horse from Boston to Lexington. After delivering the message, he continued to Concord, Massachusetts, with two other riders, but soon the British captured all three riders. Revere eventually became an officer and fought against the British in the Revolution.

1. A patriot is someone who _________ .

Ⓐ works with gold and silver
Ⓑ delivers messages
Ⓒ fought for the British
Ⓓ supports and defends his country

2. What was a major role that Revere filled with the patriot organizations?

Ⓕ He made false teeth for patriots.
Ⓖ He was a messenger between patriot organizations.
Ⓗ He protested high British taxes.
Ⓙ He was a silversmith.

3. Which of the following words is a synonym for liberty?

Ⓐ cooperation
Ⓑ respect
Ⓒ freedom
Ⓓ happiness

4. Which of the following is a way Revere demonstrated the importance of liberty in his life?

Ⓕ He joined patriot organizations.
Ⓖ He warned colonists of a planned British attack.
Ⓗ He fought in the Revolutionary War.
Ⓙ all of the above

Name ______________________________ Date ______________

Social Studies

SS3CG1–SS3CG2

For pages 139–140

Mini-Test 3

Government/Civics

DIRECTIONS: Choose the best answer.

1. **The United States _________ powers between the branches of government.**
   - Ⓐ separates
   - Ⓑ coordinates
   - Ⓒ combines
   - Ⓓ shifts

2. **You are a member of the General Assembly. For which level of government do you work?**
   - Ⓕ national
   - Ⓖ local
   - Ⓗ state
   - Ⓙ city

3. **A member of a city council is working for which level of the government?**
   - Ⓐ local
   - Ⓑ state
   - Ⓒ national
   - Ⓓ none of the above

4. **Which of the following is a branch of the U.S. government?**
   - Ⓕ representative
   - Ⓖ executive
   - Ⓗ direct
   - Ⓙ financial

5. **What is the main role of the judicial branch?**
   - Ⓐ to change the laws
   - Ⓑ to enforce the laws
   - Ⓒ to make the laws
   - Ⓓ to interpret and explain the laws

6. **Which level of government can declare war?**
   - Ⓕ state
   - Ⓖ national
   - Ⓗ local
   - Ⓙ homeland defense

7. **Laws are made in which branch of government?**
   - Ⓐ statutory
   - Ⓑ legal
   - Ⓒ judicial
   - Ⓓ legislative

8. **Which branch of government is responsible for making sure laws are obeyed?**
   - Ⓕ judicial
   - Ⓖ enforcement
   - Ⓗ executive
   - Ⓙ legislative

9. **Which of the following is responsible for collecting property taxes?**
   - Ⓐ local government
   - Ⓑ national government
   - Ⓒ state government
   - Ⓓ none of the above

10. **Thurgood Marshall, who became a Supreme Court justice, was not allowed to enter the first college to which he applied. He applied and was accepted at another college. This quest for education shows _________ .**
    - Ⓕ cooperation
    - Ⓖ respect for authority
    - Ⓗ diligence
    - Ⓙ liberty

STOP

Economics Standards

SS3E1. The student will describe the four types of *productive resources.* *(See page 143.)*

a. Natural (land)
b. Human (labor)
c. Capital (capital goods)
d. Entrepreneurial (used to create *goods* and *services*)

SS3E2. The student will explain that *governments* provide certain types of goods and services in a market economy and pay for these through *taxes.* *(See page 144.)*

a. Describe services such as schools, libraries, roads, police/fire protection, and military.

SS3E3. The student will give examples of *interdependence* and *trade* and will explain how *voluntary exchange* benefits both parties. *(See pages 145–146.)*

a. Describe the *interdependence* of *consumers* and *producers* of *goods* and *services.*
b. Describe how goods and services are allocated by *price* in the marketplace.
c. Explain that some things are made locally, some elsewhere in the country, and some in other countries.
d. Explain that most countries create their own *currency* for use as money.

SS3E4. The student will describe the *costs* and *benefits* of personal spending and *saving* choices. *(See page 147.)*

Name ______________________________ Date ______________

Social Studies

SS3E1

Economics

Productive Resources

Natural resources: resources, such as land or minerals, that exist in nature

Human resources: the human effort, or labor, involved in producing goods or services

Capital resources: resources, such as buildings, tools, or equipment, that are made by people and used to make other goods and services

Entrepreneur: a person who comes up with an idea for a product or service and sees it through to production

DIRECTIONS: Choose the best answer.

1. **A computer is an example of which type of resource?**
   - Ⓐ natural
   - Ⓑ human
   - Ⓒ capital
   - Ⓓ entrepreneurial

2. **A doctor is an example of which type of resource?**
   - Ⓕ natural
   - Ⓖ human
   - Ⓗ capital
   - Ⓙ entrepreneurial

3. **Water is an example of which type of resource?**
   - Ⓐ natural
   - Ⓑ human
   - Ⓒ capital
   - Ⓓ entrepreneurial

4. **Your teacher has invented and produced a new type of backpack. The productive resource described here is __________ .**
   - Ⓕ natural
   - Ⓖ human
   - Ⓗ capital
   - Ⓙ entrepreneurial

DIRECTIONS: Each of the following resources is used in the process of making a pencil. Write **N** if it is a natural resource, **H** if it is a human resource, or **C** if it is a capital resource.

_____ 5. **saw**

_____ 6. **cedar trees**

_____ 7. **factory**

_____ 8. **machinist**

_____ 9. **lumberjack**

_____ 10. **graphite**

STOP

Name ______________________________ Date ______________

Social Studies

Economics

SS3E2

Public Goods and Services

DIRECTIONS: Choose the best answer.

1. **Public goods and services are provided by the government and _________ .**
   - (A) benefit only the individuals who are able to pay for them
   - (B) benefit society as a whole
   - (C) can be used by only one person at a time
   - (D) are no longer available once they are used

2. **Which of the following is a reason why the government provides public goods and services?**
   - (F) to promote public safety
   - (G) to educate citizens
   - (H) to keep people healthy
   - (J) all of the above

3. **Public goods and services are paid for by _________ .**
   - (A) taxes
   - (B) commissions
   - (C) grants
   - (D) loans

4. **Which of the following is *not* a public service that your local government provides to your community?**
   - (F) police protection
   - (G) street repair
   - (H) lawn care
   - (J) snow removal

5. **The national government provides which of the following public services for our country?**
   - (A) fire department
   - (B) armed forces
   - (C) city parks
   - (D) sidewalk repair

6. **Which of the following is a public service?**
   - (F) grocery stores
   - (G) hair salons
   - (H) movie theaters
   - (J) schools

7. **Your state government provides which of the following public services?**
   - (A) Georgia State Patrol
   - (B) county libraries
   - (C) post office
   - (D) fire department

8. **Which of the following is an example of a type of tax that can be used to pay for public goods and services?**
   - (F) property tax
   - (G) income tax
   - (H) sales tax
   - (J) all of the above

Name ______________________________ Date ______________

Social Studies

SS3E3

Economics

Trading Goods and Services

DIRECTIONS: Choose the best answer.

1. Trading goods and services with people for other goods and services or money is called ________ .

- (A) division of labor
- (B) supply
- (C) exchange
- (D) scarcity

2. When two people or countries trade voluntarily, ________ .

- (F) they each have something the other one wants
- (G) they should both think they are better off after the trade than before the trade
- (H) no one forces them to make the trade
- (J) all of the above

DIRECTIONS: Examine the table below and then answer questions 3–6.

Name of country	Resources it has available to trade	Resources it needs from other countries
Erehwon	bananas, coffee, coal	wheat
Utopia	coal	rice
Mythos	wheat, rice	oil
Freedonia	wheat, coffee, rice	bananas

3. Based on the information in the table, which country is Freedonia most likely to trade with?

- (A) Erehwon
- (B) Utopia
- (C) Mythos
- (D) Freedonia is not likely to trade with any of the other countries.

4. Based on the information in the table, which country is Utopia least likely to trade with?

- (F) Erehwon
- (G) Freedonia
- (H) Mythos
- (J) Utopia is likely to trade with all of the other countries.

5. Mythos might be unwilling to trade with any of the other countries listed because ________ .

- (A) Mythos has all the resources it needs
- (B) none of them want the resources Mythos has to offer
- (C) none of them have the oil Mythos needs
- (D) no one in Mythos likes bananas

6. One way for Erehwon to get the resources it needs would be to ________ .

- (F) buy it from Mythos
- (G) trade bananas with Freedonia for it
- (H) buy it from Freedonia
- (J) all of the above

7. Each country has its own basic unit of money. The money used in a country is called its ________ .

- (A) currency
- (B) wealth
- (C) barter system
- (D) trade surplus

STOP

Name ______________________ Date ______________________

Social Studies

SS3E3

Economics

Supply, Demand, and Price

DIRECTIONS: Choose the best answer.

1. **Suppose you ran a thing-a-ma-bob factory. As the producer, at what selling price would you be most likely to produce the greatest number of them?**
   - (A) $1.00
   - (B) $2.50
   - (C) $5.00
   - (D) The same number will be produced no matter the selling price.

2. **Explain your answer to question 1.**

   ____

   ____

   ____

   ____

3. **Suppose you needed some thing-a-ma-bobs. At what price would you be most likely to purchase the greatest number of them?**
   - (F) $1.00
   - (G) $2.50
   - (H) $5.00
   - (J) The same number will be purchased no matter the price.

4. **When the price of something goes up, the number of people who want to buy the item usually ________ .**
   - (A) goes up also
   - (B) goes down
   - (C) stays the same
   - (D) drops to zero

5. **This fall, Danny decided to charge neighbors $5 per hour to rake leaves. He got a few customers, but not as many as he thought he would. What would most likely happen if Danny lowered his price to $3 per hour?**
   - (F) More people would decide to let Danny rake their leaves.
   - (G) Danny would make a lot less money.
   - (H) Danny would lose most of his customers.
   - (J) His friend Alison would start raking leaves too at $5 per hour.

6. **What happens when the supply of a product goes down but the demand goes up?**
   - (A) The price of the product stays the same.
   - (B) The price of the product goes down.
   - (C) Producers will no longer want to make the product.
   - (D) The price of the product goes up.

7. **A big winter storm knocked out power to a community for several days. A local store kept several generators in stock. The generators provided a source of electricity. However, the store did not usually sell very many because they were expensive. When the storm hit the community, the store ran out of generators and had to order more. Why do you think people wanted to purchase the generators even though they were still expensive?**

   ____

   ____

   ____

   ____

Name ______________________ Date ______________

Social Studies

SS3E4

Economics

Costs and Benefits

DIRECTIONS: Read the passage and then answer the questions.

Amanda receives a weekly allowance of $20. She allows herself to spend $10 of her allowance each week on items such as snacks or movies. She saves the other $10 for more expensive items that she wants to buy in the future.

So far Amanda has saved $80. She would like to buy two DVDs which cost $15 each. She is also thinking about buying a digital camera, which costs $80, and an MP3 player, which costs $150.

Cost can mean the price of an item, or the loss of something when another item is gained.

1. **If Amanda decides to buy the digital camera today, what will it cost her? How will this affect her ability to buy the DVDs or the MP3 player?**

2. **What benefit(s) does Amanda receive by purchasing the camera?**

3. **If Amanda does not buy the DVDs or the camera but continues to save for the MP3 player, what will it cost her? What benefit(s) will she receive?**

4. **Amanda has decided to save for the MP3 player. In order to save her money more quickly, she is only going to spend $5 of her allowance each week. This will allow her to save $15 each week. What is the cost to her of this decision?**

STOP

Name ______________________ Date ______________________

Social Studies

SS3E1–SS3E4

For pages 143–147

Economics

Mini-Test 4

DIRECTIONS: Choose the best answer.

1. **A cloth-cutting machine used in making jeans is which type of productive resource?**
   - (A) natural
   - (B) human
   - (C) capital
   - (D) entrepreneurial

2. **The cotton used in making jeans is which type of productive resource?**
   - (F) entrepreneurial
   - (G) natural
   - (H) human
   - (J) capital

3. **A seamstress who makes jeans is which type of productive resource?**
   - (A) human
   - (B) capital
   - (C) entrepreneurial
   - (D) natural

4. **The owner who started the factory where the jeans are made is which type of productive resource?**
   - (F) capital
   - (G) entrepreneurial
   - (H) natural
   - (J) human

5. **Which of the following is a form of currency in the United States?**
   - (A) pounds
   - (B) dollars
   - (C) euros
   - (D) pesos

6. **The government provides ________ goods and services that help society as a whole.**
   - (F) public
   - (G) private
   - (H) beneficial
   - (J) humanitarian

7. **The ________ you are charged when you buy an item at a store helps pay for public goods and services.**
   - (A) income tax
   - (B) sales tax
   - (C) property tax
   - (D) none of the above

8. **Not much coffee is grown in the United States. Both Costa Rica and Kenya grow coffee. One way for the United States to get coffee would be to ________ .**
   - (F) buy it from Costa Rica and Kenya
   - (G) trade another product with Kenya for coffee
   - (H) trade another product with Costa Rica for coffee
   - (J) all of the above

9. **What happens when the supply of a product goes up but the demand for the product remains the same?**
   - (A) The price goes up.
   - (B) The price goes down.
   - (C) Consumers buy less.
   - (D) Consumers buy more.

How Am I Doing?

Mini-Test 1 Page 131 **Number Correct**	**8** answers correct	**Great Job!** Move on to the section test on page 151.
	4–7 answers correct	**You're almost there!** But you still need a little practice. Review practice pages 128–130 before moving on to the section test on page 151.
	0–3 answers correct	**Oops!** Time to review what you have learned and try again. Review the practice section on pages 128–130. Then retake the test on page 131. Now move on to the section test on page 151.
Mini-Test 2 Page 137 **Number Correct**	**9–10** answers correct	**Awesome!** Move on to the section test on page 151.
	5–8 answers correct	**You're almost there!** But you still need a little practice. Review practice pages 133–136 before moving on to the section test on page 151.
	0–4 answers correct	**Oops!** Time to review what you have learned and try again. Review the practice section on pages 133–136. Then retake the test on page 137. Now move on to the section test on page 151.
Mini-Test 3 Page 141 **Number Correct**	**9–10** answers correct	**Great Job!** Move on to the section test on page 151.
	5–8 answers correct	**You're almost there!** But you still need a little practice. Review practice pages 139–140 before moving on to the section test on page 151.
	0–4 answers correct	**Oops!** Time to review what you have learned and try again. Review the practice section on pages 139–140. Then retake the test on page 141. Now move on to the section test on page 151.

How Am I Doing?

Mini-Test 4 Page 148 **Number Correct**	Score	
	9 answers correct	**Great Job!** Move on to the section test on page 151.
	5–8 answers correct	**You're almost there!** But you still need a little practice. Review practice pages 143–147 before moving on to the section test on page 151.
	0–4 answers correct	**Oops!** Time to review what you have learned and try again. Review the practice section on pages 143–147. Then retake the test on page 148. Now move on to the section test on page 151.

Name ______________________________ Date ______________

Final Social Studies Test

for pages 128–148

DIRECTIONS: Choose the best answer.

1. Which architectural element often seen in government buildings is associated with ancient Greece?

Ⓐ domes
Ⓑ columns
Ⓒ porches
Ⓓ bay windows

2. What was recorded for the first time in Greece during the sixth century B.C.?

Ⓕ a code of ethics
Ⓖ written law
Ⓗ a constitution
Ⓙ a government charter

3. A democracy is a way of governing in which the whole body of citizens takes charge of its own affairs. The concept of democracy was invented by the _________ .

Ⓐ English
Ⓑ ancient Romans
Ⓒ ancient Greeks
Ⓓ U.S. founding fathers

4. In the fifth century B.C., a man named Pericles led the city of Athens, Greece. Some people could vote. Most people, however, were not recognized as citizens and could not vote. For that reason, _________ .

Ⓕ the people of Athens had more freedom than we do in the United States today
Ⓖ Athens was a monarchy
Ⓗ Athens was not a true democracy
Ⓙ all of the above

5. A form of government in which all the citizens directly participate in the decision-making process is known as a _________ democracy.

Ⓐ legislative
Ⓑ direct
Ⓒ representative
Ⓓ republican

6. Which of the following people signed laws that ended child labor?

Ⓕ Lyndon B. Johnson
Ⓖ Franklin D. Roosevelt
Ⓗ Eleanor Roosevelt
Ⓙ Thurgood Marshall

7. Cesar Chavez helped form which of the following unions?

Ⓐ American Federation of Labor
Ⓑ Congress of Industrial Organization
Ⓒ United Farm Workers Union
Ⓓ National Migrant Workers Union

8. Which of the following people fought to get women the right to vote?

Ⓕ Mary McLeod Bethune
Ⓖ Susan B. Anthony
Ⓗ Frederick Douglass
Ⓙ Eleanor Roosevelt

9. The Mississippi River flows in which direction?

Ⓐ south to north
Ⓑ east to west
Ⓒ north to south
Ⓓ none of the above

Name ______________________________ Date ______________________

10. Which of the following rivers begins in Pennsylvania and ends at the Mississippi River?

- (F) Colorado
- (G) Rio Grande
- (H) Ohio
- (J) Hudson

11. Which of the following rivers forms a natural border between Texas and Mexico?

- (A) Ohio
- (B) Colorado
- (C) Mississippi
- (D) Rio Grande

12. Which of the following rivers ends in the Gulf of California?

- (F) Hudson
- (G) Ohio
- (H) Colorado
- (J) Mississippi

13. What is the name of the mountain range that extends from Mexico, through the western United States, and into Canada and Alaska?

- (A) Rocky Mountains
- (B) Appalachian Mountains
- (C) Sierra Nevada
- (D) Sierra Madres

14. The lines that travel in an east-west direction on a globe are called __________ .

- (F) meridians
- (G) latitude lines
- (H) longitude lines
- (J) parallel lines

15. Where on a globe is the Prime Meridian located?

- (A) 0° latitude
- (B) 0° longitude
- (C) at the Equator
- (D) at the North Pole

16. Which body of water borders Greece?

- (F) Atlantic Ocean
- (G) Pacific Ocean
- (H) Black Sea
- (J) Mediterranean Sea

17. Mary McLeod Bethune was an African American born in South Carolina in 1875. At that time, educational opportunities for African Americans were limited and she had to travel to the North to receive an education. How did this impact her life?

- (A) She was never able to complete her education.
- (B) She wanted to make sure others had educational opportunities, and she opened a school for African-American girls in Florida.
- (C) She stayed in the North for the rest of her life.
- (D) She brought a lawsuit against the state of South Carolina for discrimination in education.

18. Cesar Chavez's life in the Southwest led him to work most closely with which ethnic group?

- (F) Japanese Americans
- (G) Chinese Americans
- (H) Mexican Americans
- (J) all of the above

Name ______________________ Date ______________

19. How many levels of government are found in the United States?

Ⓐ two
Ⓑ three
Ⓒ four
Ⓓ five

20. How many branches of government are there in each level of government?

Ⓕ one
Ⓖ two
Ⓗ three
Ⓙ four

21. Which of the following is a legislative branch of local government?

Ⓐ city commission
Ⓑ Congress
Ⓒ General Assembly
Ⓓ Supreme Court

22. Which of the following branch of government is responsible for making laws?

Ⓕ executive
Ⓖ legislative
Ⓗ representative
Ⓙ judicial

23. Which level of government is responsible for maintaining armed forces?

Ⓐ state
Ⓑ interstate
Ⓒ local
Ⓓ national

24. Determining whether a law is constitutional or unconstitutional is the responsibility of which branch of government?

Ⓕ legislative
Ⓖ judicial
Ⓗ executive
Ⓙ national

25. Eleanor Roosevelt's belief in justice was illustrated when she _________ .

Ⓐ visited the sick in hospitals
Ⓑ helped write the United Nation's Universal Declaration of Human Rights
Ⓒ attended school in England
Ⓓ married Franklin D. Roosevelt

26. Land is an example of which type of resource?

Ⓕ entrepreneurial
Ⓖ capital
Ⓗ natural
Ⓙ human

27. The conveyor belt used in a bottling plant is which type of resource?

Ⓐ capital
Ⓑ natural
Ⓒ human
Ⓓ entrepreneurial

28. The labor used in making a product is which type of resource?

Ⓕ natural
Ⓖ entrepreneurial
Ⓗ capital
Ⓙ human

Name ______________________________ Date ______________

29. Which of the following is *not* a public service funded through taxes?

(A) schools
(B) highways
(C) restaurants
(D) police protection

30. What services do libraries provide that qualify them as a public service?

(F) They promote public safety.
(G) They educate citizens.
(H) They keep people healthy.
(J) none of the above

31. At a local mall, you purchase a wooden carving that was made in Kenya. What form of currency will you use to pay for your purchase?

(A) shillings
(B) U.S. dollars
(C) euros
(D) pounds

DIRECTIONS: Read the passage. Then answer the questions.

The most popular snack food in years has hit the stores recently. Everyone wants to try the new Beef-o Chips. These hamburger-flavored potato chips are so popular, the manufacturer is having a hard time keeping up with demand. Grocery stores across the nation have been mobbed by hungry customers looking to buy bags of Beef-os. The local Food Clown store reports that an entire shelf of Beef-os was cleaned out by customers yesterday in about five minutes.

32. When Beef-os first came out a couple of months ago, each bag cost $1.99. Based on the information in the passage, what do you think Beef-os might be selling for now?

(F) 25¢
(G) 99¢
(H) $1.99
(J) $2.99

33. Explain your answer to question 32.

(A) Hamburger-flavored potato chips? Yuck! Who would buy those?
(B) When supply is high and demand is low, prices usually go down.
(C) The price was $1.99 just a couple of months ago. That's too soon for any price change to occur.
(D) When supply is low and demand is high, prices usually rise.

34. Jake is saving for a new skateboard. For this reason, he chooses not to buy a pack of trading cards. What is the cost of this decision?

(F) He will be able to buy the skateboard more quickly.
(G) He will buy the trading cards.
(H) He will not have the trading cards.
(J) He will not be able to buy the skateboard.

Name ______________________________ Date ______________

Final Social Studies Test

Answer Sheet

1 Ⓐ Ⓑ Ⓒ Ⓓ
2 Ⓕ Ⓖ Ⓗ Ⓙ
3 Ⓐ Ⓑ Ⓒ Ⓓ
4 Ⓕ Ⓖ Ⓗ Ⓙ
5 Ⓐ Ⓑ Ⓒ Ⓓ
6 Ⓕ Ⓖ Ⓗ Ⓙ
7 Ⓐ Ⓑ Ⓒ Ⓓ
8 Ⓕ Ⓖ Ⓗ Ⓙ
9 Ⓐ Ⓑ Ⓒ Ⓓ
10 Ⓕ Ⓖ Ⓗ Ⓙ

11 Ⓐ Ⓑ Ⓒ Ⓓ
12 Ⓕ Ⓖ Ⓗ Ⓙ
13 Ⓐ Ⓑ Ⓒ Ⓓ
14 Ⓕ Ⓖ Ⓗ Ⓙ
15 Ⓐ Ⓑ Ⓒ Ⓓ
16 Ⓕ Ⓖ Ⓗ Ⓙ
17 Ⓐ Ⓑ Ⓒ Ⓓ
18 Ⓕ Ⓖ Ⓗ Ⓙ
19 Ⓐ Ⓑ Ⓒ Ⓓ
20 Ⓕ Ⓖ Ⓗ Ⓙ

21 Ⓐ Ⓑ Ⓒ Ⓓ
22 Ⓕ Ⓖ Ⓗ Ⓙ
23 Ⓐ Ⓑ Ⓒ Ⓓ
24 Ⓕ Ⓖ Ⓗ Ⓙ
25 Ⓐ Ⓑ Ⓒ Ⓓ
26 Ⓕ Ⓖ Ⓗ Ⓙ
27 Ⓐ Ⓑ Ⓒ Ⓓ
28 Ⓕ Ⓖ Ⓗ Ⓙ
29 Ⓐ Ⓑ Ⓒ Ⓓ
30 Ⓕ Ⓖ Ⓗ Ⓙ

31 Ⓐ Ⓑ Ⓒ Ⓓ
32 Ⓕ Ⓖ Ⓗ Ⓙ
33 Ⓐ Ⓑ Ⓒ Ⓓ
34 Ⓕ Ⓖ Ⓗ Ⓙ

Georgia Science Content Standards

¥The science section measures knowledge in five different areas:

1) Characteristics of Science
   a. Habits of Mind
   b. The Nature of Science

2) Content
   a. Earth Science
   b. Physical Science
   c. Life Science

Georgia Science Table of Contents

Habits of Mind Standards

S3CS1. Students will be aware of the importance of curiosity, honesty, openness, and skepticism in science and will exhibit these traits in their own efforts to understand how the world works. ***(See page 158.)***

a. Keep records of investigations and observations and do not alter the records later.
b. Offer reasons for findings and consider reasons suggested by others.
c. Take responsibility for understanding the importance of being safety conscious.

S3CS2. Students will have the computation and estimation skills necessary for analyzing data and following scientific explanations. ***(See pages 159–160.)***

a. Add, subtract, multiply, and divide whole numbers mentally, on paper, and with a calculator.
b. Use commonly encountered fractions—halves, thirds, and fourths (but not sixths, sevenths, and so on)—in scientific calculations.
c. Judge whether measurements and computations of quantities, such as length, weight, or time, are reasonable answers to scientific problems by comparing them to typical values.

S3CS3. Students will use tools and instruments for observing, measuring, and manipulating objects in scientific activities utilizing safe laboratory procedures. ***(See page 161.)***

a. Choose appropriate common materials for making simple mechanical constructions and repairing things.
b. Use computers, cameras, and recording devices for capturing information.
c. Identify and practice accepted safety procedures in manipulating science materials and equipment.

S3CS4. Students will use ideas of system, model, change, and scale in exploring scientific and technological matters. ***(See page 162.)***

a. Observe and describe how parts influence one another in things with many parts.
b. Use geometric figures, number sequences, graphs, diagrams, sketches, number lines, maps, and stories to represent corresponding features of objects, events, and processes in the real world.
c. Identify ways in which the representations do not match their original counterparts.

S3CS5. Students will communicate scientific ideas and activities clearly. ***(See pages 163–164.)***

a. Write instructions that others can follow in carrying out a scientific procedure.
b. Make sketches to aid in explaining scientific procedures or ideas.
c. Use numerical data in describing and comparing objects and events.
d. Locate scientific information in reference books, back issues of newspapers and magazines, CD-ROMs, and computer databases.

S3CS6. Students will question scientific claims and arguments effectively. ***(See page 165.)***

a. Support statements with facts found in books, articles, and databases, and identify the sources used.

Name ______________________________ Date ______________

Science

S3CS1

Science Practices

Habits of Mind

DIRECTIONS: Read the following story to answer the questions.

Lauren entered the science fair. For her project, she wanted to see which brand of batteries lasts longest: Everglo, Glomore, or Everlasting. She decided to place new batteries into identical new flashlights, turn on the flashlights, then wait for the batteries to run down. She wrote down the following results: Everglo—lasted 19 hours; Glomore—lasted 17 hours; Everlasting—lasted 25 hours.

She then decided to redo the experiment to confirm the results. For her second experiment, she placed new batteries in the old flashlights that her parents keep in the garage, the kitchen, and their bedroom. She then turned on the flashlights and waited for the batteries to run down. This time she wrote down the following results: Everglo—lasted 13 hours; Glomore—lasted 16 hours; Everlasting—lasted 9 hours.

Lauren was puzzled by the results of her second experiment. Because it was so similar to her first experiment, she thought she would get the same results.

1. What is the best explanation for why Lauren's second experiment had different results than her first experiment?

Ⓐ Lauren used different brands of batteries in the second experiment.

Ⓑ The second experiment used old flashlights, while the first experiment used new flashlights.

Ⓒ The second experiment was too much like the first experiment.

Ⓓ There is no good explanation; sometimes things just happen.

2. How was Lauren sure that the results of the second experiment were different from the results of the first experiment?

Ⓕ She read on the side of the battery packages how long each brand would last before it ran down.

Ⓖ She simply remembered how long it took each brand of battery to run down.

Ⓗ She recorded exactly how long it took each brand of battery to run down for each experiment.

Ⓙ She cannot be sure; her experiment was faulty.

3. Tell what Lauren did right in her experiments. Could she have done anything in a better, more scientific way?

____

____

____

____

____

____

4. You should wear eye goggles in a science lab ________ .

Ⓐ when you are working with chemicals

Ⓑ when there is a chance of flying objects

Ⓒ when you are cleaning up

Ⓓ both A and B

Name ______________________________ Date ______________

Science

S3CS2

Habits of Mind

Using Fractions in Scientific Calculations

DIRECTIONS: Choose the best answer.

1. **You plan on conducting an experiment on plant growth. You have 12 of the same plants, and plan on placing $\frac{1}{3}$ of the plants in direct sunlight, $\frac{1}{3}$ of the plants in indirect sunlight, and $\frac{1}{3}$ of the plants in shade. How many plants will receive direct sunlight?**
   - Ⓐ 3 plants
   - Ⓑ 4 plants
   - Ⓒ 6 plants
   - Ⓓ 2 plants

2. **You planted 18 seeds for an experiment. Only $\frac{1}{2}$ of them sprouted. How many seedlings grew?**
   - Ⓕ 6 seedlings
   - Ⓖ 12 seedlings
   - Ⓗ 9 seedlings
   - Ⓙ 8 seedlings

3. **There are 28 students in your science class. One-quarter of them chose to study the life of the fruit fly and $\frac{3}{4}$ chose to study the life of the honeybee. How many students chose to study the honeybee?**
   - Ⓐ 21 students
   - Ⓑ 8 students
   - Ⓒ 7 students
   - Ⓓ 14 students

4. **How many students in question 3 chose to study the fruit fly?**
   - Ⓕ 21 students
   - Ⓖ 8 students
   - Ⓗ 7 students
   - Ⓙ 14 students

5. **Your class collected 60 rocks. You determined that $\frac{2}{3}$ of them could be classified as sedimentary. How many rocks is this?**
   - Ⓐ 23 rocks
   - Ⓑ 32 rocks
   - Ⓒ 20 rocks
   - Ⓓ 40 rocks

6. **During an experiment, you mix 75 mL of liquid. You need to transfer 25 mL of this to another container to continue the experiment. What fraction of the original liquid are you transferring?**
   - Ⓕ $\frac{1}{3}$
   - Ⓗ $\frac{3}{4}$
   - Ⓖ $\frac{1}{4}$
   - Ⓙ $\frac{2}{3}$

7. **Fifteen students are in the science lab. However, there are only enough safety goggles for $\frac{2}{3}$ of the students. How many students will be able to perform the experiment?**
   - Ⓐ 5 students
   - Ⓑ 3 students
   - Ⓒ 10 students
   - Ⓓ 9 students

8. **You recorded the high temperature for the 30 days in June. During that time, $\frac{1}{3}$ of the days had temperatures of 90° or above. How many days had highs of at least 90°?**
   - Ⓕ 3 days
   - Ⓖ 13 days
   - Ⓗ 20 days
   - Ⓙ 10 days

STOP

Name ______________________________ Date ______________________

Science

S3CS2

Analyzing Measurements

Habits of Mind

DIRECTIONS: Use the information in the tables to answer the questions.

Plant Label	Number of Hours of Daily Sunlight	Height After One Month
Plant 1	2	4 in.
Plant 2	4	8 in.
Plant 3	8	16 in.

1. The above table shows the height of three bean plants after they were given a certain amount of sunlight each day. You decide to conduct your own experiment. You grow three bean plants for one month, exposing each one to the sunlight amounts given in the table above. You put labels on each plant to match the table. On the last day of your experiment, your mother moves your plants and their labels fall off. Your plants measure 9 inches, 3 inches, and 15 inches tall. Indicate how much sunlight you believe each plant received and why.

____

____

____

____

2. A friend conducts the same experiment. His results show that a plant receiving four hours of sunlight daily for one month measured 20 inches. Does this result fit with the previous data? If not, why do you think this result may have occurred?

____

____

____

____

Dolphin	Average Length	Average Weight
Adult female	7 ft.	330 lbs.
Adult male	$9\frac{1}{2}$ ft.	550 lbs.
Calf	3 ft.	30 lbs.

3. A dolphin weighs 530 pounds and measures 9 feet long. Which of the following is most likely true?

Ⓐ It is an adult male.

Ⓑ It is an adult female.

Ⓒ It is a calf.

Ⓓ There is not enough information.

4. You are given the following information on a group of dolphins. Only one is an adult female. Which of the following is most likely the adult female?

Ⓕ 5 feet, 100 pounds

Ⓖ 10 feet, 575 pounds

Ⓗ $7\frac{1}{2}$ feet, 325 pounds

Ⓙ 9 feet, 535 pounds

5. While in a boat on the ocean, a friend spots a dolphin that he estimates is 20 feet long. Is his estimate reasonable? Why or why not?

____

____

____

____

Name ______________________________ Date ______________

Science

S3CS3

Safety Practices

Habits of Mind

DIRECTIONS: Read the following statements about behaviors in a science lab. Write **S** in the blank space if the behavior is safe or **U** if the behavior is unsafe.

_____ **1. If you have long hair, tie it back when you are working with flames.**

_____ **2. Wait until the end of class to clean up any spills.**

_____ **3. For a thorough experiment, taste all chemicals before using them.**

_____ **4. Avoid using chipped glassware.**

_____ **5. Wear eye goggles when you are working with chemicals or when there is the possibility of flying objects.**

_____ **6. Do not worry about loose clothing. Clothing today is not capable of catching on fire.**

_____ **7. Leave your work area a mess at the end of class. The next class will clean it up.**

_____ **8. Wash your hands with soap and water after you finish an activity.**

_____ **9. When working with a heat source, make sure there are no materials nearby that can catch on fire.**

_____ **10. Assume that any liquid that is not boiling is cool and you can pick up the glassware with your bare hands.**

STOP

Name ______________________________ Date ______________

Science

S3CS4

Systems and Models

Habits of Mind

DIRECTIONS: Anything with parts that interact, or work together, is called a system. In the blank spaces below, write **S** if it is a system and **N** if it is not a system.

Examples:

- A tree is a system because it has roots, a trunk, limbs, and leaves that all work together to help the tree grow.
- A watch is a system because it has parts that work together to keep the correct time.
- A piece of paper is not a system because it does not have any working parts.

_____ **1. television**

_____ **2. flower**

_____ **3. plastic cup**

_____ **4. eraser**

_____ **5. automobile**

_____ **6. ant**

_____ **7. pen**

_____ **8. camera**

_____ **9. skateboard**

_____ **10. towel**

_____ **11. balloon**

_____ **12. pencil sharpener**

DIRECTIONS: Choose the best answer.

13. In the next column is a series of models that represent the size and placement of the sun in relation to Earth and the moon. Which is the best representation of the sun, Earth, and the moon, overall?

Ⓐ

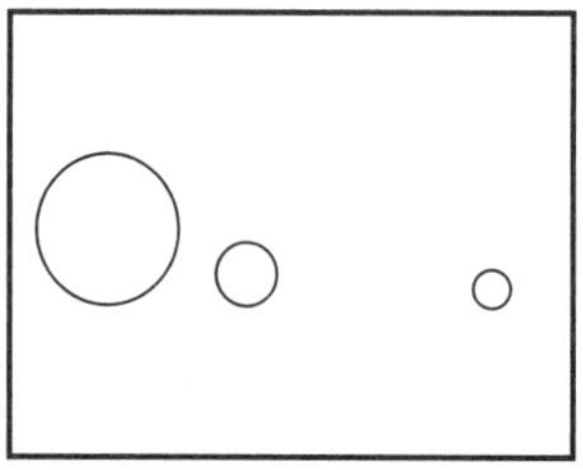

Ⓑ

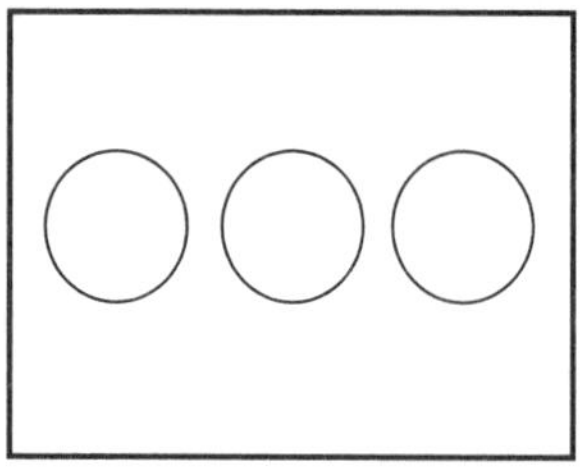

Ⓒ

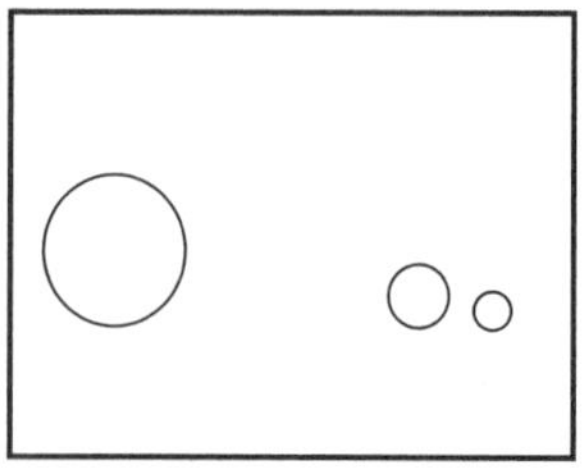

Ⓓ

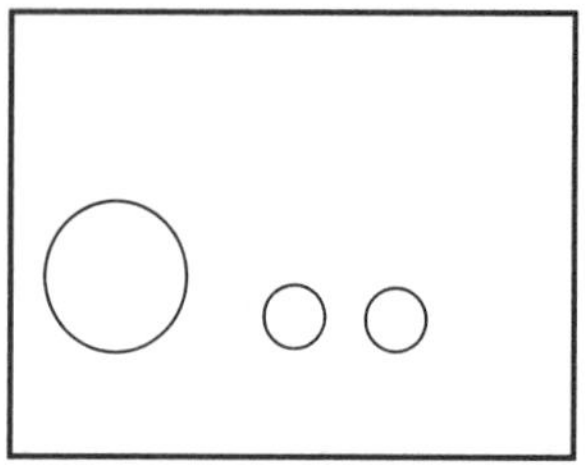

Name ______________________ Date ______________

Science

S3CS5

Habits of Mind

Illustrating With Sketches

DIRECTIONS: Your class at school has been studying the phases of the moon. Part of your homework was to record the different phases of the moon over a period of time. In the boxes below, sketch what each phase of the moon looked like.

You can use references such as books or encyclopedias to find drawings of the moon for each phase.

1. January 27—Full Moon

2. February 3—Last Quarter

3. February 10—New Moon

4. February 18—First Quarter

STOP

Name ______________________ Date ______________

Science

S3CS5

Using Data

Habits of Mind

DIRECTIONS: Read the graph showing the number of herons on Ash Pond, and then answer the questions.

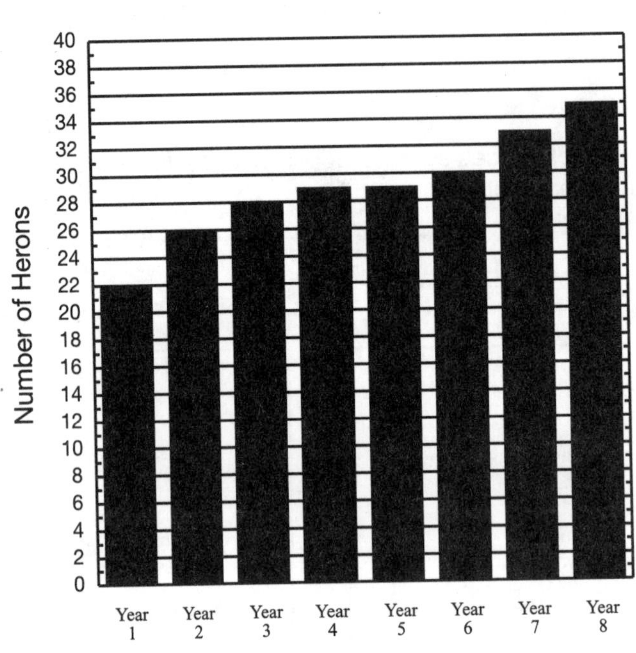

1. In which two years did the number of herons stay the same?

Ⓐ years 1 and 2

Ⓑ years 2 and 3

Ⓒ years 3 and 4

Ⓓ years 4 and 5

2. Based on the data, how much did the heron population increase between year 1 and year 8?

Ⓕ by 22

Ⓖ by 13

Ⓗ by 12

Ⓙ by 57

3. What was the average number of herons on Ash Pond over the 8 years?

Ⓐ 26 herons

Ⓑ 27 herons

Ⓒ 28 herons

Ⓓ 29 herons

4. Based on the data, what could you predict for year 11?

Ⓕ The number of herons will increase.

Ⓖ The number of herons will decrease.

Ⓗ The number of herons will stay the same.

Ⓙ Herons will become endangered.

STOP

Name ______________________ Date ______________

Science

S3CS6

Supporting Statements

Habits of Mind

DIRECTIONS: Read the passage. For each statement below, write a **Y** in the space if it is a fact supported by the passage and write an **N** if it is not a fact supported by the passage. Then answer the questions.

Why Are There Seasons? (from the book *All About Earth*)

Earth revolves around the sun. It also spins on an invisible axis that runs through its center.

It takes 365 days, or one year, for Earth to revolve once around the sun. Earth does not move in a perfect circle. Its orbit is an ellipse, which is a flattened circle, like an oval. As Earth revolves around the sun in an elliptical shape, it spins on its invisible axis.

Earth's axis of rotation is not straight up and down, it is tilted. This tilt creates the seasons on Earth. No matter where Earth is in its rotation around the sun, its axis is tilted in the same direction and at the same angle. So, as Earth moves, different parts of it are facing the sun and different parts are facing away. The North Pole is tilting toward the sun in June, so the northern half of Earth is enjoying summer. In December, the North Pole is tilted away from the sun, so the northern part of the world experiences winter.

This important relationship between Earth and the sun determines how hot and cold we are, when we plant our crops, and whether we have droughts or floods.

_____ **1. Earth's axis of rotation is tilted.**

_____ **2. Earth is the third planet from the sun.**

_____ **3. There are nine planets in our solar system.**

_____ **4. It takes 365 days for Earth to revolve once around the sun.**

_____ **5. In December, the North Pole is tilted toward the sun.**

_____ **6. The northern half of Earth experiences summer in June.**

_____ **7. The orbit of Earth is an ellipse.**

_____ **8. Earth's axis can tilt in different directions.**

9. If you used information from this article to write a report, where would you say the information came from?

____

____

____

____

____

10. Where could you find more information about this topic?

Ⓐ in an atlas

Ⓑ in a book of poems about the seasons

Ⓒ in an encyclopedia entry about seasons

Ⓓ in an essay about agriculture in the United States and Canada

Name ______________________ Date ______________

Science

S3CS1–S3CS6

For pages 158–165

Mini-Test 1

Habits of Mind

DIRECTIONS: Choose the best answer.

1. **When keeping records of your observations, it is important that you ________ .**
   - (A) do not change the records later
   - (B) change the records to reflect the results you should have gotten
   - (C) record only the results that make sense
   - (D) use red ink

2. **Of the eight tomato plants in your experiment, $\frac{1}{4}$ produced fruit. How many plants was this?**
   - (F) 1 plant
   - (G) 2 plants
   - (H) 3 plants
   - (J) 4 plants

3. **You have 100 mL of liquid in a beaker. You are told to place $\frac{1}{2}$ of this in another beaker. How much liquid should you place in the other beaker?**
   - (A) 12 mL
   - (B) 25 mL
   - (C) 50 mL
   - (D) 75 mL

4. **Which of the following is an example of unsafe behavior in a science lab?**
   - (F) cleaning up spills
   - (G) tasting chemicals
   - (H) washing up when finished
   - (J) none of the above

5. **You are having a hard time weighing your dog as she is not interested in cooperating with you. You know that an adult of her breed averages 20 pounds. Which of the following measurements that you took is most likely correct?**
   - (A) 2 pounds
   - (B) 5 pounds
   - (C) 12 pounds
   - (D) 18 pounds

6. **Which of the following is *not* a system?**
   - (F) a computer
   - (G) a human hand
   - (H) a rock
   - (J) a lamp

7. **Which of the following shapes would you use to represent the moon?**
   - (A) square
   - (B) circle
   - (C) triangle
   - (D) oval

8. **Which of the following would come first in instructions to carry out a scientific procedure?**
   - (F) Record your results.
   - (G) Observe what happens.
   - (H) Gather the required materials.
   - (J) Add the contents of the second vial to the first.

The Nature of Science Standards

S3CS7. Students will be familiar with the character of scientific knowledge and how it is achieved. ***(See page 168.)***

Students will recognize the following points.

a. Similar scientific investigations seldom produce exactly the same results, which may differ due to unexpected differences in whatever is being investigated, unrecognized differences in methods or circumstances of the investigation, or observational uncertainties.

b. Some scientific knowledge is very old and yet is still applicable today.

S3CS8. Students will understand important features of the process of scientific inquiry. ***(See pages 169–170.)***

Students will apply the following to inquiry learning practices.

a. Scientific investigations may take many different forms, including observing what things are like or what is happening somewhere, collecting specimens for analysis, and doing experiments.

b. Clear and active communication is an essential part of doing science. It enables scientists to inform others about their work, expose their ideas to criticism by other scientists, and stay informed about scientific discoveries around the world.

c. Scientists use technology to increase their power to observe things and to measure and compare things accurately.

d. Science involves many different kinds of work and engages men and women of all ages and backgrounds.

Name ______________________ Date ______________

Science

S3CS7

The Nature of Science

Scientific Results and Knowledge

DIRECTIONS: Answer the questions.

Two people carrying out the same investigation will seldom get the exact same results. This can be due to differences in what they were investigating or the way they carried out the investigation.

1. Julie and Jim spent two hours recording the number of birds visiting a bird feeder. At the end of the two hours, Julie had recorded 62 birds and Jim had recorded 55 birds visiting the feeder. What could have caused Julie and Jim to have different results?

2. In the 1660s, Sir Isaac Newton was one of the first people to begin gathering information on gravity. Newton's discoveries about gravity still apply today. Use the space below to explain how gravity affects what happens to a baseball after it is hit into the air.

STOP

Name ______________________________ Date ______________

Science

S3CS8

Types of Investigations

The Nature of Science

DIRECTIONS: For each of the following investigations, write **O** if it would best be accomplished through observation, **C** if it would best be accomplished by collecting specimens, or **E** if it would best be accomplished through doing experiments.

- When you use *observation,* you are watching what is happening. You are not creating the event.
- When you *collect specimens,* you are collecting items to be studied.
- When you *perform an experiment,* you are actively involved in finding an answer to a question, for example, what will happen if you add baking soda to vinegar. Since the baking soda cannot add itself naturally, you must add it. Therefore, you are creating the event.

_____ **1. Determine what items float in water.**

_____ **2. Chart the phases of the moon for the month of April.**

_____ **3. Determine how a horse's legs move when the horse is trotting.**

_____ **4. Categorize the types of rocks that are found in your neighborhood.**

_____ **5. Determine what happens when you mix a base and an acid.**

_____ **6. Determine how much rainfall is received in a week.**

_____ **7. Determine whether the soil in your backyard is the same as that found in a location five miles away.**

_____ **8. Determine whether a basketball, baseball, or marble falls more quickly when dropped from the same height.**

_____ **9. Determine what microorganisms live in pond water.**

_____ **10. Determine whether a plant will grow in the dark.**

_____ **11. Determine how much a plant grows over a certain period of time.**

STOP

Name ______________________ Date ______________

Science

S3CS8

The Nature of Science

Technology and Scientists

DIRECTIONS: Choose the best answer.

1. **Which of the following would you use to measure the speed of a falling object?**
   - (A) a stopwatch
   - (B) a microscope
   - (C) a balance scale
   - (D) a ruler

2. **Which of the following would be used to look more closely at a leaf?**
   - (F) a beaker
   - (G) a magnifying glass
   - (H) a barometer
   - (J) binoculars

3. **Which of the following would you use to study cells?**
   - (A) a telescope
   - (B) a magnifying glass
   - (C) a microscope
   - (D) binoculars

4. **Which of the following would you use to determine the boiling point of a liquid?**
   - (F) a barometer
   - (G) a thermometer
   - (H) a ruler
   - (J) a scale

5. **Which of the following would you use to study the stars?**
   - (A) a magnifying glass
   - (B) a microscope
   - (C) binoculars
   - (D) a telescope

6. **A person who studies the history of the earth, especially as recorded in rocks, is a ________ .**
   - (F) physicist
   - (G) geologist
   - (H) biologist
   - (J) hydrologist

7. **A person who studies stars, planets, and galaxies is a(n) ________ .**
   - (A) astronomer
   - (B) meteorologist
   - (C) geologist
   - (D) archaeologist

8. **A person who studies matter, energy, and how they are related is a ________ .**
   - (F) chemist
   - (G) biologist
   - (H) physicist
   - (J) astronomer

9. **A person who studies weather and climate is a(n) ________ .**
   - (A) archaeologist
   - (B) astronomer
   - (C) meteorologist
   - (D) biologist

10. **A person who studies living things is a ________ .**
    - (F) seismologist
    - (G) chemist
    - (H) biologist
    - (J) physicist

Name ______________________________ Date ______________

Science

S3CS7–S3CS8

For pages 168–170

Mini-Test 2

DIRECTIONS: Choose the best answer.

1. **JoLynn and Jon are conducting an experiment to determine how many seconds it takes for a ball to hit the ground when dropped from JoLynn's one-story deck. They take turns dropping the ball and running the stopwatch. When JoLynn drops the ball, Jon records that it takes 3 seconds for it to hit the ground. When Jon drops the ball, JoLynn records that it takes 6 seconds. Why might their results have been different?**
   - (A) They did not drop the ball from the same height.
   - (B) JoLynn started the stopwatch too soon.
   - (C) Jon stopped the stopwatch before the ball hit the ground.
   - (D) all of the above

2. **Which of the following types of investigation would you use to study the courting ritual of the blue heron?**
   - (F) observation
   - (G) collecting specimens
   - (H) doing experiments
   - (J) all of the above

3. **Which of the following types of investigation would you use to determine the melting rates of ice cubes under different circumstances?**
   - (A) observation
   - (B) collecting specimens
   - (C) doing experiments
   - (D) all of the above

4. **Which of the following tools would you use to study Saturn?**
   - (F) a microscope
   - (G) a telescope
   - (H) a magnifying glass
   - (J) binoculars

5. **Which of the following tools would you use to study a strand of human hair?**
   - (A) a beaker
   - (B) a telescope
   - (C) a microscope
   - (D) a barometer

6. **A person who studies plants is a __________ .**
   - (F) geologist
   - (G) physicist
   - (H) chemist
   - (J) botanist

7. **An astronomer is a person who studies __________ .**
   - (A) animals
   - (B) the weather
   - (C) stars
   - (D) water

8. **A biologist is a person who studies __________ .**
   - (F) fossils
   - (G) living things
   - (H) rocks
   - (J) energy

STOP

Earth Science Standards

S3E1. Students will investigate the physical attributes of rocks and soils. ***(See pages 173–175.)***

a. Explain the difference between a rock and a mineral.
b. Recognize the physical attributes of rocks and minerals using observation (shape, color, texture), measurement, and simple tests (hardness).
c. Use observation to compare the similarities and differences of texture, particle size, and color in top soils (such as clay, loam or potting soil, and sand).
d. Determine how water and wind can change rocks and soil over time using observation and research.

S3E2. Students will investigate fossils as evidence of organisms that lived long ago. ***(See page 176.)***

a. Investigate fossils by observing authentic fossils or models of fossils or view information resources about fossils as evidence of organisms that lived long ago.
b. Describe how a fossil is formed.

Name ______________________________ Date ______________

Science

S3E1

Earth Science

Rocks and Minerals

DIRECTIONS: Choose the best answer.

1. **Which of the following statements is true?**
   - Ⓐ All rocks are minerals, but not all minerals are rocks.
   - Ⓑ All minerals are rocks, but not all rocks are minerals.
   - Ⓒ There is no relationship between rocks and minerals.
   - Ⓓ Rocks and minerals are two different words for the same thing.

2. **Obsidian, a mineral that is also known as volcanic glass, is __________ .**
   - Ⓕ soft and shiny
   - Ⓖ hard and shiny
   - Ⓗ hard and rough
   - Ⓙ soft and rough

3. **Which of the following rocks is light, has a rough texture, and has many hollow spaces?**
   - Ⓐ granite
   - Ⓑ shale
   - Ⓒ graphite
   - Ⓓ pumice

4. **Which of the following rocks is the texture of sandpaper?**
   - Ⓕ granite
   - Ⓖ shale
   - Ⓗ sandstone
   - Ⓙ marble

5. **A rock leaves a white streak when it is scraped across a surface. It probably contains which mineral that is used to make powder?**
   - Ⓐ gold
   - Ⓑ iron
   - Ⓒ talc
   - Ⓓ graphite

6. **Which type of rock splits apart in layers, is usually gray or black, and is often used to make blackboards?**
   - Ⓕ slate
   - Ⓖ marble
   - Ⓗ sandstone
   - Ⓙ granite

7. **Which of the following minerals is the hardest?**
   - Ⓐ talc
   - Ⓑ gold
   - Ⓒ iron
   - Ⓓ diamond

8. **When a mineral breaks with rough edges, it is said to have the property of __________ .**
   - Ⓕ luster
   - Ⓖ streak
   - Ⓗ fracture
   - Ⓙ cleavage

9. **Which of the following would *not* help you identify a mineral?**
   - Ⓐ tendency to float
   - Ⓑ hardness
   - Ⓒ streak
   - Ⓓ cleavage

STOP

Name ______________________________ Date ______________

Science

S3E1

Earth Science

Soil

DIRECTIONS: Use the table below to help answer the questions.

Type of Soil	Characteristics
Sand	Largest particle in soil; feels rough; drains quickly
Silt	Forms from the weathering of rocks; particles are between the sizes of sand and clay; feels smooth and powdery when dry; feels smooth but not sticky when wet
Clay	Smallest particle in soil; feels smooth and very hard when dry; feels sticky when wet; does not let air or water move through
Humus	Made up of decayed organic matter; has large amounts of plant nutrients; holds water well

Organic matter is material that is made up of decayed plant and animal life, such as decayed leaves.

1. Decayed organic matter that holds large amounts of plant nutrients and moisture is called __________ .

- (A) clay
- (B) humus
- (C) sand
- (D) silt

2. Which type of soil becomes extremely hard when dry?

- (F) sand
- (G) clay
- (H) silt
- (J) humus

3. Which type of soil contains the largest particles?

- (A) silt
- (B) sand
- (C) clay
- (D) humus

4. Which type of soil feels smooth and powdery to the touch?

- (F) clay
- (G) sand
- (H) humus
- (J) silt

5. Which type of soil contains the smallest particles?

- (A) sand
- (B) humus
- (C) silt
- (D) clay

6. Which type of soil drains quickly?

- (F) sand
- (G) silt
- (H) clay
- (J) humus

STOP

Name ______________________ Date ____________

Science

S3E1

Earth Science

Effects of Wind and Water

DIRECTIONS: Choose the best answer.

1. **The changes shown in the pictures below are probably due to __________ .**

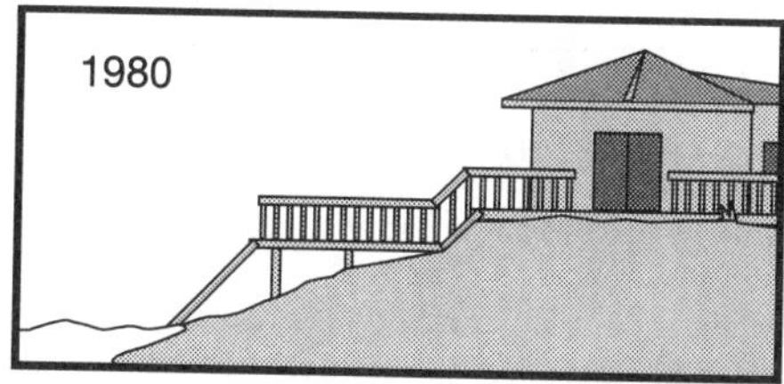

Ⓐ pollution
Ⓑ erosion
Ⓒ tornadoes
Ⓓ condensation

2. **Christopher was looking at pictures of different mountain ranges in the United States. He was surprised to see that the Appalachian Mountains were smaller and more rounded than the Rocky Mountains. The Appalachian Mountains looked old and worn compared to the Rocky Mountains. Why?**

Ⓕ The effect of wind and water caused weathering, wearing away the mountains.
Ⓖ Too many people and animals traveled across the mountains, causing them to wear away.
Ⓗ All of the snowfall was so heavy that it weighted down the mountains and caused them to shrink.
Ⓙ The water that used to cover the earth wore away parts of the mountains.

3. **During the Ice Age, most of the state of Illinois was covered by a huge glacier that changed the landscape. Which of the following was *not* an effect of the glacier on the landscape of that state?**

Ⓐ New mountains were made.
Ⓑ The peaks of hills were scraped off.
Ⓒ Many deep valleys were filled in.
Ⓓ Soil was transported miles away from its origin.

4. **Which characteristic is common to all agents of erosion?**

Ⓕ They carry sediments when they have enough energy of motion.
Ⓖ They are most likely to erode when sediments are moist.
Ⓗ They create deposits called dunes.
Ⓙ They erode large sediments before they erode small ones.

5. **Study the pictures below. Which of the following most likely caused the change shown in the two pictures?**

Ⓐ a tornado
Ⓑ a flood
Ⓒ wind
Ⓓ friction

STOP

Name ______________________________ Date ______________

Science

S3E2

Earth Science

Fossils

DIRECTIONS: Choose the best answer.

1. Fossils are usually found in which type of rock?

- (A) igneous
- (B) sedimentary
- (C) metamorphic
- (D) craggy

2. What is the least number of years it takes for a fossil to form?

- (F) 10 years
- (G) 100 years
- (H) 1,000 years
- (J) 10,000 years

3. Which part of an animal is least likely to be preserved as a fossil?

- (A) bone
- (B) tooth
- (C) skin
- (D) claw

4. The body of an animal is more likely to become fossilized if it ________ .

- (F) is left on the surface of the ground
- (G) does not contain hard body parts such as bones
- (H) is buried deeply in the ground
- (J) Fossilization is equally likely with all of the above.

5. Fossils may also be found in ________ .

- (A) amber
- (B) tar deposits
- (C) frozen earth
- (D) all of the above

6. A trace fossil is ________ .

- (F) part of the original organism that has been preserved
- (G) a mark left behind by a living organism
- (H) a hollow print left by the outside of an organism
- (J) a very small part of a fossil

7. A woolly mammoth found frozen in a glacier is an example of a ________ .

- (A) body fossil
- (B) trace fossil
- (C) mold fossil
- (D) cast fossil

8. During an archaeological dig, you excavate through four layers of rock that contain fossils. Where are the oldest fossils located?

- (F) in the first, or top, layer
- (G) in the second layer
- (H) in the third layer
- (J) in the fourth, or bottom, layer

Name ______________________________ Date ______________

Science

S3E1–S3E2

For pages 173–176

Mini-Test 3

Earth Science

DIRECTIONS: Choose the best answer.

1. All ________ are ________ .

Ⓐ minerals, rock
Ⓑ rocks, fossils
Ⓒ rocks, minerals
Ⓓ fossils, minerals

2. Luster describes a mineral's ________ .

Ⓕ color
Ⓖ hardness
Ⓗ surface shine
Ⓙ weight

3. Which of the following is the name for volcanic glass?

Ⓐ obsidian
Ⓑ gold
Ⓒ sandstone
Ⓓ marble

4. A rock that has a sparkly luster and can appear in many different colors is ________ .

Ⓕ sandstone
Ⓖ marble
Ⓗ pumice
Ⓙ shale

5. Which of the following minerals might be pink?

Ⓐ pyrite
Ⓑ emerald
Ⓒ iron
Ⓓ quartz

6. What occurs when weathered rock and organic matter are mixed together?

Ⓕ Compost breaks down.
Ⓖ Soil erodes.
Ⓗ Soil forms.
Ⓙ Minerals form.

7. Which of the following types of soil holds the largest amount of moisture?

Ⓐ clay
Ⓑ humus
Ⓒ silt
Ⓓ sand

8. What two forces cause erosion?

Ⓕ water and gravity
Ⓖ sun and wind
Ⓗ wind and water
Ⓙ gravity and wind

9. A geologist finds a rock sample that contains a fossil. What can she conclude from this?

Ⓐ It is a mineral.
Ⓑ It is a sedimentary rock.
Ⓒ It was formed in the recent past.
Ⓓ The fossil shows a plant that is now extinct.

10. Why do hard parts of an organism help fossils to form?

Ⓕ Hard parts are less likely to decompose.
Ⓖ Hard parts are less likely to be eaten.
Ⓗ Hard parts are less likely to be broken.
Ⓙ all of the above

Physical Science Standards

S3P1. Students will investigate how heat is produced and the effects of heating and cooling, and will understand a change in temperature indicates a change in heat. ***(See page 179.)***

a. Categorize ways to produce heat energy such as burning, rubbing (friction), and mixing one thing with another.
b. Investigate how insulation affects heating and cooling.
c. Investigate the transfer of heat energy from the sun to various materials.
d. Use thermometers to measure the changes in temperatures of water samples (hot, warm, cold) over time.

S3P2. Students will investigate magnets and how they affect other magnets and common objects. ***(See page 180.)***

a. Investigate to find common objects that are attracted to magnets.
b. Investigate how magnets attract and repel each other.

Name ______________________________ Date ______________

Science

S3P1

Physical Science

Heat

DIRECTIONS: Choose the best answer.

1. A log fire represents heat energy produced by __________ .

Ⓐ burning
Ⓑ friction
Ⓒ mixing one thing with another
Ⓓ none of the above

2. Rubbing your hands together briskly is an example of heat energy produced by __________ .

Ⓕ burning
Ⓖ friction
Ⓗ mixing one thing with another
Ⓙ none of the above

3. An insulated beverage container will __________ .

Ⓐ keep hot beverages hot
Ⓑ keep cold beverages cold
Ⓒ cool hot beverages
Ⓓ both A and B

4. How can you insulate your skin from the cold air when you go outside during the winter months?

Ⓕ wear sunscreen
Ⓖ wear lotion
Ⓗ wear layers of clothing
Ⓙ none of the above

5. What is the name of energy from the sun?

Ⓐ solar
Ⓑ polar
Ⓒ nuclear
Ⓓ lunar

6. Energy from the sun is transferred to the earth by __________ .

Ⓕ conservation
Ⓖ conduction
Ⓗ radiation
Ⓙ convection

7. Simon left a cube of ice in a glass on a windowsill during a sunny day. What would you expect to happen over the next hour?

Ⓐ The ice cube will melt.
Ⓑ The ice cube will evaporate.
Ⓒ The ice cube will become larger.
Ⓓ none of the above

8. You are sitting outside on a sunny day. What effect will you feel from the sun on your skin?

Ⓕ You skin will feel cooler.
Ⓖ You skin will feel warmer.
Ⓗ You skin will feel softer.
Ⓙ You skin will feel the same.

9. You boil a cup of water in the microwave. When you use a thermometer to check the temperature, it reads 100°C. If you leave the water on the counter and check it 30 minutes later, what would you expect the temperature to be?

Ⓐ greater than 100°C
Ⓑ less than 100°C
Ⓒ exactly 100°C
Ⓓ 0°C

STOP

Name ______________________________ Date ______________

Science

S3P2

Physical Science

Magnets

DIRECTIONS: Review the list of items below. For each item, write **Y** for yes if the item would be attracted to a magnet. Write **N** for no if would not be attracted to a magnet.

_____ **1. penny**

_____ **2. iron needle**

_____ **3. rubber band**

_____ **4. plastic spoon**

_____ **5. steel paper clip**

_____ **6. notebook paper**

_____ **7. aluminum foil**

_____ **8. leather glove**

_____ **9. metal screw**

_____ **10. cotton ball**

_____ **11. nail**

_____ **12. ice cube**

DIRECTIONS: Choose the best answer.

13. In which direction does a magnetic compass always point?

- (A) north
- (B) south
- (C) east
- (D) west

14. What are the north and south ends of a magnet called?

- (F) borders
- (G) caps
- (H) poles
- (J) tips

15. Which of the following must occur for two magnets to be attracted to each other?

- (A) The north pole of one magnet should be placed next to the north pole of the other magnet.
- (B) The south pole of one magnet should be placed next to the south pole of the other magnet.
- (C) The north pole of one magnet should be placed next to the south pole of the other magnet.
- (D) Magnets are never attracted to one another.

16. What will happen between these two magnets?

N S		S N

- (F) attract
- (G) repel
- (H) not move
- (J) none of the above

STOP

Name ______________________________ Date ______________

Science

S3P1–S3P2

For pages 179–180

Mini-Test 4

Physical Science

DIRECTIONS: Choose the best answer.

1. **Which of the following is a way to produce heat energy?**
   - (A) by burning
   - (B) by friction
   - (C) by mixing one thing with another
   - (D) all of the above

2. **Which of the following is *not* a form of energy?**
   - (F) solar
   - (G) solid
   - (H) nuclear
   - (J) electrical

3. **A burning candle gives off __________ .**
   - (A) no energy
   - (B) only light
   - (C) only heat
   - (D) both light and heat

4. **The temperature of a cup of water taken from the refrigerator is recorded at 38°F. After sitting on the counter for 30 minutes, the temperature is recorded at 62°F. What has happened?**
   - (F) The water has gotten colder.
   - (G) The water has gotten warmer.
   - (H) There is no change in the water.
   - (J) The water has evaporated.

5. **What effect does an insulated lunch bag have on cold foods placed inside it?**
   - (A) It helps keep them cool.
   - (B) It warms them up.
   - (C) It makes them colder.
   - (D) It has no effect.

6. **Jonathan puts a magnet into a pile of metal paper clips. What will happen?**
   - (F) The magnet will repel the paper clips.
   - (G) The paper clips will be attracted to the magnet.
   - (H) The magnet will be attracted to the paper clips.
   - (J) Nothing will happen.

7. **Why would a nail be attracted to a magnet?**
   - (A) It is made of steel or iron.
   - (B) It weighs less than the magnet.
   - (C) It is thinner than the magnet.
   - (D) all of the above

STOP

Life Science Standards

S3L1. Students will investigate the habitats of different organisms and the dependence of organisms on their habitats. ***(See page 183.)***

a. Differentiate between habitats of Georgia (mountains, marsh/swamp, coast, Piedmont, Atlantic Ocean) and the organisms that live there.
b. Identify features of green plants that allow them to live and thrive in different regions of Georgia.
c. Identify features of animals that allow them to live and thrive in different regions of Georgia.
d. Explain what will happen to an organism if the habitat is changed.

S3L2. Students will recognize the effects of pollution and humans on the environment. ***(See pages 184–185.)***

a. Explain the effects of pollution (such as littering) to the habitats of plants and animals.
b. Identify ways to protect the environment (conservation of resources, recycling of materials).

Name ______________________________ Date ______________

Science

S3L1

Life Science

Habitats

DIRECTIONS: Choose the best answer.

1. In which of Georgia's habitats will you find the highest elevation?

Ⓐ swamp
Ⓑ mountains
Ⓒ Piedmont
Ⓓ Atlantic Ocean

2. In which habitat does the manatee live?

Ⓕ mountains
Ⓖ Atlantic Ocean
Ⓗ coast
Ⓙ swamp

3. In which habitat will you find wet, peaty soil?

Ⓐ Piedmont
Ⓑ Atlantic Ocean
Ⓒ swamp
Ⓓ coast

4. In which habitat will you find the highest rainfall?

Ⓕ Atlantic Ocean
Ⓖ swamp
Ⓗ mountains
Ⓙ Piedmont

5. Carnivorous plants, which trap and eat insects, are often found in swamps where the __________ lacks nutrients.

Ⓐ air
Ⓑ rainfall
Ⓒ soil
Ⓓ none of the above

6. Which of the following features of the river otter allow it to stay in its habitat during the winter months?

Ⓕ long tail
Ⓖ webbed feet
Ⓗ flaps that cover the nose and ears under water
Ⓙ dense fur

7. A raccoon's diet may consist of nuts, fruits, berries, beetles, mice, frogs, fish, and reptile and chicken eggs. In which habitat would you find raccoons living?

Ⓐ coast
Ⓑ mountains
Ⓒ Piedmont
Ⓓ all of the above

8. Which of the following do alligators need to survive?

Ⓕ freshwater areas
Ⓖ saltwater areas
Ⓗ mountainous areas
Ⓙ forests

9. What might happen to a water-loving plant should the rainfall decrease for a long period of time?

Ⓐ The plant will thrive and grow.
Ⓑ The plant might adapt to the decreased rainfall if the change is gradual.
Ⓒ The plant will wither and die.
Ⓓ both B and C

STOP

Name ______________________________ Date ______________

Science

S3L2

Life Science

Protecting the Environment

DIRECTIONS: Study the chart that shows how much one school has helped the environment. Then answer the questions.

Conservation Efforts at Coe School			
Year	Pounds of Paper Recycled	Pounds of Cans Recycled	Number of Trees Planted
2002	550	475	120
2003	620	469	250
2004	685	390	320

1. **Which sentence is true about paper recycling at Coe School?**
   - (A) Students recycled more paper each year.
   - (B) Students recycled less paper each year.
   - (C) Students never recycled paper.
   - (D) Students recycled the same amount of paper each year.

2. **Which conservation project did not show better results each year?**
   - (F) recycling paper
   - (G) recycling cans
   - (H) planting trees
   - (J) They all showed better results each year.

3. **Which of the following is the most likely reason for the decrease in can recycling at Coe School?**
   - (A) Students reduced the amount of canned beverages they were drinking.
   - (B) Students found new uses for their cans.
   - (C) Students saved their cans.
   - (D) Students began recycling their cans at home.

DIRECTIONS: Choose the best answer.

4. **Which resource could be conserved by recycling a stack of newspapers?**
   - (F) rocks
   - (G) trees
   - (H) plastic
   - (J) oil

5. **Which of the following is an example of *recycling* to conserve resources?**
   - (A) walking to the store rather than riding in a car
   - (B) taking newspapers to a facility where they will be made into another paper product
   - (C) using a glass jelly jar as a pencil holder
   - (D) throwing aluminum cans in the trash

6. **The best example of a way to conserve natural resources is __________ .**
   - (F) regulating toxic emissions from cars
   - (G) the greenhouse effect
   - (H) cutting down on packaging used in consumer goods
   - (J) keeping garbage dumps away from residential areas

Name ______________________________ Date ______________

7. Which of the following is an example of *reusing* to conserve resources?

- (A) walking to the store rather than riding in a car
- (B) taking newspapers to a facility where they will be made into another paper product
- (C) using a glass jelly jar as a pencil holder
- (D) throwing aluminum cans in the trash

8. Which of the following is *not* a good water conservation practice?

- (F) taking short showers
- (G) fixing leaky faucets
- (H) leaving the water running while brushing your teeth
- (J) using the water you have cooked vegetables in to water your plants

9. Which of the following is *not* a conservation activity?

- (A) replace
- (B) reuse
- (C) recycle
- (D) reduce

10. An example of the opposite of reducing is over-packaging. Which of the following is an example of over-packaging?

- (F) filling a cereal box completely
- (G) putting an item in a cardboard box, then putting that box in another box
- (H) putting foam packing material around a fragile item
- (J) packing an item in the smallest possible box

11. Pollution can have a negative impact on the ________ .

- (A) air
- (B) water
- (C) land
- (D) all of the above

12. Which of the following will most likely suffer due to an oil spill in an ocean bay?

- (F) whales
- (G) waterfowl
- (H) squirrels
- (J) robins

13. Explain how the oil spill would affect the animal you chose in question 12.

____

____

____

____

____

____

____

____

____

____

STOP

Name ______________________ Date ______________

Science

S3L1–S3L2

For pages 183–185

Mini-Test 5

Life Science

DIRECTIONS: Choose the best answer.

1. In which of Georgia's habitats would you find the saw palmetto plant, also known as a palm shrub?

Ⓐ mountains
Ⓑ swamp
Ⓒ coast
Ⓓ Piedmont

2. In which habitats would you expect to find aquatic life?

Ⓕ swamp
Ⓖ Atlantic Ocean
Ⓗ coast
Ⓙ all of the above

3. A desert cactus is transplanted in the mountains of Georgia and dies. What is the most likely reason that this happened?

Ⓐ It was not used to the colder environment.
Ⓑ It received too much rain.
Ⓒ both A and B
Ⓓ neither A nor B

4. Trees are conserved when cardboard and newspapers are _________ .

Ⓕ hauled to a dump
Ⓖ burned
Ⓗ kept in storage
Ⓙ recycled

5. Which of the following contributes to pollution?

Ⓐ car exhaust
Ⓑ littering
Ⓒ dumping sewage waste that has not been treated
Ⓓ all of the above

6. Which of the following is *not* a benefit of conserving natural resources?

Ⓕ better air quality by reducing pollutants
Ⓖ protecting natural areas for future generations
Ⓗ making fossil fuels last longer
Ⓙ making bigger, more expensive cars

7. Walking or riding a bicycle to a store rather than driving a car is an example of _________ .

Ⓐ replacing
Ⓑ recycling
Ⓒ reducing
Ⓓ reusing

8. Some companies release pollutants into the air. These pollutants return to the earth as acid rain. How does acid rain change the environment?

Ⓕ Acid rain helps clean buildings and roads.
Ⓖ Acid rain harms plants and animals.
Ⓗ Acid rain returns valuable nutrients to the soil.
Ⓙ Acid rain helps clean polluted water.

How Am I Doing?

Mini-Test 1 Page 166 **Number Correct**	**8** answers correct	**Great Job!** Move on to the section test on page 189.
	4–7 answers correct	**You're almost there!** But you still need a little practice. Review practice pages 158–165 before moving on to the section test on page 189.
	0–3 answers correct	**Oops!** Time to review what you have learned and try again. Review the practice section on pages 158–165. Then retake the test on page 166. Now move on to the section test on page 189.
Mini-Test 2 Page 171 **Number Correct**	**8** answers correct	**Awesome!** Move on to the section test on page 189.
	4–7 answers correct	**You're almost there!** But you still need a little practice. Review practice pages 168–170 before moving on to the section test on page 189.
	0–3 answers correct	**Oops!** Time to review what you have learned and try again. Review the practice section on pages 168–170. Then retake the test on page 171. Now move on to the section test on page 189.
Mini-Test 3 Page 177 **Number Correct**	**9–10** answers correct	**Great Job!** Move on to the section test on page 189.
	5–8 answers correct	**You're almost there!** But you still need a little practice. Review practice pages 173–176 before moving on to the section test on page 189.
	0–4 answers correct	**Oops!** Time to review what you have learned and try again. Review the practice section on pages 173–176. Then retake the test on page 177. Now move on to the section test on page 189.

How Am I Doing?

Mini-Test 4 Page 181 **Number Correct**	**7** answers correct	**Great Job!** Move on to the section test on page 189.
	4–6 answers correct	**You're almost there!** But you still need a little practice. Review practice pages 179–180 before moving on to the section test on page 189.
	0–3 answers correct	**Oops!** Time to review what you have learned and try again. Review the practice section on pages 179–180. Then retake the test on page 181. Now move on to the section test on page 189.
Mini-Test 5 Page 186 **Number Correct**	**8** answers correct	**Awesome!** Move on to the section test on page 189.
	4–7 answers correct	**You're almost there!** But you still need a little practice. Review practice pages 183–185 before moving on to the section test on page 189.
	0–3 answers correct	**Oops!** Time to review what you have learned and try again. Review the practice section on pages 183–185. Then retake the test on page 186. Now move on to the section test on page 189.

Name ______________________ Date ______________

Final Science Test

for pages 158–186

DIRECTIONS: Choose the best answer.

1. Why should you keep a record of an investigation?
   - Ⓐ so you can see exactly what was done during the investigation
   - Ⓑ so others can repeat the investigation
   - Ⓒ both A and B
   - Ⓓ neither A nor B

2. **When should observations be recorded?**
   - Ⓕ at the time of the observation
   - Ⓖ within a day of the observation
   - Ⓗ a week following the observation
   - Ⓙ There is no reason to record observations.

3. **In a recent experiment with 18 samples, $\frac{1}{3}$ of them did not give the expected results. How many sample results surprised the students?**
   - Ⓐ 3 results
   - Ⓑ 6 results
   - Ⓒ 9 results
   - Ⓓ 12 results

4. **You have a beaker containing 200 mL of solution. You are asked to transfer $\frac{3}{4}$ of this to another beaker. How much solution will remain in the original beaker?**
   - Ⓕ 150 mL
   - Ⓖ 75 mL
   - Ⓗ 50 mL
   - Ⓙ 125 mL

5. **You know that the average adult female giraffe is 13 to 16 feet tall and weighs 1,200 to 2,600 pounds. The average adult male is 15 to 18 feet tall and weighs 1,700 to 4,200 pounds. The average newborn giraffe is 7 feet tall and weighs 100 to 150 pounds. Which of the following should be true about a giraffe that is 10 feet tall and weighs 900 pounds?**
   - Ⓐ It is an adult male.
   - Ⓑ It is not a newborn, but it is not yet an adult.
   - Ⓒ It is an adult female.
   - Ⓓ It is a newborn.

6. **Which of the following should you do when working near flames in a science lab?**
   - Ⓕ Tie back long hair.
   - Ⓖ Secure loose clothing.
   - Ⓗ Check that there are no materials nearby that can catch fire.
   - Ⓙ all of the above

7. **How does a keyboard interact with the computer system?**
   - Ⓐ It allows data to be printed.
   - Ⓑ It allows data to be viewed.
   - Ⓒ It allows data to be input.
   - Ⓓ It allows data to be stored.

8. **Which of the following shapes would you use to represent a chicken egg if you were creating a model?**
   - Ⓕ rectangle
   - Ⓖ oval
   - Ⓗ circle
   - Ⓙ square

Name ______________________________ Date ______________

9. Which of the following types of investigation would you use to determine what happens when water and vinegar are mixed?

Ⓐ observation
Ⓑ collecting specimens
Ⓒ experimentation
Ⓓ all of the above

10. Which of the following tools would you use to watch birds hatching in a nest in your backyard?

Ⓕ a microscope
Ⓖ a telescope
Ⓗ a magnifying glass
Ⓙ binoculars

11. Which of the following tools would you use to measure how far a ball rolled?

Ⓐ a stopwatch
Ⓑ a measuring tape
Ⓒ a barometer
Ⓓ a scale

12. An archaeologist is a person who studies ________ .

Ⓕ remains of past civilizations
Ⓖ living things
Ⓗ stars and planets
Ⓙ rocks

13. A meteorologist is a person who studies ________ .

Ⓐ water
Ⓑ weather and climate
Ⓒ rocks
Ⓓ meteors

14. Which of the following tests can help you to identify a mineral?

Ⓕ hardness
Ⓖ luster
Ⓗ cleavage
Ⓙ all of the above

15. A scientist scratches a mineral with her fingernail, a penny, and a nail. What property is she testing?

Ⓐ luster
Ⓑ cleavage
Ⓒ weight
Ⓓ hardness

16. Which of the following minerals is the softest?

Ⓕ diamond
Ⓖ gypsum
Ⓗ quartz
Ⓙ silver

17. Which type of soil feels the smoothest to the touch?

Ⓐ clay
Ⓑ silt
Ⓒ sand
Ⓓ humus

18. Which type of soil is made up of decayed organic matter?

Ⓕ sand
Ⓖ clay
Ⓗ humus
Ⓙ none of the above

19. The two forces of erosion are water and ________ .

Ⓐ sun
Ⓑ wind
Ⓒ gravity
Ⓓ ice

Name ______________________________ Date ______________

20. What conditions help preserve a fossil?

Ⓕ exposure to air and water
Ⓖ rapid burial
Ⓗ the presence of scavengers
Ⓙ none of the above

21. Which part of an animal is most likely to be preserved as a fossil?

Ⓐ lung
Ⓑ eye
Ⓒ blood
Ⓓ tooth

22. Which of the following activities does not produce heat energy?

Ⓕ rubbing your hands together briskly
Ⓖ using sandpaper to sand wood
Ⓗ burning coal
Ⓙ sitting in the sun

23. An item that prevents the transfer of heat has which property?

Ⓐ insulation
Ⓑ radiation
Ⓒ friction
Ⓓ refrigeration

24. What will happen to hot soup that is put into a thermos?

Ⓕ It will become hotter.
Ⓖ It will stay warm.
Ⓗ It will cool quickly.
Ⓙ It will become icy.

25. __________ is the measure of heat or thermal energy.

Ⓐ Mass
Ⓑ Density
Ⓒ Temperature
Ⓓ Force

26. The temperature of a glass of water sitting on your kitchen counter is 68°, the same as the temperature in the room. What will be the temperature of the water when you measure it an hour later?

Ⓕ It will be warmer than room temperature.
Ⓖ It will be colder than room temperature.
Ⓗ It will be the same as room temperature.
Ⓙ There is no way to predict this.

27. A magnet cannot move which of the following objects?

Ⓐ a paper clip
Ⓑ a nail
Ⓒ a toothpick
Ⓓ a staple

28. Magdalena has dropped a box of antique needles into a haystack. Some of the needles are made of wood, some are made of iron, and some are made of bone. If she runs a magnet over the haystack, which needles will she be able to find?

Ⓕ the wooden needles
Ⓖ the iron needles
Ⓗ the bone needles
Ⓙ none of the needles

29. What will happen if the north pole of one magnet is placed near the south pole of a second magnet?

Ⓐ The magnets will attract.
Ⓑ The magnets will repel.
Ⓒ The magnets will not move.
Ⓓ none of the above

Name ______________________________ Date ______________

30. Which of the following is a habitat found in Georgia?

- (F) mountain
- (G) swamp
- (H) coast
- (J) all of the above

31. Plants that thrive in peaty soil would most likely be found in which of Georgia's habitats?

- (A) Atlantic Ocean
- (B) Piedmont
- (C) swamp
- (D) all of the above

32. Causing harm to the natural environment by introducing waste products is called __________ .

- (F) conservation
- (G) pollution
- (H) recycling
- (J) protection

33. Which of the following are conservation practices?

- (A) replace, recycle, reuse
- (B) reduce, recycle, reuse
- (C) reduce, recycle, recall
- (D) recycle, replace, recall

34. Using old holiday cards in a craft is an example of __________ a resource.

- (F) reusing
- (G) rotating
- (H) replacing
- (J) reducing

35. Which of the following is an example of conserving energy?

- (A) turning on all the lights in your home
- (B) leaving the computer on overnight
- (C) turning off the television when you are not watching it
- (D) none of the above

36. Which of the following is an example of recycling to conserve resources?

- (F) throwing tin cans in the trash
- (G) using a tin can to hold nuts and bolts
- (H) taking tin cans to a facility where they can be processed for use in steel mills
- (J) not buying food in tin cans

STOP

Name ______________________________ Date ______________

Final Science Test

Answer Sheet

1 (A) (B) (C) (D)
2 (F) (G) (H) (J)
3 (A) (B) (C) (D)
4 (F) (G) (H) (J)
5 (A) (B) (C) (D)
6 (F) (G) (H) (J)
7 (A) (B) (C) (D)
8 (F) (G) (H) (J)
9 (A) (B) (C) (D)
10 (F) (G) (H) (J)

11 (A) (B) (C) (D)
12 (F) (G) (H) (J)
13 (A) (B) (C) (D)
14 (F) (G) (H) (J)
15 (A) (B) (C) (D)
16 (F) (G) (H) (J)
17 (A) (B) (C) (D)
18 (F) (G) (H) (J)
19 (A) (B) (C) (D)
20 (F) (G) (H) (J)

21 (A) (B) (C) (D)
22 (F) (G) (H) (J)
23 (A) (B) (C) (D)
24 (F) (G) (H) (J)
25 (A) (B) (C) (D)
26 (F) (G) (H) (J)
27 (A) (B) (C) (D)
28 (F) (G) (H) (J)
29 (A) (B) (C) (D)
30 (F) (G) (H) (J)

31 (A) (B) (C) (D)
32 (F) (G) (H) (J)
33 (A) (B) (C) (D)
34 (F) (G) (H) (J)
35 (A) (B) (C) (D)
36 (F) (G) (H) (J)

Answer Key

Page 8
1. A
2. G
3. D
4. Answers will vary. The sign might say "Quiet, please! Testing in progress."
5. The author is nervous about taking tests.

Page 9
1. A
2. G
3. B
4. J
5. C

Page 10
1. C
2. J
3. C
4. H
5. C
6. G
7. D
8. G

Page 11
1–6. Answers will vary. Students should list three synonyms for each word.

7–12. Answers will vary. Students should list three antonyms for each word.

13. too, two
14. scent, sent
15. fore, four

Page 12
1. ice
2. a snowstorm
3. kite
4. the night
5. mice

Answers will vary for questions 6–10.

Examples include:

6. a lunch as cold as ice
7. a friend like a sister
8. a coat as warm as a soft blanket
9. a winter day like a beautiful painting
10. with a smile that sparkled like sunshine

Page 13
1. C
2. F
3. C
4. J
5. A
6. H
7. B
8. J
9. B
10. J

Page 14
1. B
2. G
3. B

Page 15
1. D
2. F
3. C
4. H

Page 16
1. A
2. F
3. C

Page 17
1. B
2. G
3. A
4. J
5. B
6. H

Page 18
1. A. Dylan
   B. Danny
   C. Danny
   D. Dylan
2. Dylan's day
3. Students should tell whether their reactions would be most like Danny's or Dylan's.

Page 19
1. C
2. G
3. C

Page 20
Many insects find a **warm** place to spend the **winter.**

Details:
- Ants try to dig deep into the ground.
- Some beetles stack up in piles under rocks or dead leaves.
- Female grass-hoppers lay their eggs and die.
- Honeybees gather in a ball in the middle of their hive.

Page 21
1. She began skating at a young age and her family supported her.
2. There were no skates small enough for Bonnie's small feet.
3. Bonnie won five Olympic gold medals.

Pages 22–23
1. A
2. H
3. B
4. F
5. D
6. G
7. C
8. J

Page 24
1. D
2. G
3. C
4. J
5. C
6. G
7. A

Page 25
1. A
2. The author said that he or she is sad when whales beach themselves.
3. J

Page 26
1. B
2. G
3. A
4. J
5. A

Page 27
1. D
2. H
3. A
4. H
5. B
6. H
7. D

Pages 28–29
Mini-Test 1
1. A
2. H
3. A
4. F
5. D
6. H
7. D
8. G
9. B
10. H
11. D
12. F
13. C

Alice while they make pizza.

three reasons for their positions. Students should construct their letters with an appropriate greeting and closing and use correct punctuation and spelling.

7. A
8. H
9. C

Page 31

1. Jason's teacher; he or she asked Jason what was wrong and made a phone call.
2. Jason; he forgot his lunch.
3. Jason's mother; she brought Jason's lunch to school.
4. All three passages describe the morning that Jason forgot to bring his lunch to school.

Page 32

1. Answers will vary. Students should write a paragraph that describes how to make or do something. They should include transitional words between each step of the process.
2. Answers will vary. Students should write the procedure using numbered steps.

Pages 33–34

1. C
2. F
3. Answers will vary. Red Queen—triumphant, anxious; White Queen—unfriendly, not bright; Alice—eager, cautious, serious.
4. D
5. Answers will vary. Students should write dialogue that could take place between the Queens and

Page 35

1. Students should describe their main characters and use adjectives in their description.
2. Students should discuss where and when their stories take place. They should use adjectives to describe the setting.
3. Students should present the main problems that will be introduced in their stories and how they will be resolved by the main characters.
4. Verbs: looked, paced, wondered, raced, smiled, started talking. The verbs show that Juan was feeling anxious about Bill's visit but was relieved when their friendship still felt the same as it did in the past.

Page 36

1. D
2. H
3. A
4. G
5. C
6. J
7. C
8. J
9. D

Page 37

Letters should explain why the students should be allowed to do something of their choosing and provide

Page 38

Students should enter the main topic in the center circle. Ideas about the main topic should connect to the center circle. Further breakdown of these ideas should be connected to the appropriate idea.

Page 39

1. A
2. J
3. B
4. G
5. C
6. F
7. A

Page 40
Mini-Test 2

1. Students should use prewriting strategies to organize their thoughts, such as web diagrams or graphic organizers.
2. Students should use their notes to create drafts of their reports.
3. Students should edit and revise their drafts.
4. Students should write organized final reports.

Page 42

1. D
2. H
3. B
4. G
5. C
6. J

Page 43

1. D
2. F
3. C
4. H
5. B
6. G
7. D
8. H

Page 44

1. S
2. PS
3. P
4. P
5. PS
6. S
7. P
8. S
9. PS
10. P
11. S
12. PS
13. P

Page 45

1. B
2. F
3. C
4. G
5. C
6. F
7. D
8. J
9. D
10. H

Page 46

1. D
2. H
3. B
4. H
5. B
6. J
7. B
8. J
9. C

Page 47

1. A
2. F
3. C
4. H
5. B
6. J

7. B
8. H
9. A

Page 48
1. D
2. G
3. D
4. H
5. C
6. J
7. C
8. F
9. D
10. H
11. C

Page 49
1. C
2. J
3. C
4. F
5. C
6. G
7. D
8. H
9. C

Page 50
1. C
2. F
3. D
4. F
5. A
6. J
7. C
8. F
9. B

Pages 51–52
Mini-Test 3
1. D
2. F
3. C
4. J
5. A
6. H
7. A
8. J
9. A
10. G
11. D
12. H
13. B
14. F
15. C
16. F
17. C

Pages 55–60
Final English/
Language Arts Test
1. A
2. G
3. A
4. H
5. D
6. J
7. D
8. G
9. C
10. G
11. B
12. H
13. B
14. G
15. C
16. G
17. A
18. G
19. A
20. F
21. C
22. J
23. D
24. F
25. C
26. F
27. C
28. G
29. A
30. H
31. D
32. G
33. D
34. H
35. C
36. F
37. C
38. H
39. B
40. H
41. D
42. J
43. C
44. G
45. D
46. F
47. D

Page 65
1. 4
2. 3
3. 3
4. 8
5. B
6. F
7. D
8. 4,037
9. 42,513
10. 16.3
11. 5.5
12. 2.1
13. G
14. D
15. J

Page 66
1. 832 vowels, 832 − 254 = 578
2. 218 acorns, 218 + 627 = 845
3. $1.98, $1.98 + 3.27 = $5.25
4. 198 minutes, 198 − 120 = 78
5. 119 cards, 119 + 39 = 158
6. 1,020 butterflies, 1,020 − 562 = 458

Page 67
1. **a.** Thomas needs $43.75 ($60 − $16.25 = $43.75)
   b. Thomas has $25.00. He still needs $35.00.
   c. The check was for $17.50. (1/2 of $35.00 = $17.50)
   d. $42.50 has been saved. ($25.00 + $17.50 = $42.50)
   e. He still needs $17.50. ($60 − $42.50 = $17.50)

Page 68
1. A
2. G
3. C
4. H
5. D
6. G

Page 69

x	0	1	2	3	4	5	6	7	8	9	10
0	0	0	0	0	0	0	0	0	0	0	0
1	0	1	2	3	4	5	6	7	8	9	10
2	0	2	4	6	8	10	12	14	16	18	20
3	0	3	6	9	12	15	18	21	24	27	30
4	0	4	8	12	16	20	24	28	32	36	40
5	0	5	10	15	20	25	30	35	40	45	50
6	0	6	12	18	24	30	36	42	48	54	60
7	0	7	14	21	28	35	42	49	56	63	70
8	0	8	16	24	32	40	48	56	64	72	80
9	0	9	18	27	36	45	54	63	72	81	90
10	0	10	20	30	40	50	60	70	80	90	100

1. 48 sports books
2. 120 fiction books
3. 36 tables
4. 85 customers
5. $70

Page 70

1. $(2 \times 6) + (2 \times 3)$
   $2 \times 9 = 12 + 6$
   $18 = 18$
2. $(3 \times 4) + (3 \times 3)$
   $21 = (4 + 3)3$
   $21 = 21$
3. $(4 \times 9) - (4 \times 1)$
   $4 \times 8 = 36 - 4$
   $32 = 32$
4. $(9 \times 2) - (3 \times 2)$
   $12 = (9 - 3)2$
   $12 = 12$
5. $2 \times 15 - 2 \times 3$
   $12 \times 2 = 30 - 6$
   $24 = 24$
6. $(7 \times 8) + (5 \times 8)$
   $12 \times 8 = 56 + 40$
   $96 = 96$

Page 71

1. B
2. H
3. A
4. F
5. C
6. G
7. B
8. J

Page 72

1. 50
2. 500
3. 1,200
4. 5,600
5. 54,000
6. 8,000
7. 18,000
8. 28,000
9. 16,000
10. 15,000
11. 2,500
12. 1,000
13. 4,000
14. 1,800
15. 7,500
16. 4,800
17. 9,000
18. 2,800
19. 6,000
20. 9,000

Page 73

1. A
2. G
3. C
4. G
5. C
6. H
7. C
8. F

Page 74

1. C
2. F
3. D
4. J
5. B
6. G
7. C
8. F
9. C
10. G

Page 75

1. 5 R3
2. 4 R3
3. 3 R2
4. 6 R3
5. 8 R2
6. 9 R1
7. 8 R3
8. 7 R2
9. 6 times
10. 4 postcards per family member, 4 postcards for the scrapbook
11. 15 moose per herd, 1 extra moose placed in the first herd
12. 9 tourists

Page 76

1. 27
2. 73
3. 4
4. 21
5. 9
6. 3
7. 16
8. 42
9. 6
10. 40

Page 77

1. 0.7
2. 0.6
3. 0.8
4. 0.9
5. 0.1
6. 0.5
7. any 4 parts should be shaded
8. any 3 parts should be shaded
9. any 2 parts should be shaded

Page 78

1. A
2. J
3. B
4. H

Pages 79–80

1. D
2. H
3. C
4. F
5. B
6. H
7. 9.4
8. 7.8
9. 10.9
10. 7.9
11. 6.9
12. 2.7
13. 1.1
14. 5.3
15. 2.5
16. 2.4
17. 4.8
18. 3.3
19. B
20. J
21. B
22. H

Pages 81–82
Mini-Test 1

1. C
2. J
3. A
4. H
5. C
6. G
7. D
8. H
9. B
10. J
11. A
12. H
13. C
14. F
15. D
16. J
17. D
18. G
19. A

Page 84

1. 90 degrees
2. 180 degrees
3. 360 degrees
4. 270 degrees
5. 180 degrees
6. 180 degrees
7. 90 degrees
8. 270 degrees
9. 360 degrees
10. 15 minutes
11. 15 minutes
12. 60 minutes
13. 30 minutes
14. 30 minutes
15. 45 minutes
16. 15 minutes
17. 60 minutes
18. 45 minutes

Page 85

1. 3.218 km
2. Tanner
3. 12 miles
4. $\frac{1}{2}$ mile
5. 526 miles
6. 846 km
7. 715 km
8. 5,000 m
9. 10 km

Page 86

1. $1\frac{3}{4}''$
2. $2\frac{3}{4}''$
3. $3\frac{3}{4}''$
4. $1\frac{1}{4}''$
5. $2\frac{1}{2}''$
6. $3\frac{1}{2}''$
7. $1\frac{1}{2}''$
8. 2''
9. 17 mm
10. 70 mm
11. 53 mm
12. 65 mm

Page 87

1. 21
2. 2
3. 2

4. 52,800
5. 5
6. 10
7. 62
8. 36
9. 340 mm
10. yes
11. 300 cm
12. no
13. 1,000 cm × 1,200 cm

Page 88

1. 12 cm
2. 36 in.
3. 89 ft.
4. A
5. F
6. C
7. F

Page 89

1. 10 square units
2. 6 square units
3. 6 square units
4. 9 square units
5. 9 square units
6. 7 square units
7. B
8. J

Page 90
Mini-Test 2

1. B
2. F
3. B
4. H
5. C
6. J
7. A
8. G

Page 92

1. C
2. G
3. C
4. G
5. D
6. G
7. A
8. F
9. C
10. H
11. B
12. H

Page 94

1. B
2. F
3. B
4. H
5. A
6. J

Page 95

1. B
2. H
3. D
4. H
5. B
6. J
7. A
8. G

Page 96
Mini-Test 3

1. B
2. G
3. D
4. J
5. B
6. J
7. B
8. H
9. D

Page 98

1. B
2. F
3. B
4. H
5. C
6. G

Page 99

1. A
2. G
3. D
4. F
5. C
6. H
7. C

Page 100

1. B
2. H
3. D
4. H
5. A
6. G
7. C
8. J
9. D
10. H

Page 101
Mini-Test 4

1. C
2. H
3. B
4. G
5. C
6. G
7. A

Page 103

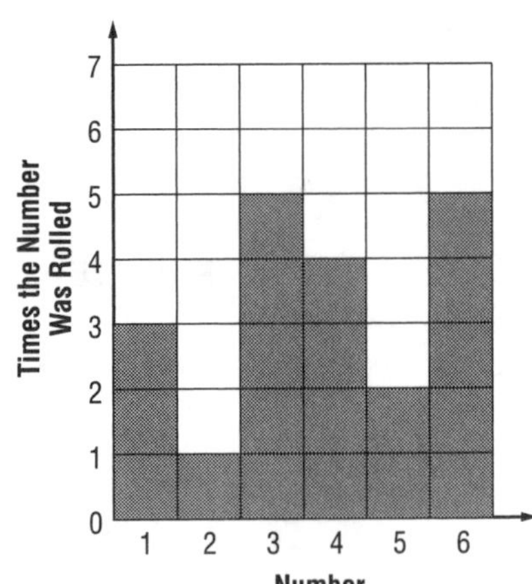

1. C
2. G
3. A
4. G
5. A
6. H
7. D

Page 104

1. A
2. J
3. B
4. J

Page 105
Mini-Test 5

1. A
2. J
3. B
4. G
5. C

Page 107

1. B
2. F
3. C
4. G
5. D
6. H
7. A
8. H

Page 108

1. C
2. J
3. B
4. G
5. A
6. J
7. A

Page 109

1. B
2. G
3. A
4. F
5. A

Pages 110–111

1. B
2. H
3. D
4. J
5. B
6. J
7. C
8. F
9. B
10. F
11. D
12. F

Page 112

1. C
2. F
3. D
4. J
5. B
6. H

Pages 113–114

1. D
2. F
3. C
4. F

For numbers 5–8, students should write the directions or show the steps they used to solve each problem.

5. B
6. F
7. C
8. H

Pages 115–116
Mini-Test 6

1. A
2. G
3. C
4. J
5. C
6. F
7. A
8. F
9. A
10. J
11. C
12. F
13. A

Pages 119–124
Final Mathematics Test

1. A
2. J
3. C
4. H
5. C
6. F
7. C
8. F
9. C
10. G
11. C
12. J
13. B
14. J
15. A
16. H
17. A
18. F
19. C
20. J
21. C
22. J
23. B
24. J
25. B
26. H
27. A
28. H
29. D
30. H
31. D
32. G
33. D
34. F
35. B
36. H
37. B
38. H
39. A
40. H
41. A
42. J
43. B
44. F
45. C
46. J
47. B
48. J
49. B
50. H
51. C

Page 128

1. C
2. F
3. B
4. G
5. D
6. F
7. B
8. J
9. C

Page 129

1. B
2. H
3. A
4. J

Page 130

1. C
2. J
3. B
4. G
5. A
6. H
7. B

Page 131
Mini-Test 1

1. C
2. H
3. C
4. F
5. A
6. G
7. B
8. H

Page 133

1. G
2. E
3. B
4. A
5. F
6. C
7. D

Page 134

1. D
2. H
3. B
4. F

Page 135

1. A
2. G
3. C
4. J

Page 136

1. B
2. J
3. D
4. Answers will vary. Students may mention that after losing their farm and then experiencing the drought in the southwest, the Chavez family had few options as Mexican Americans but to become migrant farm workers in California. The conditions his family faced as migrant workers led to Chavez's interest in improving the conditions for these workers.

Page 137
Mini-Test 2

1. D
2. G
3. D
4. F
5. D
6. F
7. C
8. F
9. D
10. J

Page 139

1. D
2. H
3. B
4. G
5. A
6. G
7. B
8. F
9. C

Page 140

1. D
2. G
3. C
4. J

Page 141
Mini-Test 3

1. A
2. H
3. A
4. G
5. D
6. G
7. D
8. H
9. A
10. H

Page 143

1. C
2. G
3. A
4. J
5. C
6. N
7. C

8. H
9. H
10. N

Page 144

1. B
2. J
3. A
4. H
5. B
6. J
7. A
8. J

Page 145

1. C
2. J
3. A
4. F
5. C
6. J
7. A

Page 146

1. C
2. Producers would be more likely to produce more thing-a-ma-bobs at the highest price because they would make a higher profit, which is why all companies are in business.
3. F
4. B
5. F
6. D
7. Answers will vary. Most students will conclude that people wanted to purchase the generators because they needed another source for their electricity since their normal source was unavailable.

Page 147

Answers will vary. Sample answers are provided here.

1. The camera will cost Amanda \$80. She will not be able to buy the DVDs today, and it will take her much longer to save for the MP3 player.
2. Amanda will have a camera she can use to take photos of her friends and family.
3. Amanda will not own the DVDs or the camera. However, she will be able to own the MP3 player much sooner than if she had bought these items.
4. Amanda's cost is that she will have to cut back on the things she normally spends money on each week. For example, she may not be able to go to a movie.

Page 148
Mini-Test 4

1. C
2. G
3. A
4. G
5. B
6. F
7. B
8. J
9. B

Pages 151–154
Final Social Studies Test

1. B
2. G
3. C
4. H
5. B
6. G
7. C
8. G
9. C
10. H
11. D
12. H
13. A
14. G
15. B
16. J
17. B
18. H
19. B
20. H
21. A
22. G
23. D
24. G
25. B
26. H
27. A
28. J
29. C
30. G
31. B
32. J
33. D
34. F

Page 158

1. B
2. H
3. Answers may vary. Possible answer: Lauren made accurate, detailed records of the result of her experiment. However, she should have used either new flashlights or the same old flashlights for both experiments. This would have given her a clearer idea of how long the batteries last under specific conditions.
4. D

Page 159

1. B
2. H
3. A
4. H
5. D
6. F
7. C
8. J

Page 160

1. 3 inches—2 hours, 9 inches—4 hours, 15 inches—8 hours; these heights are very close to the averages given in the table.
2. Sample answer: No, this plant is $2\frac{1}{2}$ times taller than the average given. The measurement may not be accurate, the plant may have received more sunlight than 8 hours per day, he may have grown a different kind of plant, or the plant may have been taller at the beginning of the experiment.
3. A
4. H
5. Because this length is over two times the given data, it is likely that this is not true and the friend is not very good at estimating length.

Page 161

1. S
2. U
3. U
4. S
5. S
6. U
7. U

8. S
9. S
10. U

Page 162
1. S
2. S
3. N
4. N
5. S
6. S
7. S
8. S
9. S
10. N
11. N
12. S
13. C

Page 163

1. 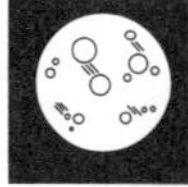
2. 
3. 
4. 

Page 164
1. D
2. G
3. D
4. F

Page 165
1. Y
2. N
3. N
4. Y
5. N
6. Y
7. Y
8. N
9. The information came from the book *All About Earth.*
10. C

Page 166
Mini-Test 1
1. A
2. G
3. C
4. G
5. D
6. H
7. B
8. H

Page 168
1. Answers will vary. Students should mention that either Julie counted some birds twice or Jim missed some of the birds in his tally.
2. Students should mention that no matter how high the baseball may be initially hit, gravity means it must return to the ground.

Page 169
1. E
2. O
3. O
4. C
5. E
6. O
7. C
8. E
9. C
10. E
11. O

Page 170
1. A
2. G
3. C
4. G
5. D
6. G
7. A
8. H
9. C
10. H

Page 171
Mini-Test 2
1. D
2. F
3. C
4. G
5. C
6. J
7. C
8. G

Page 173
1. A
2. G
3. D
4. H
5. C
6. F
7. D
8. H
9. A

Page 174
1. B
2. G
3. B
4. J
5. D
6. F

Page 175
1. B
2. F
3. A
4. F
5. B

Page 176
1. B
2. J
3. C
4. H
5. D
6. G
7. A
8. J

Page 177
Mini-Test 3
1. C
2. H
3. A
4. G
5. D
6. H
7. B

8. H
9. B
10. J

Page 179
1. A
2. G
3. D
4. H
5. A
6. H
7. A
8. G
9. B

Page 180
1. N
2. Y
3. N
4. N
5. Y
6. N
7. N
8. N
9. Y
10. N
11. Y
12. N
13. A
14. H
15. C
16. G

Page 181
Mini-Test 4
1. D
2. G
3. D
4. G
5. A
6. H
7. B

Page 183
1. B
2. G
3. C
4. H
5. C
6. J
7. D
8. G
9. D

Pages 184–185
1. A
2. G
3. A

4. G
5. B
6. H
7. C
8. H
9. A
10. G
11. D
12. G
13. Answers will vary. Students may state that the oil may coat the birds' feathers, which will cause them to lose their ability to float and to retain heat and drown or freeze to death.

Page 186
Mini-Test 5

1. C
2. J
3. C
4. J
5. D
6. J
7. C
8. G

Pages 189–192
Final Science Test

1. C
2. F
3. B
4. H
5. B
6. J
7. C
8. G
9. C
10. J
11. B
12. F
13. B
14. J
15. D
16. G
17. A
18. H
19. B
20. G
21. D
22. J
23. A
24. G
25. C
26. H
27. C
28. G
29. A
30. J
31. C
32. G
33. B
34. F
35. C
36. H

NOTES

NOTES

NOTES

NOTES

NOTES

NOTES